Police as
Problem Solvers

Police as Problem Solvers

Hans Toch

Distinguished Professor
State University of New York
Albany, New York

and

J. Douglas Grant

President Emeritus
Social Action Research Center
Nicasio, California

Plenum Press • New York and London

Library of Congress Cataloging-in-Publication Data

Toch, Hans.
    Police as problem solvers / Hans Toch and J. Douglas Grant.
        p.   cm.
    Includes bibliographical references and index.
    ISBN 0-306-43845-3
    1. Police. 2. Police social work. 3. Police--United States.
I. Grant, James Douglas, 1917-   . II. Title.
HV7921.T636   1991
362--dc20   91-10619
                                                                 CIP

ISBN 0-306-43845-3

© 1991 Plenum Press, New York
A Division of Plenum Publishing Corporation
233 Spring Street, New York, N.Y. 10013

Printed in the United States of America

To the memory of Donald J. Newman

This cardinal,
Though from an humble stock, undoubtedly
Was fashion'd to much honour. From his cradle,
He was a scholar, and a ripe, and good one;
Exceeding wise, fair spoken, and persuading:
Lofty, and sour, to them that lov'd him not;
But, to those men that sought him, sweet as summer.

—Shakespeare, *King Henry VIII* (Act IV, Scene II)

Preface

This book is about police and police reform and about a movement called "problem-oriented policing," which is sweeping the country.

The problem-oriented approach has been labeled "a philosophical revolution" and "the cutting edge of policing" (Malcolm, 1989). Two observers, Wilson and Kelling (1989), have written that the approach "constitutes the beginning of the most significant redefinition of police work in the past half century" (p. 48). Such an esteemed development matters, and one expects knowledgeable persons to observe it and think about it.

Our mission in this book is different from that of some observers, those concerned with management practice and philosophy. Ours is a more person-centered book, which views the problem-oriented movement from the trenches where battles, not wars, are waged. We are concerned with what an erstwhile colleague of ours dubbed the "nitty-gritty" and what others have called the "human equation." This is so because the core of our interest is on the experience of being problem oriented and how one engenders this experience. Coincidentally, such grass roots analysis happens to fit problem-oriented policing, which delegates thinking and planning to those on the frontlines.

In the battles won by problem-oriented policing, ordinary police officers become generals or, at least, strategists of policing. The jobs that such men and women do are expanded, and we shall center on this expansion of the job.

Over the years we have been interested in human service work as work that we thought could be enriched. We became involved in problem-oriented policing before its broader, community-centered consequences were recognized, but service to the public always seemed to us the most likely arena in which police could be more inventive so that they and the public would benefit.

Outsiders have long been obsessed with the need to "control" the police and reduce their discretion to keep them from abusing their power. What we thought should be done, and what we think should be done now, is that the role of police officers be professionalized by enhancing their discretion. We see professional judgment exercised when persons are trusted to think about what they do after learning contextual facts. We feel that officers do a better job by making informed decisions about policing, and we know from experiences (such as those we shall record) that police find mindful work more meaningful and enhancing than the standard routines that occupy their time.

Though these views are key assumptions of problem-oriented policing, the approach evolved from a different perspective. First, questions centered on the definition of police work and its increasingly questionable effectiveness. The problem was to change organizational goals, and approaches to goals, so that police could make more of a difference.

Concerns about who was to plan and implement this process came later. To the student of policing, however, process-related concerns matter, because they bear on the question of whether one's goals are achievable. If one is to take a trip, it helps to anticipate one's mode of transportation and prospective itinerary, which is the way one gets from here to there.

This book pays attention to these details. This is not to say that our presentation will be devoid of conceptual content and empty of ideas. We shall be concerned with issues—some even substantial issues—but our main interest is in making the process of problem-oriented activity come alive and make sense. We feel that practitioners and interested observers of police might benefit from getting a sense of what problem-oriented policing means to those who engage in its exercise. To convey such feeling, we have drawn on some of our previously reported experiences, which we can now see in a new light. We have also drawn on reports by pioneers in problem-oriented policing who confirm our impressions of why the process works and why it matters that it works.

The experiment we have reported in Chapters 6–10 of this book was an exercise in problem-oriented police reform conducted by ourselves and a group of police officers. We published this study 15 years ago and reprint parts of it now. The work was supported by the Center for Studies of Crime and Delinquency (now the Center for Studies of Antisocial and Violent Behavior) of the National Institute of Mental Health. The opinions expressed, however, are ours, and we hope that some of these impressions will continue to stand the test of time.

Hans Toch
J. Douglas Grant

Albany, and Nicasio, CA

Acknowledgments

We would not have written this book if we had not been involved in a police intervention and if this experiment had not succeeded. We owe much to our colleagues in this project: Raymond Galvin (the coauthor of our original report) and Officers John Dixon, Roy Garrison, Carl Hewitt, Larry Murphy, Mike Nordin, Robert Prentice, and Mike Weldon. Our sponsor was Chief Charles Gain, who was a chief of vision and a reformer ahead of his time. Dr. Saleem Shah of NIMH monitored the project and was a source of helpful advice.

Given the passage of years since our involvement, we have had to restudy the police field. Among our tutors were Herman Goldstein of the University of Wisconsin, John Eck of the Police Executive Research Forum, and James Fyfe of American University. All three have reviewed our chapter drafts and have helped improve them. We have also learned from key written sources, which we have quoted freely. We are especially grateful to the following for permission to reprint excerpts from their works:

The American Sociological Association and Egon Bittner for text used from "The Police on Skid Row: A Study in Peace Keeping," published in *American Sociological Review*, Volume 32, 1967.

The National Council on Crime and Delinquency and Herman Goldstein for excerpts from "Improving Policing: A Problem-Oriented Approach," which appeared in *Crime and Delinquency*, Volume 25, 1979.

Police Executive Research Forum and John Eck for permission to excerpt Eck and Spelman, *Solving Problems: Problem-Oriented Policing in Newport News*, and Taft, *Fighting Fear: The Baltimore County C.O.P.E. Project*, and to reproduce *Key Elements of Problem-Oriented Policing*.

Praeger and the Greenwood Publishing Group for quotes from *Community Policing: Rhetoric or Reality,* edited by J. R. Greene and S. D. Mastrofski, published by Praeger Publishers in 1988.

Transaction Publishers for excerpts from *Two Cultures of Policing: Street Cops and Management Cops,* by E. Reuss-Ianni.

Parts of Chapter 10 of this book have been adapted (with permission) from J. D. Grant, J. Grant, and H. Toch, "Police-citizen conflicts and decisions to arrest," in V. J. Konecni and E. B. Ebbesen (Eds.), *The Criminal Justice System: A Social–Psychological Analysis,* San Francisco: W. H. Freeman and Company, 1982. Other portions of Chapter 10 and Chapters 6–9 are drawn from H. Toch, J. D. Grant, and R. T. Galvin, *Agents of Change: A Study in Police Reform,* Cambridge: Schenkman Publishing Company, 1975. This case material describes a process now known as problem-oriented policing.

We are finally indebted—as usual—to Joan Grant; also, to Sally Spring, the best book typist in the country.

Contents

1

The Advent of Problem-Oriented Policing

Problem-oriented policing was officially born in April 1979, as a phrase in the subtitle of an essay. The author of the article, Herman Goldstein, was a redoubtable academic, but his essay was the kind of prescription scholars often advance with no expectation of impact. If Goldstein's concept took hold, it was because it was immensely timely and made sense to many students of policing and administrators of police departments.

Goldstein started with some history: He noted that police chiefs had for decades tried to shape up casually run police organizations in the name of "professionalization." The ideal officer had been seen by the chiefs as clean-cut, educated, corruption-free, quick to obey orders, and technically up-to-date. The department in which such an officer worked was presumed to look well-managed, busy, and efficient.[1] By the same token, there was little concern with whether any of this well-oiled competence translated into tangible benefits for the communities that the police ostensibly served. The goal of the administrators was seemingly to improve means for the achievement of unexamined end results.

Goldstein (1979) implied that the disjuncture between enhanced means and neglected ends became obvious with attainment of efficiency. It was one thing for a sloppy and inefficient organization to not accomplish much and quite another for a model enterprise to do similarly badly. Awareness of limited impact was also painful because of assumptions that had been made and taken for granted, which new research findings cast in doubt.

A case in point pertains to the practice of randomized, motorized patrolling, which takes up most of the time most police officers spend at

1

work. The practice was first instituted—as were many others—to take advantage of technological advances.

Before 1920, policemen walked through neighborhoods on (flat)foot, getting to know residents and settings in which they lived and worked.[2] The advent of the automobile and telephone made it possible to place officers in cars, contacting them when they were needed and directing them to the sites of complaints.[3] Dispersal of motorized units placed any unit in rough proximity to any call, thus ensuring rapid response, and even (on well-publicized occasions) to a sensational arrest. The motorized officers cruised the streets between calls, hoping for a complaint that would direct them to a "good bust." A consequence of this avocation, which was at first disregarded, was that "by staying in their cars, patrol officers lost contact with the residents of their beats who were neither offenders nor victims. Their knowledge of community problems became more and more limited" (Eck and Spelman, 1987a, p. 13).

At first, there was no reason for the officers to stay in cars between calls.[4] Randomized patrol gave them a reason. The reason was a hoped-for intimidating effect of police presence and a presumed capacity for strategic surveillance. The visibility of police cars was said to deter contemplated crime, and eyeballing by officers was presumed to pinpoint offenses in the process of being committed. Randomization was of assistance to both these goals, since malefactors would be unable to predict when a randomly cruising officer (or at times, two officers) would appear.

The shining benefits of preventive patrol looked self-evident until they were called into question by an experiment in Kansas City (Kelling, Pate, Dieckman, and Brown, 1974), which suggested that police presence might not make much difference in practice, either to citizens or offenders. In the experiment, doubling or tripling the number of police cars on patrol did not affect neighborhood crime rates or attitudes toward police. Worse, after the experimenters discontinued patrols altogether, there was no increase in crime or demand from the public for restoration of service. These findings were buttressed by other studies that showed that few serious crimes are committed where officers could physically observe them (Skogan and Antunes, 1979; Kansas City Police Department, 1980; Eck and Spelman, 1987a).

A related question pertained to what the public regards as good police work. Goldstein (1979) felt that the criteria the public uses have to do with the outcome of police services the consumers expected. He wrote:

Those concerned about battered wives, for example, could not care less whether the police who respond to such calls operate with one or two officers in a car, whether the officers are short or tall, or whether they have a college education. Their attention is on what the police do for the battered wife. (p. 240)

Goldstein's point was that citizens are not impressed by efficiency of operation but by effectiveness of response. What the citizens want is police activity that addresses the concerns they are experiencing and ameliorates the difficulties they have called to the attention of police.

Police have no problems with reforms that make the public happy, though they object to the way reforming is sometimes done.[5] The officers know that in many reforms they tend to be seen as in need of shaping up and that they become targets, rather than participants, in change. This does not mean that officers will oppose all changes. The sort of innovations they may not oppose are precisely those in which they are enlisted to help improve quality of services to the public. Officers in New York City supported an experiment, for example, that improved their skill in handling domestic disturbances (Bard, 1969). More recently, community policing (see Chapter 11) has found wide acceptance in police departments.

THE "END PRODUCT" OF POLICING

Goldstein asks what police work is supposed to accomplish. Observers who have not thought about this question do not understand it, because they equate police work with "law enforcement." But to what end would the law be enforced? Would one continue to enforce misdemeanors promiscuously if there were no visible benefit beyond keeping the police busy and jails congested with harmless violators? And how much of what police do in the course of a day is classifiable under the "enforcement" heading?

Goldstein's aim in reviving these questions was not only to underline the fact that police do a great deal more than fight crime, but to point out that crime fighting and other services of police can be similarly defined as problem-oriented activities, in the sense that they address problems that are brought to the police by consumers of services. Goldstein (1979) explains that

by problems, I mean the incredibly broad range of troublesome situations that prompt citizens to turn to the police, such as street robberies, residential burglaries, battered wives, vandalism, speeding cars, runaway children, accidents, acts of terrorism, even fear. These and other similar problems are the essence of police work. They are the reason for having a police agency. (p. 242)

Goldstein notes that police are unique in a number of respects. They are available 24 hours a day and they have no sharply delimited mandate that circumscribes what they do. They carry considerable authority. Police also function as last resorts, and are called by citizens when no one else can help them. As a result, the challenges the police face are often difficult ones. Goldstein notes that

> Many of the problems coming to the attention of the police become their responsibility because no other means has been found to solve them. They are the residual problems of society. It follows that expecting the police to solve or eliminate them is expecting too much. It is more realistic to aim at reducing their volume, preventing repetition, alleviating suffering, and minimizing the other adverse effects they produce. (Goldstein, 1979, p. 243)

If police must somehow respond to a variety of problems, including crime problems, one cannot assess the effectiveness of police work by counting the number of arrests police make, ascertaining their clearance rate, or measuring the time it takes for the average officer to answer the average call. Such a numbers-oriented accounting system "is somewhat like that of a private industry that studies the speed of its assembly line, the productivity of its employees, and the nature of its public relations program, but does not examine the quality of its product" (Goldstein, 1979, p. 243). A police quality control system would have to be based on a study of problems to which the police respond, so as to pose the question of how effectively these problems are solved.

PROBLEMS AS BEHAVIOR PATTERNS

One difficulty is that police problems are usually defined in terms of a criminal code, which is a list of uninformative legalistic labels. One reason rosters of crimes are misleading is that

> they frequently mask diverse forms of behavior. Thus, for example, incidents classified under "arson" might include fires set by teenagers as a form of vandalism, fires by persons suffering severe psychological problems, fires set for the purpose of destroying evidence of a crime, fires set by persons (or their hired agents) to collect insurance, and fires set by organized criminal interests to intimidate. Each type of incident poses a radically different problem for the police. (Goldstein, 1979, p. 245)

A second difficulty is more obvious and has to do with the fact that there are many situations that require attention, though no crime has been committed. The taxonomy of offenses draws attention to alcohol offenders, for example, but not to drunks who freeze to death if police do not pick them up. Offense-centered categories also imply that the solution to a problem is to make an arrest, and there is no provision for other activities that have to do with crime, such as the counseling of victims.

Goldstein favors subdividing behavior to which police respond into categories that involve similar people (e.g., suspects) doing things for similar reasons in similar situations. The advantage of viewing human behavior in this way is that it makes it possible to think of a response that is uniquely applicable to the behavior, rather than to the statute that subsumes it. Robbery is a broad label that does not define a meaningful subset; neither does purse snatching, which is an appreciably better category. What defines a problem is a category such as "teenagers snatching the purses of elderly women waiting for buses in the downtown section of the city during the hours of early darkness" (Goldstein, 1979, p. 246). Analysis of this sort of delimited behavior helps one to search for solutions, and it might even help to consider further subdivision, such as offenses by gang-affiliated and non-gang-affiliated teenagers.

Behavioral categories can reveal problems that are obfuscated by being buried under formalistic labels. An example of such a problem that is cited by Goldstein is being subjected to irritating noise. Noise complaints are routinely handled by police, but are distributed under inconsequential offense headings that obscure the fact that noise occasions a great deal of misery, that "sleep is lost, schedules are disrupted, mental and emotional problems aggravated. Apartments become uninhabitable" (p. 247). For the person whose quality of life is thus adversely affected, "improved policing would mean a more effective response to the problem of noise created by her neighbors" (p. 247).

Once problems (such as "noise complaints") have been defined, information must be collected that makes sense of the problems. This information includes data that officers have acquired by answering complaints. Experienced officers, in particular, "are an extremely rich source of information that is too often overlooked by those concerned about improving the quality of police service" (Goldstein, 1979, p. 249). Some of what the officers already do might in fact solve the problem and could be emulated by other officers.

Researching a problem means gathering statistics: In the case of noise, what is the number and source of the complaints? Does noise more frequently occur in given types of locations? What types of persons are responsible for creating noise and what do they do to produce it? How is the problem currently being responded to and are any of the current responses effective? Such facts permit the posing of strategic questions, which have to do with alternative ways of addressing the problem.

To address a problem one must think creatively, but the solutions one considers must be grounded in the facts one has gathered. Substantial solutions often involve cooperative endeavors between police and other service providers in which a problem is solved because the police "take the initiative, as a sort of community ombudsman, in getting others to address it" (Goldstein, 1979, p. 254). Police can in such ways help create innovative modes of service delivery that fill unmet needs. They can also inspire ordinances and regulations to provide new remedies to control resistant and persistent problems. On the other hand, less difficult problems may be solved by disseminating information or providing reassurance. Sometimes simple gadgets help: locks on doors or street lights can reduce burglary calls in some neighborhoods.

Goldstein concludes that this sort of problem-centered approach should appeal to police. After all, "the approach calls for the police to take greater initiative in attempting to deal with problems rather than resign themselves to living with them" (p. 257). And as for frontline officers, Goldstein (1979) suggests that they have reason to welcome "an innovation that is cast in the form of a new response to an old problem — a problem with which they have struggled for many years and which they would like to see handled more effectively" (p. 258).

EVOLUTION OF THE PROBLEM-ORIENTED APPROACH

Since 1979, the approach first outlined by Goldstein has taken on dimensions that have rounded out the model and to some extent supplemented it. One such refinement is in the definition of problems and nonproblems. From this definitional perspective, a non-problem-oriented approach is one that focuses on *incidents*. When a complaint is received, the police respond to the complaint; when a suspect has been identified, the suspect is arrested. Specific situations (incidents) are addressed, but conditions that underlie them are not addressed. If we assume that such conditions are at work, there will be more complaints and more offenses, and nothing much will have been accomplished. The net effect can even be destructive if the unaddressed conditions get worse and the impotence of the police is thereby highlighted.

From the problem-oriented perspective, incidents are symptoms. A problem exists where a set of conditions produces a proliferation of incidents. To keep incidents from further multiplying, one must address the underlying conditions, which must be identified. To pinpoint causes or conditions, one must examine incidents for clues. Such clues are garnered by looking at the *patterning* of incidents. Patterning has to do with common characteristics of incidents, such as who does what to whom, and under what circumstances. It also has to do with how people respond to interventions that have been tried. The pickpockets referred to above, for instance, may have been sobered by a tour of a maximum-security penitentiary.

To look for patterns does not mean that a police department's incident-driven business must be curtailed. Policing must always remain reactive, just as medicine must deal with irritating symptoms of diseases. But both professions must do more than cope with symptoms where knowledge permits them to do more. A pattern that can be isolated does not guarantee a cure, of course (since not all conditions are curable), but it helps define the disease so that we can think in terms of curing it. Where police incidents group—where complaints and offenses aggregate—the question "why?" becomes easier to ask, and a problem-centered solution becomes conceivable.

Traditional policing at times approximates this definitional stance, since enforcement activities (such as stakeouts) are often targeted based on analyses of crime statistics that highlight concentrations of incidents. This approach recognizes that a problem (say, robbery) exists, but responds to it by assaulting its symptoms. The approach also has a second feature that is at variance with problem-oriented policing, which is that analysis of the problem is done by one set of people—for example, the crime analysis section of a police department—and the responding by another group of people who have no hand in the analysis.

In problem-oriented policing, as we mostly see it today, police—rank-and-file officers—do the problem solving. It is this dramatic feature (which we shall deal with in the next two chapters) that distinguishes the approach most clearly from other approaches and makes it particularly exciting. Goldstein himself has pointed out that

> by drawing on the expertise of officers and involving them in devising solutions, the problem-solving approach increases the potential for more effective police responses. It also challenges the officer's imagination and creativity, generating new enthusiasm for the job. (Goldstein, 1987, p. 17)

If police officers are assigned to an exercise in problem-oriented policing, they may attack a wide-spectrum problem that is of concern to a whole police department or a circumscribed problem that is sharply localized. Whichever they do, they must first try to carefully define the problem and the kind of information that is needed to illuminate it. They must preliminarily collect existing information, such as available incident-related and demographic statistics, and published research that bears on their problem. They may next interview all sorts of people who have firsthand information—including victims, fellow officers, knowledgeable civilians, and sometimes offenders—to help them make sense of the problem. They can also interview service providers who have tried to solve the problem, to gain an idea of how well the problem has been addressed. They may even do formal surveys, but these will tend to be modest, since officers mostly have limited resources.

The next task of the officers would be to "uninhibitedly explore" solutions, which includes talking to people who can help assess solutions or who might be enlisted in their implementation. Problem-oriented policing is not seen as a grandstanding enterprise; it places a premium on solutions that involve persons other than the police in their final implementation. The approach also prizes alternatives to enforcement as the means to solve problems.

Once solutions, whatever these are, are devised and have been proposed and approved, they must be implemented by the officers. Solutions must also be evaluated as they are implemented to determine the extent to which they solve problems. A crucial step for the officers is that of deciding what data they will collect to evaluate the program they have decided to implement.

TIMELINESS OF THE PROBLEM-ORIENTED MODEL

As Goldstein pointed out in his seminal article, the management focus of police was to reduce sloppiness, inefficiency, and corruption, including political interference. To the extent to which this effort succeeded, it became an advance on sloppy, inefficient, and corrupt policing. But the enterprise also had serious liabilities, both for officers and citizens. The officers often experienced the approach as demoralizing because they felt tainted by a broad brush of accusations. The officers also knew that while their discretion was seen as circumscribed, they were forced to exercise it daily. They were in practice on their own (except for sporadic encounters with sergeants), which meant that their ostensibly tight supervision was a fiction.

A result of ambiguity and authoritarian management was bitterness, which contributed to the genesis of an alienated officer subculture. One sophisticated group of observers (Kelling, Wasserman, and Williams, 1988) describes this process as follows:

> First, use of individual discretion has been driven underground; creativity and productive adaptations go unrecognized and unrewarded. Second, police departments often fail to tap the potential abilities of their officers. An ethos of "stay out of trouble," which has developed in many departments, stifles officers who are otherwise resourceful and abets officers who "perch" in their positions. Finally, a police culture has developed that maintains

> values that are alien to both police departments and communities. This police culture is characterized by suspiciousness, perceptions of great danger, isolation from citizens, and internal solidarity (the "blue curtain"). (pp. 2–3)

The alienated police officer is likely to view himself as misunderstood and rejected; he may feel that others (particularly in the criminal justice system) bend their efforts to undo his work. He may feel unappreciated, uncompensated, and disrespected. He may also have little respect for large numbers of citizens (whom he may characterize as intrinsically incorrigible) and may have contempt for his superiors, whom he may view as removed from police work, subject to political manipulation, and imprisoned by minority group concerns.

The alienated officer may view himself as going through motions. Conversely, he may see himself as engaged in a thankless crusade, unappreciated by others, which necessitates disguising his conduct, deceiving, prevaricating, and circumventing instructions that circumscribe.

In the meantime, citizens have become alienated for a different reason. The management approach that had developed to policing confronted citizens with a "full enforcement crime-fighting model" that presumed that laws are to be enforced to the hilt and all those who violate laws will be arrested. The formula was in fact intrinsically unworkable, but it created pressure on police to find violators so as to meet high arrest quotas. This meant that citizens who had needs that could not be met by making an arrest acquired nuisance status and received short shrift in delivery of services. Another result was that many borderline transgressors were arrested. These persons invariably knew other borderline violators who had not been arrested and regarded themselves as unfairly singled out. The problem was compounded when suspects who were arrested were black or Hispanic and the officers were predominantly white.

Proactive policing of this period was an unfriendly, negative activity, and police who specialized in this activity were seen by spectators as negative and unfriendly. Ordinarily such reputation might be a small price to pay, but it became a serious matter in the context of cumulating ethnic and class grievances that colored perceptions of the police to the point where it contributed to riots, many of which started with a routine effort by the police to arrest a minor transgressor.

To add injury to insult, crime fighting had not reduced crime. This became increasingly obvious as police failed to keep pace with burgeoning crime rates and communities felt decreasingly safe. The result, even prior to the drug crisis (Chapter 12), was that the police not only lost popularity but a great deal of public confidence.

The public also sensed the disjuncture between efficiency and effectiveness to which we have referred. As police became more efficient in deploying cars, answering calls, and reducing their response time, it also became clearer that much of this activity was wasted, in the sense of not accomplishing hoped for results. More carefully targeted, discriminating practices—handling some calls by telephone, for instance—eventually helped, but the means–end issue had been placed on the table, and became even more salient as task forces and street sweeps failed to deter drug trading. An ironic development (to which we shall return) was a demand for the rebirth of foot patrol, which chiefs had regarded as a Stone Age practice.

New challenges also occasioned new thinking. A plethora of community problems—homelessness, the decay of inner cities, the deinstitutionalized mentally ill—posed unfamiliar difficulties for the police, and raised questions that had not been dealt with before. New difficulties joined more familiar challenges (what to do about drunks, runaways, graffiti, public housing projects, rape victims, domestic fights, child abuse, the safety of parks and playgrounds, and so forth), which had already called for problem-centered strategic thinking in the past, had required coordination with other parties concerned with the same problems and caused deviations from a crime-fighting definition of the police mission.

OLD WINE WITH NEW LABEL?

The view that problem-oriented policing represents a revolution is not enthusiastically accepted by everyone. There are experts who convincingly argue (sometimes in aggrieved tones) that "problem oriented" is simply a new label for old police wine in a more fashionable bottle.

As is usually the case with such controversies, the accusation is not true or false but hinges on matters of definition. Many policemen in the past have found themselves self-consciously responding to "problems" in their communities. They have done this with strategies containing mixes of enforcement and nonenforcement options, after careful study (or, at least, familiarization with facts). The similarities between such ventures and problem-oriented policing are real. There are also differences, however, and it may be well to consider these differences using a carefully conducted police study as example.

The study is by Egon Bittner (1967) and centered on policing in skid rows. Skid row is a designation first applied to logging terminals in which serious drinking occurred, and has come to be used to describe certain deteriorated sections of cities. According to Winick (1979),

Many large cities have a Skid Row, an older area where homeless and up-rooted men, who are frequently alcoholics, live. The area usually has deteri-orated housing, sleazy bars and restaurants, and a generally blighted appearance. The indigent drinking man on Skid Row is often serviced by a variety of public institutions, going to which may be called "making the loop" or "making the circle." (pp. 351–352)

Wiseman (1970), who is an expert on skid rows, notes that skid rows have presented an enduring and consistent set of problems that center around homelessness, subculturally supported inebriation, and sub-stantial deterioration of neighborhoods. She writes that

not only has Skid Row proved tenacious as a continuing urban pattern but the area and its culture are strikingly similar from city to city and from time period to time period. In fact, the descriptions of Skid Row have been re-markably stable over the 50 years: the filth and stench of the hotels, the greasy cheapness of the restaurants, the litter in the streets, the concentration of "low-type" bars, or "dives." All of these aspects are mentioned again and again in both the research and the romantic literature from the 1920's until today.

This consistency overrides the changes in Skid Row demographic com-position from itinerant workers to more stable local spot jobbers and retired men living on social security. The social silhouette of these men has not changed to any degree—idle, ill-kempt, living hand to mouth. Even the special jargon used by the habitués of Skid Row is amazingly consistent from city to city and through time. (p. 4)

Given this discouraging profile of skid rows, the policing of such neighborhoods provides a daunting challenge to officers who are as-signed to work in them and must cope with their junglelike attributes. What should such officers do and what should be their goals? It is obvious that the answer cannot be "accumulate high-arrest records," which would be indecently easy. Arresting chronic alcoholics would make officers look ridiculous and would serve no constructive purpose. Most jails are already full of alcohol offenders (who have traditionally made up the bulk of jail populations), and such persons take up space needed for clients who pose more substantial threats to society.

Bittner notes that officers on skid row see themselves as keeping the peace in the area, which is an admittedly vague goal. "Peace keeping," writes Bittner (1967), "appears to be a solution to an unknown problem arrived at by unknown means" (p. 701). In pursuing this solution, more-over, officers have a great deal of latitude. In the skid row studied by Bittner (1967), he found that

the prevailing method of carrying out the task is to assign patrolmen to the area on a fairly permanent basis and to allow them to work out their own ways of running things...patrolmen are supposed to know what to do and are free to do it. (p. 704)

The officers were viewed as skid row specialists, who exercise judgments based on their professional expertise. In the words of a sergeant interviewed by Bittner (1967), "A good man has things worked out in his own ways on his beat and he doesn't need anybody to tell him what to do" (p. 715).

Bittner found that the officers regard their expertise as deriving from "experience and practice" which gives them a reservoir of "street sense" or "common sense." When officers act, they tend to maintain that they "play it by ear." This self-characterization suggests that they have no underlying premises, but it means something different. According to Bittner (1967),

> What the seasoned patrolman means, however, in saying that he "plays by ear" is that he is making his decisions while being attuned to the realities of complex situations about which he had immensely detailed knowledge. This studied aspect of peace keeping generally is not made explicit, nor is the tyro or the outsider made aware of it. (p. 715)

In making their seemingly instantaneous decisions, the officers rely (they say) on cues whose significance becomes obvious to them because they know what to look for. Bittner (1967) reports that

> patrolmen maintain that some of the seemingly spur-of-the-moment decisions are actually made against a background of knowledge of facts that are not readily apparent in the situations. Since experience not only contains this information but also causes it to come to mind, patrolmen claim to have developed a special sensitivity for qualities of appearances that allow an intuitive grasp of probable tendencies. In this context, little things are said to have high informational value and lead to conclusions without the intervention of explicitly reasoned chains of inferences. (p. 712)

Skid row officers acquire their self-styled expertise by getting to know the denizens of their beat. "Getting to know" in this context is not a scientific enterprise. It does not mean taking surveys or collecting statistics. It means "the establishment and maintenance of familiar relationships with individual members of these groups" (p. 707), an endeavor to which the officers dedicate a good deal of time. For example,

> the rounds include entering hotels and gaining access to rooms or dormitories, often for no other purpose than asking the occupants how things are going. In all this, patrolmen address innumerable persons by name and are in turn addressed by name. The conversational style that characterizes these exchanges is casual to an extent that by non-skid-row standards might suggest intimacy. (Bittner, 1967, p. 708)

An officer who behaves in this fashion acquires a great deal of particularistic knowledge:

As a general rule, the Skid Row patrolman possesses an immensely detailed factual knowledge of his beat. He knows, and knows a great deal about, a large number of residents. He is likely to know every person who manages or works in the local bars, hotels, shops, stores, and missions. Moreover, he probably knows every public and private place inside and out. Finally, he ordinarily remembers countless events of the past which he can recount by citing names, dates and places with remarkable precision. Though there are always some threads missing in the fabric of information, it is continuously woven and mended even as it is being used. New facts, however, are added to the texture, not in terms of structured categories but in terms of adjoining known realities. In other words, the content and organization of the patrolman's knowledge is primarily ideographic and only vestigially, if at all, nomothetic. (pp. 707–708)

That the skid row officers' knowledge is highly detailed does not mean that the officers lack the ability to generalize about skid row inhabitants and their outlook on life. Bittner (1967) points out, for example, that officers feel that on skid row

the dominant consideration governing all enterprise and association is directed at the occasion of the moment. Nothing is thought of as having a background that might have led up to the present in terms of some compelling moral and practical necessity...No venture, especially no joint venture, can be said to have a strongly predictable future in line with its initial objectives. It is a matter of adventurous circumstance whether or not matters go as anticipated...The places the residents occupy, the social relations they entertain, and the activities that engage them are not meaningfully connected over time...Of course, everybody's life contains some sequential incongruities, but in the life of a Skid Row inhabitant, every moment is an accident. (pp. 705–706)

This is not only an immensely sophisticated portrayal, but turns out to be an accurate one. Jacqueline Wiseman (1970) painstakingly reconstructed the skid rowers' perspective, and talks of their psychological world in the same terms as the officers. Moreover, policemen are particularly voluble in discussing victimization on skid row, which they are dedicated to preventing. Unlike less sophisticated observers, they see vulnerability and predatory propensities as coexistent in the same individuals and varying with situations. This view not only is plausible but is an advance on conventional social science theory.

In addressing skid row peacekeeping problems, the officers engage in a great deal of activity that borders on social work and that falls under the heading of service delivery. Bittner (1967) reports that

patrolmen note that they frequently help people to obtain meals, lodging, employment, that they direct them to welfare and health services, and that they aid them in various other ways. Though patrolmen tend to describe such services mainly as the product of their own altruism, they also say that their colleagues who avoid them are simply doing a poor job of patrolling...Hotel

clerks normally call policemen when someone gets so sick as to need attention; merchants expect to be taxed, in a manner of speaking, to meet the
pressing needs of certain persons; and the inhabitants do not hesitate to
accept, solicit, and demand every kind of aid. The domain of the patrolman's
service activity is virtually limitless, and it is no exaggeration to say that the
solution of every conceivable problem has at one time or another been attempted by a police officer. (p. 709)

Skid row officers do arrest persons, but they do not do so as an end
in itself. Bittner (1967) asked one officer why he had not apprehended an
intoxicated participant in a conflict. To no one's surprise, "the officer
explained that this would not solve anything" (p. 720). The officers
arrest some participants in disturbances to prevent escalations of violence. They also arrest some persons "for their own good," especially
when they are helpless or self-destructive. A skid row officer explained
to Wiseman (1970) that

we pick them up for their own protection—they'd die on the streets if we
didn't. I think it should be unlawful to incarcerate an alcoholic... but without
other facilities to take care of them, it's inhuman not to incarcerate them.
Some men here admit they're alive today because we picked them up and
dried them out. (p. 77)

When skid row officers arrest skid row denizens, it is because an
arrest serves some other purpose. "It is the rare exception," writes Bittner (1967), "that the law is invoked merely because the specifications of
the law are met." The law is used, says Bittner, "as a resource to solve
certain pressing practical problems in keeping the peace" (p. 710).

Officers generally prefer to use constructive alternatives to arrests
where such alternatives are available:

This fact becomes partly visible when one views the treatment of persons who are not arrested even though all the legal grounds for an arrest are
present. Whenever such persons are encountered and can be induced to
leave, or taken to some shelter, or remanded to someone's care, then patrolmen feel, or at least maintain, that an arrest would serve no useful purpose.
That is, whenever there exist means for controlling the troublesome aspects
of some person's presence in some way alternative to an arrest, such means
are preferentially employed, provided, of course, that the case at hand involves only a minor offense. (Bittner, 1969, p. 710)

Wiseman (1970) makes comparable observations, and she provides
illustrations such as the following:

If a man looks like he can make it home and he lives in the neighborhood, he is told to "take a hike down the pike."

Police will actually deliver men to the mission or some other halfway
house rather than arrest them. If they look clean and have been at the Christian
Missionaries before, we might take them there to see if they can get in. (p. 69)

Officers at times even refrain from arresting where there is active external pressure for them to make arrests, provided that inaction serves problem-centered ends. Wiseman (1970) cites one such incident from an interview with an officer:

> We also have to deal with places where these men congregate, get tanked up, and then go out and make trouble. The Blue Sky cafe used to be a haven for these guys. The owner didn't care. He wouldn't cooperate. We busted guys there regular, but it didn't do much good. Finally, after trying to get the cafe owner's license revoked, we hit on putting him out of business by giving him *no* police protection. He'd blow his whistle and call for the police and we'd just stand across the street and pretend we didn't hear. The alcoholics got in fights, broke the place up. He was out of business in three weeks. (p. 70)

Wiseman (1970) does not take a propolice stance, but points out that the seasoned skid row patrolman is "proud of the empathy he has for the Skid Row residents and their problems." One officer confided to her that

> you have to know how they feel. We know the hangovers and the dry heaves ourselves. Consequently, we know them and have compassion for them. (p. 69)

One reason why Wiseman sees policing as a double-edged enterprise is that the particularistic criteria the policemen use in making enforcement decisions are inexplicit, which means that the offenders who are arrested may not understand why they have been selected as suspects. Wiseman (1970) writes:

> Once the chronic drunkenness offender becomes aware of the manner in which the drunk ordinance is applied, he is inclined to become angry that almost all of the police criteria for arrest seem extraneous to whether he is, in fact, really drunk. He knows that danger of arrest is highly dependent upon geographic, social, and bureaucratic factors, and the knowledge galls him. (p. 78)

Once skid row denizens have been jailed in this fashion, Wiseman portrays their processing as less than humane. Such injustices loom large in the eyes of the homeless alcoholics and contribute to the salience of the policemen's reputation as rabid law enforcers. Simultaneously, the officers get insufficient credit for peacekeeping activities, which are mostly taken for granted.

Before the advent of the problem-oriented policing movement, police human service activities were also not credited by other service workers, who persisted in seeing all police officers as crime fighters rather than as partners in service delivery. This observation was first made by Cumming, Cumming, and Edell (1965), who concluded from a careful study that the policeman's supportive acts are not only the latent and hence amateur part of his role, they are also latent in not being recognized and legitimated by the other agents in the integrative system. These others, our own studies show, prefer to recognize the policeman's professional controlling function, which they both need and often call upon. Thus, it is as an agent of control that the policeman participates in a divided labor with social workers, doctors, clergymen, lawyers and teachers in maintaining social integration. The problems he faces appear to be a *failure of integration within the integrative system*, so that he cannot mobilize the other agents when he needs them. (p. 286; emphasis in the original)

FROM NATIVE WISDOM TO PROBLEM SOLVING

From the details we have provided, it should be clear that it makes no sense to ask whether skid row policing is problem oriented or not. In one sense, the answer is "skid row policing is clearly problem oriented," but we must add, "not quite in the way we nowadays use the phrase." What we can next ask is how we could make skid row policemen problem-oriented officers in the current sense of the term.

At least part of the answer to this question pertains to the agency in which the officers work. The skid row officers are distinctly permitted to work without encumbrance or interference. Middle managers (sergeants) seem to respect their work and approve of what they do. Other managers who were interviewed by Bittner seem sympathetic. But peace keeping is almost impossible to measure. Arrests can be counted, but the events the skid row officer has prevented (such as escalated confrontations and victimized drunks) are accomplishments he cannot claim in the absence of baseline measurements. Even more intangible achievements (such as persuading incapacitated individuals to call it a night) must stand unrecorded, and thus unrecognized.

The police department in which the skid row officers work clearly accommodates them, but we have no way of telling how it recognizes their achievements and rewards them. Does the police department define skid row peace keeping as "real policework" at the explicit core of its organizational mission? Are the skid row officers prized intrapreneurs, or just a valued sideshow?

Similar issues pertain to the officers themselves, who know they do a good job but cannot verbalize what it is. The officers have evolved informal group norms. Bittner (1967) points out, for example, that "patrolmen who are 'not rough enough,' or who are 'too rough,' or whose roughness is determined by personal feelings rather than situational exigencies, are judged to be poor craftsmen" (p. 701). These rudiments of definition tell us what quality peace keeping is not, as the officers see it. But what makes for a quality cop on skid row and how can colleagues spot such a cop when they see him?

The officers try hard to avoid this sort of question, and the reason for their reticence is instructive. On the one hand, the officers believe there are constructive solutions for problems and that one's experience supplies them. One's experience is (instantaneously) available where it is relevant, and it supplies answers. It dictates a correct course of action to the officer who is experienced — even paradoxically, to the rookie — but it cannot be communicated to the inexperienced. By the same token it cannot be dissected because a review would destroy it and you can always know it when you see it.

But a fly in this ointment is that not all officers are infallible. And if experience is a reliable guide, how can some experienced officers be less competent than others, and react emotionally, for instance, oversentimentally, angrily, inflexibly, or harshly? If undesirable traits of undesirable officers (such as skewed law enforcement philosophy or sentiment) can neutralize the benefits of their experience, why are more beneficent traits (such as compassion) irrelevant to the deployment of experience? And if varying dispositions can dictate different actions to different officers, how can experience in general serve as an infallible guide to correct decisions? The officers sense this inconsistency, and try to beg it, because it means that there must be other ways of defining the correctness of decisions than the experience of their originator. Such thoughts are threatening because they open the prospect of second-guessing decisions, which is unwelcome.

The second issue pertains to the nature of police experience itself. The officers make rounds, ask questions, and garner a great many facts. They assume (as did Sergeant Friday) that the facts they collect speak for themselves. But they intuit at some level that facts cannot speak for themselves: Facts (Sergeant Friday notwithstanding) must be interpreted and must be culled when they get applied. The process entails more than careful storage and instantaneous retrieval, which the officers prize.

The officers prize blind intuition, but no one doubts their capacity to theorize about the problems they encounter. For some reason, the officers do not credit themselves with insights, perspectives or premises for action, articulated conceptions or preconceptions, goals or objectives.

The officers have skills, but deny that they could describe them. They clearly exercise options when they act, but pretend that they have no rationale for these options. And though the officers prize learning (a word that means "to profit from experience") they cannot learn from each other, because they do not seriously discuss their work.

Officers have awesome knowledge, but cannot fully perfect it. They can repeat mistakes (which are "experience"), assuming successes. Typical encounters are experienced, but so are atypical ones. To tell the difference between typical and atypical experiences one must check experiences against those of others. Better still, one must seek knowledge other than experience to gain added perspective.

Street knowledge is solid knowledge, and it is unquestionably valuable. Those of us who lack it (academics concerned with the real world) must get it second hand. But street knowledge has to be pooled to achieve reliability and it must be supplemented to attain validity. Only after reliability and validity are secured does experience become the ideal basis for rational decisions and problem solving.

Skid row presents many police problems, and the skid row officers address them. There are individual problems, such as stopping a fight or securing medical care for a person who needs it. There are larger-scale problems, such as incipient riots and the proliferation of aggressive mendicants. Still other problems are composite problems that can best be addressed in patterned fashion. Soup kitchens may be ill-attended, for example, and men may go hungry for lack of knowledge or transportation. Both problems might be solved if one circulates information and arranges busing.

Skid Row officers solve problems mostly tactically, which is not the same as solving them strategically. The officers intervene mostly individually, or in ad hoc groups. They do not team up, or invoke other resources (community agencies, for instance) as partners in joint ventures. Actions are only patterned in the sense that officers may independently pursue similar results in comparable ways.

Problem-oriented skid row policing would require the officers to formulate their goals based on careful analysis of skid row problems. It would force the officers to discuss policing strategies for achieving their goals. And it would require them to choose among their options those that make most sense. In other words, the officers would have to surface their knowledge and face the problem-solving processes they employ.

The officers might usefully peruse a roster published by the Police Executive Research Forum (no date), which is entitled "The Key Elements of Problem-Oriented Policing." If they did so, they would discover that that approach is not alien to them, but simply a more systematic way of going about the peace-keeping venture in which they are engaged. The officers would discover that if they followed the prescription (with support from their agency), they could have greater impact. They could better ameliorate skid row problems that now concern them and could do so in a more thoughtful and thought-provoking way. The roster reads as follows:

- A problem is the basic unit of police work rather than a crime, a case, a call, or an incident. A problem is a group or pattern of crimes, cases, calls, or incidents.
- A problem is something that concerns or causes harm to citizens, not just the police. Things that concern only police officers are important, but they are not problems in this sense of the term.
- Addressing problems means more than quick fixes; it means dealing with conditions that create problems.
- Police officers must routinely and systematically investigate problems before trying to solve them, just as they routinely and systematically investigate crimes before making an arrest. Individual officers and the department as a whole must develop routines and systems for investigating problems.
- The investigation of problems must be thorough even though it may not need to be complicated. This principle is as true for problem investigation as it is for criminal investigation.
- Problems must be described precisely and accurately and broken down into specific aspects of the problem. Problems often aren't what they first appear to be.
- Problems must be understood in terms of the various interests at stake. Individuals and groups of people are affected in different ways by a problem and have different ideas about what should be done about the problem.
- The way the problem is currently being handled must be understood and the limits of effectiveness must be openly acknowledged in order to come up with a better response.
- Initially, any and all possible responses to a problem should be considered so as not to cut short potentially effective responses. Suggested responses should follow from what is learned during the investigation. They should not be limited to, nor rule out, the use of arrest.
- The police must proactively try to solve problems rather than just react to the harmful consequences of problems.
- The police department must increase police officers' and detectives' freedom to make or participate in important decisions. At the same time, officers must be accountable for their decision making.
- The effectiveness of new responses must be evaluated so these

results can be shared with other police officers and so the department can systematically learn what does and does not work.

A HYPOTHETICAL EXAMPLE

Let us assume that the officers have decided to become a problem-oriented skid row police team. Led by their supportive and kindly sergeant, they review, discuss, and prioretize some of the problems they see on skid row. The problem they decide to start with (after taking a vote) is the victimization of skid row alcoholics by skid row alcoholics. They all have some theories about this problem, which they would like to test. They also think alternatives are needed, because they feel that the offenders in these incidents are not standard muggers and assaulters, for whom prison would be the remedy of choice.

The officers decide to collect information about patterns of robberies and assaults. They divide into two subgroups, one of which is charged with studying data from arrest reports. This group obtains statistics from the Crime Analysis Section that provide them with demographic profiles of the offenders and victims in skid row incidents. The profiles show that the groups are similar except in age, with the offenders being younger than the victims (neither are spring chickens). The task force is also interested in the location of incidents; they discover, among other things, that assaults tend to take place on the street and in furnished rooms after bouts of congenial drinking. Many muggings occur in shelters, which offer dormitory accommodations.

The task force draws a smaller sample of arrest reports and reviews narratives for clues as to why incidents arise. Minor disputes often have to do with issues of proprietorship relating to bottles of wine. One issue that frequently arises is that skid row norms about the sharing of beverages can break down at critical junctures. Other issues have to do with the discontinuance of drinking bouts by individuals who are classified as "kill joys."

The second task force is charged with interviews, and it concentrates on victims of recent incidents. Special interviews are conducted with repeat victims. The task force concludes that these men are often of low intelligence and gravitate into ill-chosen groups in search of acceptance. Predators may see the victims as socially undesirable but associate with them because they are easy marks. The task force notes that some victims claim memory lapses that seem genuine. Other victims list skid row figures they have learned to fear and point to locations they have learned to avoid. Other interviews center on staff who are attached to locations (such as shelters) cited as high-risk locations and those (such as missions) in which few incidents occur. The high-risk staff complain about manpower shortages that keep them from monitoring their charges. They also blame the police for offering inadequate protection. Low-risk staff cite rules they enforce, such as the following:

- Curfew is at 11 o'clock every night and a man who leaves the Center (to go to a movie, visit a friend, etc.) and returns after that time will find himself locked out.
- Men must have passes to visit relatives, to stay away from the Center overnight, to go job hunting, or see the doctor during the day. All time away from work must be made up. No weekend passes are issued until a man has been in the Center for 30 days.
- All private property, such as typewriters, radios, and electric shavers, must be checked in upon arrival and stored until the beneficiary leaves or rooms alone.
- Once a man has left his room in the morning, he may not return until 5:00 P.M. (This rule holds even when the weather turns cold or there is unexpected rain and he is without a jacket.)
- There must be no drinking on or off the premises.
- Lockers are inspected periodically for stolen goods. "Girlie" magazines or liquor are forbidden. (cited in Wiseman, 1970, p. 17a)

Having completed their research, the task forces get together to discuss their findings and to explore ways of addressing the problems they have highlighted. Among the diverse intervention options they discuss, some are enthusiastically tabled. These include proposals to

1. Publish a "Crumb of the Month" poster with a picture of a known predator containing the message, "If you drink with this man, your life may not be worth a plug nickel."
2. Run seminars for drunks on party etiquette, covering topics such as "being a good host–guest" and "how you can gracefully adjourn while you can still stand up."
3. Run a program of interpersonal skills training for socially inept alcoholics, which would be mandatory for repeat victims.
4. Define unconsciousness of victims as contributory negligence when they are mugged, and deprive such victims of the right to file complaints.
5. Use decoy officers in high-risk locations who look scraggly and shopworn and are entitled to reimbursement for alcohol they consume.

More consequential suggestions are also advanced, and two are selected for implementation. The first program aims at preventing incidents in the single-residence hotels and shelters that have shown higher-than-average rates of muggings and assaults. The program calls for a meeting with all the managers of the facilities. This meeting would focus on steps the managers might be prepared to take, such as rules that they might be willing to institute governing social interactions, drinking, and the disposition of possessions. The assumption would be that these rules could vary in restrictiveness but would be made firmly known to residents when they check in, with the intention of being enforced. In turn, police would supply intensive backup such as increased patrolling (for instance, periodic checks of dormitories) and an eviction service covering rule violators. The latter would be housed in makeshift lockups, assuming minimal cooperation. More recalcitrant individuals would be arrested and taken to jail.

There would be a lead-in period during which the managers would keep logs of incidents in their facilities and the police would keep track of complaints. These data would be one of the sources of documentation in evaluating the program. Records would be additionally kept of number and types of eviction, arrests and dispositions.

The second program the officers adopt involves enlisting residents in a Crime Prevention Task Force. In organizing the task force, the officers would canvas the "better elements" among their constituents for expressions of interest. The officers would carefully explain that task force membership would provide the opportunity to help prevent victimization among skid row residents. A second advertised goal of the task force would be to devise nonpunitive means of social control, so that one could confine arrests to situations in which there is no choice except to send someone to jail.

Among the incentives for task force membership would be an armband the skid row resident could wear while certifiably sober and engaged in task force business. Given these same contingencies, the task force members could ride as passengers in police cars, and they would have restricted use of police facilities.

The first order of business for the task force would be a joint meeting of the officers and members to discuss future plans in general terms. Subsequent meetings would be restricted to those who commit themselves to participate. These meetings would be brainstorming sessions aimed at originating proposals for action. The officers would start by describing the victimization problem, using the data they have collected plus relevant illustrations. Other task force members could add experiential details to this picture, relying on their knowledge and impressions.

Any proposals the participants regard as sensible would be thoroughly discussed. The discussion would focus on issues of ethics, practicality, and effectiveness. To be adopted, a proposal would have to be humane and have short-term payoff and some means to assess it. It would also have to provide tasks for officers and residents who are members of the task force.

After proposals are approved, responsibilities would be allocated to individuals who express interest in the interventions, and they would form project-related subgroups. These subgroups would report to periodic meetings of the task force convened to review their progress. Backup projects would also be available in case some of the interventions turn out to be impracticable or ineffective.

All proposals that are approved by the task force would be described to the Chief of Police. The chief would have to attend a plenary task force meeting for this purpose. Successful projects would also be publicized and participating task force members would receive recognition for their efforts. It would further be assumed that if short-term interventions are completed, longer-term programs would be considered by the task force.

BUILDING ON A FOUNDATION

Our hypothetical program is more than a "pipe dream" because it is compatible with the style of policing extant on skid row. One important fact is that the officers are not tied to their radios, nor are they under pressure to accumulate arrests and citations. They have autonomy, which they use with self-conscious verve, both in the way they patrol skid row (circulating through favored hot spots) and in the actions they take. The officers view skid row as a unique but familiar world, which has unique but familiar attributes. They do not apply preconceived categories—such as legal definitions of offenses—to incidents they encounter, nor of offenders, to people.

The enterprise in which the officers see themselves engaged (keeping the peace) is compatible with problem solving. Whereas police often prize a fraction of their activities—playing cops and robbers—and deemphasize the rest of their work, skid row officers see everything they do as relevant to their mission. They boast of samaritan acts and of ingenious alternatives to arrests. And where the officers do arrest, it is because the offenses are serious or arrests achieve other ends, such as preventing injury or violence. The context in which the arrest takes place tends to define its purpose, which means that this context (and/or the dispositions of the offender) must be assessed before one intervenes.

Assessments take place in terms that sound very problem oriented. Police evaluate categories of contexts—such as disputes apt to degenerate unless the parties are separated—or categories of persons—such as men too intoxicated to take care of themselves. Such categories cannot be formulated without some preconception of causation or understanding of processes, such as the escalation of alcohol-infused conflicts. These understandings and preconceptions are in no way different from social science theory, except in the reluctance of the officers to theorize. Nor are the officers' interventions different from social science-based interventions, other than in the modesty ("We simply use street sense") with which they are characterized.

Molière once wrote of a man who became a self-styled intellectual after he discovered that he had spent his life talking prose. The officers could have a similar experience vis-à-vis problem-oriented policing. To become problem oriented, the officers would have to surface the problem solving they inchoately do, and begin to do it consciously. The remainder of what is called for is simply the systematizing of the assessment and analysis process, the pooling and supplementing of knowledge, the invoking of resources, and last but not least, the documenting of impact. None of this should be alien to the officers nor should it threaten their department. It carries benefits for both the officers and their employers, and contributes to the professionalization of police.

The contention that this is the case will be one of the subjects of our next chapter, Chapter 2, which will summarize experiences that are recognized problem-oriented "classics." We shall contrast these experiences with problem-solving efforts that do not engage officers as social scientists, and explore how experiential wisdom and formal knowledge can be combined.

In Chapter 3 we discuss problem-oriented policing as an example of work reform and show how this approach is congruent with what industrial psychologists know about work motivation and how to raise it. Two trends—job enrichment and industrial democracy—seem particularly applicable to interventions such as problem-oriented policing.

Chapter 4 deals with change issues, which have to do with introducing innovations such as problem-oriented experiments into organizations such as police agencies, which often resist change. Chapters 5–10 deal with a problem-oriented experiment whose results are available for review. This experiment can be traced step by step, because we tried to keep track of what happened as the process unfolded.

In the last chapters we return to current trends—including community-oriented policing and combinations of policing concepts—that strike us as particularly useful if applied to the drug crime problem, which defies more conventional solutions.

NOTES

1. Progressive reformers wanted educated officers who were versed in science and concerned with social welfare. MacNamara (1977) writes about Vollmer—the father of the professional police movement—that "(his) prototype police officer would be at home with the microscope or polygraph, courageous and physically capable of handling street disorders, trained in fingerprinting and photography, adept at first aid, a marksman of military bearing and skills, yet so certain of his manhood as to be able to deal humanely, effectively, and sympathetically with lost children, beaten wives, and bereaved parents" (p. 180).

   Vollmer and his contemporaries envisioned "professional" management for their "professional" officers. They prized the prospect of streamlining agencies, instituting centralized reporting, and efficient chains of command. Paradoxically, they thus reinforced bureaucratization trends that stifle the initiative of officers. Walker (1977) points out that

   > Bureaucratization entailed the development of formal and elaborate internal procedures (civil service, training programs, etc.) that subjected the police officer to more direct control and supervision. The control of the rank and file was in fact regarded as the great accomplishment of police reform. But this was not the same as professionalization, if by that concept we mean enhancing the independent judgment of the practitioner. The police in the 1920s, however, were not evolving in the same direction as the recognized professions. Rather, police officers were regarded as objects to be controlled and directed by chief administrators. If anything, it was the police chiefs who were professionalizing, and doing so at the expense of the rank and file. (p. 136)

2. Foot patrol was preferred because of this attribute. An expert of the time (Graper, 1921) points out that "the policeman patrolling on foot has greater opportunities of studying his post and of becoming acquainted intimately with its peculiar needs than has the man who is burdened with a horse or a bicycle. He cannot cover quite as much ground in the same time, but he can cover it more thoroughly" (p. 130). Other perceived advantages included the fact that a patrolman could sneak up on a malefactor, whereas the clatter of hoofs "gives ample warning of his approach" (pp. 131–132).

3. Graper (1921) refers to the first experiment involving motorized officers. He writes that

   > A novel system of patrol has been inaugurated by Chief Vollmer in Berkeley, California, from whose police department so many progressive ideas have come during recent years. Every member of the force is required to own a gasoline driven automobile and to operate it in the course of his daily work. The men are assigned to regular posts but cover them differently every day. The policeman's automobile is equipped with policeman's implements, ropes and hooks to be of aid to the fire department and to help stalled teams and motor vehicles. For the purchase and upkeep of the automobiles the city allows each policeman $27.50 in addition to his monthly salary and furnishes gasoline and oil besides. An ingenious signal system enables the members of the force in a few minutes' time to surround any block from which trouble is reported at any time of the day. This radical departure from the ordinary methods of patrol indicates that in some cities at least, new methods are being tried and attempts are being made to lift police service to a higher state of efficiency. Reports indicate that the system in use is giving entire satisfaction. (p. 133)

4. As recently as the 1950s, it was assumed that officers would *not* remain in their cars between calls, but would be foot patrolmen a good portion of the time. O. W. Wilson (1952), for example, insisted that

> In some respects the distinction between foot and motorized patrol is unfortunate. All patrolmen should be thought of as being foot patrolmen and should be required to perform the usual routine patrol duties including inspectional tasks...The vehicle transports the patrolman from one task to another, brings him to the scene with greater speed and less fatigue, and enables him to capture a fleeing criminal.
>
> When the patrolman with an automobile performs all the duties of a foot patrolman, he must spend a large part of his time on foot. This provides opportunity for observation and for contact with citizens and thus enables the patrolman to serve as the eyes and ears of the department...The patrolman who remains in his vehicle hidden in a secluded spot when he is not driving is not providing patrol service. The officer who spends all his time driving neglects his duty to make inspections, to observe, to make himself available for public service, and to make contacts with citizens. Protection against weather and relief from fatigue by occasional periods spent in driving from one location to another are to be used with discretion. (pp. 84–85)

5. Most technical innovations in policing have given managers greater control over the behavior of subordinates, and subordinates have exercised ingenuity to evade such control. Walker (1977), in discussing the introduction of two-way radios, mentions that "patrolmen developed ingenious techniques for subverting the effect of the new communications system and preserving for themselves an important degree of autonomy" (p. 136).

An earlier innovation was the patrol box, which the officers had to contact at prescribed intervals. This strategy was viewed as inadequate by officials because it "does not necessarily mean that patrolmen are performing their duties for they may loaf in cigar stores, barber shops, restaurants and other places between pulls of the box" (Graper, 1921 p. 152). To such concerns of managers and reformers, the officers reacted with understandable hostility. Walker (1977) explains that "much of police history could be told in terms of a cat and mouse game between patrolmen and their supervisors. From the earliest call boxes to the modern two-way radio, administrators have sought some means of monitoring the activities of their men. Patrolmen, for their part, have been equally ingenious in their efforts to nullify and subvert the latest technological innovations" (p. 13).

2

Police Officers as Applied Social Scientists

The role of the problem-oriented officer is a new role (see Chapter 1) and, to some, a threatening role (see Chapter 4). It is also a vaguely defined role, which means that the incumbents have to be brave, risk-taking pioneers who must conquer unexplored terrain, however strongly they may be backed by innovative superiors. The accounts we have available of problem-oriented experiments reflect this pioneering flavor and the uncertainty it brings. These accounts, however, also provide a sense of what it means for the adventure to culminate in a colonized frontier.

A case in point is the Baltimore County COPE project, one of the first self-styled problem-oriented police experiments. It took place in a traditional police department ("If you didn't bust heads or lock them up, you called social services"), which had acquired a new chief in 1977. The chief was a progressive administrator ("a risk taker from the start") who was interested in engendering reform. He saw his opportunity in 1981, when he encountered strongly felt community concerns that had been sparked by violent crimes. These community concerns had prompted county executives to authorize hiring 45 new police officers for the chief to deploy as he saw fit.

The chief decided to organize his new officers into a patrol force to fight fear. He appointed a project team, who organized the officers into three smaller units, comprising 15 men each. The units were to patrol their areas on motorcycles (a compromise between car and foot) to "have more direct contact with citizens." They were instructed to conduct "fear surveys" and "use any means within their power to quell fear" (Taft, 1986, p. 10). The three units had no other predefined mission and received no further guidance as to what they should do. They consequently embarked on the running of crime fear surveys ("like Fuller Brush salesmen"), which did not satisfy them. They also ran crime prevention meetings in their neighborhoods and complained of boredom. They proclaimed that they felt nostalgic about conventional police work, and "became frustrated by what they perceived to be severe limitations on traditional tactics being imposed from on high" (p. 12). The overt frustration level of the officers was now worrisome and the survival of the experiment was in doubt. At this juncture—six months into the project—the chief's advisors decided that "it seemed like an ideal time to bring in Herman Goldstein" (p. 13).

Herman Goldstein's 1979 article (see Chapter 1) was a prescription for managers, not policemen. The officers, fortunately, did not catch on to this distinction and applied the prescription to themselves. They liked the notion of doing research, brainstorming, and preparing action plans based on research results. "We needed a light at the end of the tunnel," one of them testified, "and this was our light" (Taft, 1986, p. 14).

A pair of the more enterprising officers descended on a housing project that had been noted for hostility to police. The officers conducted door-to-door surveys, compiled crime statistics, photographed potholes, and measured the borders of playgrounds. Their statistics showed that most crimes occurred after dark, and the officers decided to arrange for street lights to be repaired. They used their photographs to inspire the county to do road repair. They hypothesized that youth leisure was a crime-related problem and "badgered county park and recreation officials until a dormant rehabilitation and construction project was approved for a local park" (p. 15). The chief and his staff approved of the officers' predations ("By God, I think they got it") and rewarded them, and the COPE model was institutionalized.

Institutionalization of COPE (Citizen-Oriented Police Enforcement) meant that the officers had to perfect routines and procedures for studying and addressing problems in their neighborhoods. Taft (1986) reports that

> brainstorming sessions became longer and more spirited. "We would do action plans on a blackboard and argue about them for two days," says Off. Sam Hannigan of the central COPE unit. "We felt like we were in one of those self-improvement courses where they wouldn't let you go to the bathroom." Action plans grew thicker and more detailed. Officers grew more savvy in their negotiations with other agencies. "It got to the point where we came to expect the runaround," said Off. Blair Melvin of the central COPE unit. "We learned real quick to say, 'Let me speak with your supervisor.' " (p. 17)

One of the problems tackled by COPE was an apartment complex that had been terrorized by street robberies. The officer first assigned to the project did a survey of the residents and reported to his colleagues that

> he found that most of the residents were elderly women who felt particularly vulnerable to street attacks. Most were unwilling to leave their apartments after dark. Their feelings were exacerbated by the conditions of the complex: many street and building lights were broken; unkempt trees and shrubs created many hiding places; rats, stray dogs, and unrepaired structural damage all contributed to the feeling—widespread among residents—that they were trapped. (Eck and Spelman, 1987b, p. 40)

The COPE officers set out to get senior citizens organized. Neighborhood organizations provided technical assistance and the apartment residents soon had their own local association. A church provided meeting facilities, a baker supplied donuts, and a printer donated printing services.

The officers also arranged for street lights to be repaired and for buildings to be inspected. After the inspectors had made unflattering reports "the apartment manager bowed to accumulated pressures, and began to refurbish the buildings" (Eck and Spelman, 1987, 1987b, p. 41). In the wake of this flurry of actions, the string of robberies stopped and residential burglaries were sharply curtailed. Equally relevant as an outcome, "COPE provided the residents with better living conditions and a new Community Association that can help them obtain further improvements" (p. 41).

Another problem the officers tackled was a localized skid row population (see Chapter 1) of men who were enthusiastically involved in aggressive panhandling and who had become increasingly unpopular with area merchants. The chamber of commerce demanded police action. The officers drafted a no-nonsense panhandling statute, but "knew that even stiffer sentences would not prevent the vagrants from returning" (p. 18). In considering more enduring solutions, they turned to a model that had been devised by several police departments in the late 1960s, starting with a Vera Foundation experiment, the Bowery Project, in New York City. The most ambitious of these projects had been instituted by the St. Louis Police Department (1970), who went into the alcoholic treatment business. The St. Louis Department set up a Detoxification and Diagnostic Evaluation Center to which police officers brought chronic alcoholics they had picked up for counseling and therapy.

In communities in which police-sponsored detoxification centers had been established, experts had designed the programs and municipal executives had implemented them. In Baltimore County, for the first time rank-and-file officers did the spade work and the designing. They interviewed hospital officials, Salvation Army officers, welfare workers, and legal authorities and they questioned vagrants "to determine if they would use such a facility" (p. 18). They studied the services available to alcoholics and reviewed laws relating to drunkenness and vagrancy. As they did this work, they expressed incredulity ["At times we turned to each other and said, 'can you believe we are doing this?' " (p. 19)], but gained enthusiasm and considerable knowledge. When they presented their implementation steps, starting with a "Task Force on the Homeless" (which was instituted), they sounded convincing and authoritative.

COPE received prestigious awards, but was less successful in overcoming peer resistance. Taft (1986) observed that "often riding motorcycles and wearing leather jackets, COPE officers are considered 'glory boys' by their counterparts on patrol" (p. 21). He noted that the officers were viewed as something other than "real cops" who did "real police work" (p. 21). The sticking point was that COPE was not a crime-fighting unit. As one of the founders of COPE observed, "Let's face it: no matter what you say, people join police departments to chase criminals. It's cops and robbers. And it will be very hard to break that stereotype" (Taft, 1986, p. 29).

Patrol officer resistances of this kind have struck police experts as ironic because the experts see projects such as COPE as advancing the officers' interests. In the case of COPE, they saw impact "on the amount of power and responsibility that is vested in the individual officer...the...approach encourages the imagination, resourcefulness and intelligence of each officer...exploits the enormous amount of practical experience most officers possess" (p. 22). They also noted that projects such as COPE dilute the military hierarchy of police. As reported by Taft (1986),

> In at least one COPE unit, commanders and line officers have established such a good working relationship that, they insist, rank has become almost superfluous. "As far as I can see, the lieutenant and the sergeant are both one of us," says Off. Sam Hannigan of the central COPE unit. "We do surveys together. We go over action plans together. You could get rid of the titles 'lieutenant' and 'sergeant' and call them 'supervisor' and 'foreman.' " Says Ernie Bures, Hannigan's sergeant, pointing to his stripes, "I don't need these anymore." (pp. 23–24)

Projects such as COPE also garner esteem for the police. The citizens who came in contact with the problem-oriented officers said things like "talking to a COPE officer is like talking to a regular human being" (p. 26). A study that was done by an outside researcher showed increased citizen satisfaction in COPE precincts (16%), decreased fear (10%), fewer police calls (11%), and fewer offenses reported to the police (12%) (Cordner, 1986). On the other side of the ledger, bureaucrats declared themselves ambivalent and some of them "complained that COPE officers overstepped their bounds while tinkering with community affairs in their neighborhoods. 'It's the tail wagging the dog,' complained one....The lines of authority and responsibility start getting very gray" (Taft, 1986, p. 25).

Baltimore County established four COPE units and teaches problem solving in its police academy. It does not claim to have a problem-oriented police department. A police department in Newport News, Virginia has embarked on a direction that gets us closer to this objective.

THE NEWPORT NEWS EXPERIMENT

Darrell Stephens, ex-chief of the Newport News Police Department, said that "instead of creating a special unit or function, we asked line officers and supervisors to work problem solving into their daily routine" (Eck and Spelman, 1987a, p. vi). The premise of his department's effort was that "problem-solving can be applied by officers throughout the agency as part of their daily work" (p. xvii). The definition of problem orientation adopted in Newport News was that it is "an agency-wide strategy to encourage and guide all its members to engage in problem-solving" (p. 5).

Newport News started by setting up a task force "to develop and implement the problem-solving process" (p. 7). A task force is usually a group that represents a cross-section of an organization, which has been assembled to think through a specific topic. In the case of Newport News, the task force consisted of 11 "volunteers," ranging in rank from patrol officers to deputy chiefs (the chief sat in). The group also included a consultant from the Police Executive Research Forum, a member of the Federally-sponsored team that helped the police department with its project. One way in which this team helped was that it located promising police experiments that the task force visited and compared. An important outcome of these reviews was that "agencies that documented program effectiveness were more convincing to Task Force members than those agencies that only provided opinions" (p. 7).

The task force subdivided problem solving into a four-stage process, from problem identification to assessment of solutions. The group spent most of its time on the second stage, which it defined as "analysis, or learning the problem's causes and consequences." They developed a very detailed analysis guide, listing attributes of actors (offenders, victims, and third parties), incidents (including sequence of events and contextual factors), and responses to incidents (community and institutional responses) that they felt should be covered in a study of any problem the police might run across.

The task force next embarked on two ambitious problem-solving ventures. This shift from sandbox to battlefield was intended as a tangible demonstration and as an inspiration to the rest of the department's troops. In the words of Eck and Spelman (1987a),

> Work on these two problems accomplished three objectives. First, the two problems provided sources of information about the "real world" of problem-solving that could be used to develop the process and guide. Second, officers working on these problems received a great deal of recognition from senior officials. The experience provided by working on these problems demonstrated that department members would be rewarded for innovative approaches. Third, the successes in addressing the two problems convinced members of the Task Force, as well as other members of the department, that problem-oriented policing could work. (p. 7)

In the first project, a patrol officer was assigned to study thefts from the parked cars of shipbuilding workers in lots that surrounded the Newport News shipyards. In recent years, between 700 and 800 thefts annually had been reported; these thefts accounted for 10% of index crimes in Newport News. Yet, car thefts were not taken particularly seriously, since individual damage was low. Eck and Spelman (1987a) report that "when the problem was first posed for study by a member of the Task Force who had once patrolled the parking areas, the idea was met with much joking and criticism" (p. 73).

The officer the task force assigned to the project, Paul Swartz, started with offense and arrest reports covering a three-year period. He obtained a printout from the city's computer, and "hand tabulated the data in literally dozens of ways, focusing on three characteristics: when the thefts were committed, where they were committed, and who (probably) committed them" (p. 74). One result of the officer's painstaking analysis was that he was able to pinpoint "theft-prone" areas. Using spot maps, he identified seven vulnerable lots that invited the highest break-in rates.

Next, Swartz picked the brains of fellow officers and experienced detectives who worked the area, and talked to members of the shipyard's security force. Thereafter, he did something innovative: he "interviewed several thieves convicted and sentenced for breaking into vehicles in these parking lots. He promised the offenders that nothing said in the interviews would be used against them" (Eck and Spelman, 1987b, p. 43).

The offender interviews yielded rich information about the stealing habits of two clusters of geographically separated thieves:

> Swartz learned that drugs were a prime target of the northern thieves, but stereo equipment and car parts were also targets. They especially looked for "muscle" cars, cars with bumper stickers advertising local rock and roll radio

stations, or cars with other evidence that the owner might be a marijuana smoker or cocaine user. (Thrush [an interview subject] related that a roach clip or a feather hanging from the rearview mirror, or a corner of a plastic bag sticking out of the glove compartment were dead giveaways.) Thrush confirmed that the northern thieves worked together...

Further interviews confirmed and extended Thrush's testimony. The southern thieves were after money, rather than drugs; as a result, they concentrated on car stereo equipment, auto parts, guns, and other goods that could be fenced easily. Although they worked independently, they did know one another. (Eck and Spelman, 1987a, p. 75)

Swartz was now armed with a mine of information, which he disseminated in the form of crime analysis bulletins and talks at patrol lineups. Within weeks, three prime suspects were arrested *in flagrante delicto*, and the theft rate in parking lots dropped. This short-term result was regarded as a testimonial to a problem-oriented inquiry, in that

...the police department's response to the theft from vehicles problem involved mostly traditional tactics—interception patrol, plainclothes stakeouts, and the like. But these tactics were directed in nontraditional ways, through extensive analysis of police records, through the pooling of the street information known to individual officers, and through development of a new data source, the offenders themselves. As a result, patrol officers knew where and when to look, and for whom. Their efforts led to the arrest and eventual incarceration of the thieves many regarded as the most active. (p. 76)

The results of the intervention were also assessed by studying incident rates. The analysis was sophisticated and confirmed that the experiment could be deemed successful:

Time-series analysis of 39 months of reported thefts prior to the intervention and 16 months after...shows that the *number of reported thefts has been reduced by more than half* since the directed patrol tactics began in April 1985. This works out to a reduction of nearly one theft per day, or nearly 450 thefts prevented as of July 1986. (p. 76, emphasis in the original)

However, these low incident rates would be expected to jump back (and in fact, did) with diminishment of pressure. Swartz knew that he had to consider longer-term solutions and "suspected that other agencies and businesses would need to be involved if the long-run response was to be effective" (Eck and Spelman, 1987a, p. 75). His campaign yielded mixed (and, at times, amusing) results. The plant security force was willing to help, but they could only do so by disseminating information. Insurance companies argued that the problem was not "serious." Swartz found that

Although they paid a substantial amount in claims to their clients, the amount was small relative to other claims. Moreover, it was stable, so they were able to charge high premiums for comprehensive insurance and gain a tidy profit each year. A one-year reduction in thefts would mean a windfall profit for the insurers; but this would force them to reduce premiums, and they might lose money the next year if thefts returned to their earlier levels. (pp. 75–76)

A more favorable development occurred serendipitously: City Planning—which had never heard of Officer Swartz—studied parking as part of an ambitious urban renewal effort that included a plan for multi-level garages. A police detective with his ear to the ground learned of this venture. The detective had himself assigned to the site review board. There, he became the resident expert on "crime prevention through environmental design of parking lots and other...buildings" (p. 76).

THE BATTLE OF NEW BRIARFIELD

The second task force target problem was a low-income project "generally regarded as the worst housing in Newport News" (Eck and Spelman, 1987a, p. 66). This housing project had the highest burglary rate in the city, which was defined as a problem to be addressed. The police opened an office in a vacant apartment and and as a result the burglary rate dropped, but it jumped back when police moved out of their office. This failure of conventional enforcement became a challenge for the task force, which was looking for worthy problems to address.

The task was first assigned to a detective with civilian research assistants. This team went to work and found, among other things, that idle teenagers congregated in the development during school hours. These young truants were reputed (by residents) to pass their self-assigned vacations committing burglaries and acts of vandalism. Officers who were interviewed described a more comprehensive problem, which they called the "death cycle" of apartments:

First, a tenant moves out of the unit. Kids break in, remove anything of value, and vandalize the unit. This leaves the apartment unprotected: doors remain ajar, windows are broken. Unless the unit is quickly boarded up (and until recently, the apartment maintenance crew rarely did so), addicts and drinkers begin to take refuge there to get high, and kids continue to play in the structure. The unit deteriorates more quickly, now that it is exposed to the elements. The combination of weather and vandalism create structural defects in the exterior walls, floors, and ceilings; over time, these defects get worse, and may spread to adjacent units. Sometimes the unsavory users intimidate the legitimate residents next door. In any case, residents of neighboring units are likely to leave. This creates opportunities for other units to be broken into, pillaged, and made uninhabitable...In the end, the entire row of units becomes vacant. (p. 67)

What did remaining residents think of all this? To explore this issue the team ran a survey, after they pretested questions and moved mountains to obtain a high-response rate. The respondents in this survey spoke freely, and the picture they painted was bleak. They said that crime and the fear of crime had circumscribed their lives. For instance, "one young mother stated that she was so afraid of a break-in that she did not even keep food in the unit. Instead, she kept it at her mother's home and took a bus three miles whenever she had to prepare a meal" (p. 68). There were residents who did not go outdoors, and most adults never went out after dark.

Physical conditions were the residents' next most pressing concern. This concern was not only expressed in general terms, but was documented with illustrative instances:

Some told (and showed) interviewers real horror stories: in some units, roofs or floors had caved in and the residents left to the elements for up to six weeks; a water main had recently broken, flooding parts of the complex for nearly a month before it was repaired; cold drafts blew through large cracks in numerous door and window frames. (p. 69)

The sense of stark disillusionment and resignation that pervaded survey responses impressed the task force and reinforced its resolve to act. Eck and Spelman (1987a) point out that "prior to the survey, Task Force members were more likely to blame the residents for their plight than to sympathize with them. But after the survey the Task Force members became much more concerned about the community" (p. 71). The survey also had undergirded observations that had been made by officers about the intimate causal link between deterioration and criminal offenses:

It became apparent that the physical condition of the complex contributed substantially to the burglary problem. In fact, the poor and deteriorating conditions were one of the causes of the burglaries, as well as one of the consequences. (p. 69)

Officer Haddix, one of the members of the task force, "took it upon himself to improve the physical conditions at New Briarsfield" (p. 71). He persuaded the reluctant manager to have all trash removed, including from a swimming pool that had become an unsightly garbage dump. He arranged for streets to be cleaned, and for abandoned cars — which littered the area — to be towed.

The detective who had started the project now became a real estate detective. With the help of brokers and other experts on the machinations of tax deduction rackets, the detective located successive partnerships that owned and milked the deteriorated complex. He filed a detailed report of his findings with the chief, who relayed the document to the heads of city agencies, inviting them to attend a meeting under police sponsorship. This meeting was unique in that it became "the first combined action by Newport News city departments on any issue of its kind" (p. 71). The actions of the group were strong and decisive: Owners of the development were given 30 days to bring their buildings into code compliance or have the units demolished. HUD took over the complex, with the understanding that a new development was to be built. Two years later, the city bought the complex, which was finally demolished in 1989 (Police Executive Research Forum, 1989a).

A third officer, Officer Lyons, had moved into the area as a foot patrol officer and became a community organizer. He expanded a crime watch group and formed a second organization to lobby for tenant rights.

In the meantime, outcome data were collected. They showed a 35% drop in the local burglary rate, which had previously been going up. They also showed improvement in attitudes toward the police, and "a great deal of cooperation from the residents" (Eck and Spelman, 1987a, p. 72). Physical changes had occurred, and the complex "remained relatively trash free since the initial police cleanup efforts" (p. 72).

EXPANDING THE PROCESS

Task force members undertook problem-solving efforts and inspired other officers to join them to the extent to which their schedules permitted. Among the many projects that were initiated in this way were studies of domestic homicides, gas station driveoffs, assaults on officers, DWI (driving while intoxicated), disturbances at convenience stores, localized drug dealing, robberies in office buildings, commercial burglaries, vacant buildings, rowdiness in a skating rink, dirt bikes, and disturbances at a shopping center.

The assault project was typical of the smaller-scale efforts. It was a study conducted by a sergeant (female) in the internal affairs division, who reviewed a large sample (seven months) of police assault incident reports. The sergeant discovered one fact that was surprising: half of the incidents had occurred in the booking room of the headquarters building. On a hunch, the sergeant visited booking rooms in other police departments and concluded that "the layout of the room needlessly put arresting officers at risk of assault" (Eck and Spelman, 1987a, p. 91). The sergeant persuaded architecture students from a local university to redesign the room, which was later renovated.

The sergeant had simultaneously discovered that some of the younger officers appeared assault-prone, and that several of the offenders had been repeatedly involved. Based on these facts, she decided "to look at the problem from a psychological perspective, again with the help of local universities" (p. 92).

Activities such as these gave officers new and different experiences. Eck and Spelman (1987a) point out that Newport News policemen "have conducted literature reviews, interviewed prostitutes and thieves, surveyed businesses, held conferences with local public and private officials, photographed problem sites, and searched title and tax records" (p. xxiii). Most of the officers who had done such things testified that they enjoyed the activities and prized the knowledge they acquired. They said that they found research tasks "more interesting than chasing calls for service or investigating reported crimes, especially when problem-solving periods were interspersed with periods of doing more traditional police work" (p. 93). Some officers, on the other hand, "[became] impatient with analysis of problems for which the proper responses seem[ed] obvious to them" (p. 93). In fact, "the tendency to act before analyzing," according to Eck and Spelman (1987a), "still pervades the department" (p. 94). Eck and Spelman (1987a) also note that "there have been occasional grumblings from officers not assigned to solve problems that their problem-solving comrades have not pulled their fair share of incident-driven weight" (pp. 95–96).

According to the results of a police department survey, 60% of the Newport News force (and its entire top brass) found the problem-solving approach to be personally useful. This did not mean, of course, that the process had been institutionalized. Only a third of those who were involved in projects felt that "I have received the recognition I deserve for my efforts" (p. 98). This fact makes sense because, "although personal satisfaction from serving the public well is in itself a strong incentive, most officers rely on their fellow officers and supervisors when judging whether their efforts are worthwhile" (p. 100). A reward system of this kind was not systematically instituted and is difficult to design. Time budgeting was another constraint, since incident-driven policing makes peremptory demands. Assignments also proved too inflexible to allow all problem solvers to remain with problems until they were solved. Time pressures invite shortcuts so that "officers often skip the analysis step and jump directly into proposing the solution" (p. 101). Last, it is hard to change public perceptions of the police, and "explaining problem-oriented policing may be difficult" (p. 109).

APPLIED SOCIAL RESEARCH

Examples of problem-oriented policing in action help us to consider questions about its principal attributes. One of these questions pertains to the form the problem-oriented enterprise should take. An obvious option is to set up problem-solving teams, such as the COPE units in Baltimore; another is to encourage problem solving within an entire organization (such as the Newport News police department) by creating a climate that promotes it. Each of these choices has risks, and we shall review these in some detail in Chapter 4. We have seen that COPE had peer approval problems, which is a risk for compartmentalized innovations. By contrast, Newport News has problems that are usual where systemic innovations intersect with preexisting cultures.

A second question pertains to the officer's new role in problem-oriented change, as we shall discuss this in Chapter 3. The examples we have reviewed show officers shaping police activities, which means that they helped set organizational policy. The examples also describe activities that are unusual for police officers, such as organizing tenants, drafting statutes, and pioneering treatment programs. These activities are often more intellectually demanding than ordinary police activities and provide enrichment to the police officer's job.

A third set of issues will concern us now in the remainder of this chapter and pertain to research (knowledge acquisition) and reform. The link between these two lies at the core of problem-oriented policing, which assumes underlying conditions can be illuminated and solutions can be inferred from inventories of facts. This type of enterprise, which is applied social science, has been the purview of academics. Their success rate in implementing solutions has been low, but academics have to "sell" their suggestions while officers can implement theirs. Police also have power, which social scientists lack. As in the commercial about the broker, when police speak, people listen, since it is wise not to argue with a person who can make arrests.

Some problems of academics, however, apply to the police. One such problem is that of gaps between diagnoses and prescriptions, or between data and suggested implications for action. Social scientists and officers are well-intentioned people who want to see improvements in undesirable social conditions. Humane developments are intrinsically worthy, but this does not mean that one has data that document their desirability. All kids should have playgrounds, for example, and to promote the building of a playground is a noble and satisfying endeavor. But one may not have data that support the need for such projects, such as inventories of extracurricular pursuits of neglected children or observations that show playground sites (or prospective sites) converted into hotbeds of nefarious misdeeds. Such data tell us that one can solve two crime-related problems (the need for constructive play activities and the dismantling of a crime site) with a combinatory intervention. No such rationale applies where a disused lot is photographed on general principle with the preexisting intent of shaming a parks department into building a playground.

A caveat applies where previous data, collected elsewhere, have led to an inference that can be invoked because it covers the situation one has encountered. Such has been the case with the "broken windows hypothesis" (Wilson and Kelling, 1982), which holds that deterioration of a neighborhood leads to community disorganization, which very much includes high rates of crimes. This assumption justifies standard problem-oriented moves, such as cleanups, disposal of abandoned cars, new street lights, road repairs, and so forth. The approach makes more sense, however, with follow-up assessment to prove that the hypothesis applies. It is possible, for example, that steps taken have locally evanescent results, which suggests that cultural norms must be simultaneously addressed as physical improvements are effected. In other cases an empirically derived theory may be applicable, but there is no evidence that the appliers (the officers) have heard of it. Simply doing something because it has worked before does not qualify as buttressing. Conditions may be similar, but may also be in essential respects unique. Senior citizens, for instance, do not benefit from playgrounds and may find them offensive.

In several examples we have reviewed, the data undergird short-term interventions, which means crime fighting based on pattern description. Such is the case in the car theft arrests, in which analysis pinpointed types of violators. "Underlying conditions" are nowhere in evidence, and when such conditions are broached (by the detective arguing for architectural design) there are no data to support them.

New Briarfield is different because a data-based causal model is available. It is supplied by officers who observe crime–deterioration links in the "death" of apartment units. It is buttressed by survey data that describe trapped tenants and their disengagement. Subsequent police actions plausibly interrupt causal chains, which predict the effects of crime-infested abandoned buildings on the lives of remaining tenants. The project is a rare and sophisticated example of what the problem-oriented model looks like when all the inferential leaps can be made.

One difficulty is that the questions the typical analysis poses (who? where? how? to whom?) do not necessarily answer the question (why?) that pertains to causation. And it is not obvious that if we could answer this question, we have the means to neutralize causes, which are usually long-term, obdurate, complex, and linked to other causes. Detoxification, for example, does not neutralize causes of alcoholism and has no chance of curing hard-core alcoholics. But that is not really the point. A problem-oriented approach is not designed to remedy structural problems, but to make sure that one does not ignore them. And the first step to this end is to recognize that symptoms occur in groups, and have common origins. It also helps to get a feel for the human consequences of causal chains, as did the task force that reviewed the New Briarfield survey and sensed the alienation it depicted. Richer problem definition leads to more substantial responses, which can cumulatively make a difference that improves people's lives.

The best problem definition links experiential data with descriptive statistics, so that problems can be pinpointed and explored in depth. Officers may have a "feel" for a problem through close familiarity with persons who manifest it, but cannot distinguish typical from atypical manifestations of the problem. Managers may know the scope of a problem in quantitative terms, but have no sense of what it means in human terms when one meets it live on the streets. Each perspective requires supplementation from the other perspective, but each views the other as irrelevant. The problem has been described by Elizabeth Reuss-Ianni (1983), who writes:

> Reduced to its essentials, however, the conflict over how best to identify organizational or managerial problems and to seek data necessary for problem solving and decision making embodies a tension between those who look to the folklore of the job and those who seek scientific or rational solutions to management problems.
>
> Each method may be valid, but each also has its limitations. The experiential empiricism of conventional folk-wisdom or "war stories" of practice provide an existential mode of problem identification, at least of the practical problems of day-to-day policing. It does not, however, provide a means of systematic data seeking or of generalizing beyond individual experience, and is consequently easily dismissed by those looking for scientific solutions. Many established police procedures and practices thereby escape serious questioning or attention. Routine data collected, including activity logs, arrest and crime coding sheets, and statistics on response time, provide standardized means of gathering information on the job. But field personnel frequently dismiss the data and the findings derived from them as irrelevant to their problems. As a result, many practitioners fail to use any research-generated data for improving practice or setting policy. (pp. 18–19)

SCIENCE AND EXPERIENCE

Among plausible copouts (no puns) for an officer who is not interested in problem-oriented policing is to point out he is not qualified to do social science research. Officers who make this argument are either trying to be funny or needlessly diffident, since research design and statistics are communicable skills and other assistance—computer programming, for instance—can be rented. Specialized expertise, such as knowledge about real estate or architecture in Newport News, is also available in town or at campuses. Teaming officers and civilians carries fringe benefits in the form of cross-fertilization among interestingly different backgrounds.

Officers also have an advantage over social scientists. They have firsthand experience, which is combinable with other data to the benefit of both. Often, experience helps make sense of data, while data ratify experiences. But combining experience and data requires translation of one information source into terms that are assimilable by the other. This means that officers cannot maintain that their experience is ineffable and that their premises must remain unexamined. They cannot advance arguments such as:

> It's hard to explain why I did that and why it worked. I've been here a long time, and I've learned what makes these people tick. They know me too. I know that's no answer, but if you watch a pizza baker throw dough in the air and asked him what he did to make it come down in a circle all the time, he probably couldn't tell you either. It's just something you learn over time, is all. (J. Fyfe, personal communication)

There is no way of combining knowledge, defined in this fashion, with scientific findings, because science assumes that facts must be checked, while the officer argues that "the unique conditions and nuances of any police field situation cannot be precisely replicated" (J. Fyfe, personal communication). This is a self-serving assumption and must be challenged because it is not only antithetical to science but to rational problem solving. If police situations are unique, they call for unique responses, and there is no point looking for patterns among incidents or solutions to groups of situations.

Science must also accommodate experience. The scientist cannot argue, as some do, that "You cannot move from data such as crime statistics, to questions such as 'What does this tell me about Joe Blow?' And don't expect me to pay attention to war stories, though I'll grant that some are entertaining, in a repulsive sort of way." Cross-fertilization of knowledge presupposes that we recognize that

1. *Experiences are respectable data.* Experiences can be pooled; if some

are unrepresentative, this fact emerges (and can be corrected for) when we compare experiences. If experience tells me that people explode when I appear on the scene, yet other people elicit courteous responses in the same situation, this suggests that there may be reasons (such as my own behavior) for the difference between my experience and that of most people. If, on the other hand, others make observations comparable to mine, this suggests that we experience a reliable phenomenon which can be subjected to analysis.

Experiences always become data once they are recorded. The arrest report that memorializes my ineffable experience can be combined with other arrest reports. Items that may not have struck me as noteworthy (such as the age of the suspect or the presence of spectators) may emerge in tabulations as variables that help explain the outcome of my encounters.

The difference between experiences and data may be such that the former are an improvement on the latter. A questionnaire response suffers from brevity and may be biased by the question to which it responds. A narrative is richer and redolent with nuances that may illuminate a problem. Combined with the questionnaire response, the narrative aids interpretation and adds flesh to bones. Thrush the Booster (the Newport News car thief) may be worth hundreds of arrest reports, and—more critically—helps make sense of them.

2. *Experiences can be source of hypotheses.* The Newport News officers who described the "death cycle" of tenement dwellings advanced an experience-based theory, which was a richer theory than most social scientists can manage. This theory describes conditions that the officers had observed in revisiting the same locations over time. The theory portrayed stages corresponding to these conditions and made sense of them. We can verify whether these stages occur in the same order in other housing complexes and ask ourselves whether the same process is at work. If a hypothesis is not experience generated, it must stand the test of experience as a first check if it is to apply to real life. If I have a theory about car boosting that does not make sense to Thrush, chances are that I am wrong.

3. *Doing social science is experience.* Gathering data gives one a feel for the subject one is gathering data about, which explains why it is important for officers to do research themselves, rather than having it done for them. In doing a fear survey, the officer gets an intimate sense of the experience of fear and an enhanced appre-

ciation of why he should be concerned about fear. Doing research educates and changes attitudes and is used for this purpose in problem-oriented policing. Questioning citizens in living rooms provides officers with experiences that involve citizens as consumers of service rather than as suspects or complainants. Citizens who are surveyed have counterpart experiences, which involve officers as people-who-care. An equivalent benefit arises from questioning other officers, which places respondents in the role of experts, whose experiences and observations are valued. Other contacts—such as with bureaucrats—provide officers with a sense of how citizens must feel when their needs are unattended to.

FINDING RESEARCHABLE PROBLEMS

One way of introducing problem-oriented policing is to select entry points that are compatible with the premises of the model. One way of doing this has been a "soft" approach to goals, which opts for an area (such as fear) that invites a public relations rather than a crime-fighting perspective. A liability of this strategy (which we shall return to in Chapter 4) is that it reduces the credibility of the experiments to those who have a traditional view of the police mission.

A less risky criterion for selecting entry points is to ask whether the police face problems that they find puzzling and whether inferences can be drawn from research that would enhance police understanding of the problem. A second criterion would be whether enhanced understanding would help the police address the problem more sensibly and/or effectively.

Any police department knows of areas in which officers feel they could use greater understanding or where they respond with guarded confidence. In a review of problem areas that face a state police department, one such problem area had to do with citizens who react with unexpected hostility (and sometimes with violence) when they are stopped for violations. It would be of help to officers if they could better anticipate escalations and defuse them if possible. Data are available about this problem, particularly pertaining to extreme incidents, in which officers have been assaulted.

Another example facing the same agency has to do with an army base that has been opened in a remote rural setting. Officers who have dealt with farmers suddenly face a panoply of problems, some of which are enforcement related, and others service related. These problems

require networking arrangements that link the police force with municipal government and military authorities. Unfamiliar challenges face
these authorities, and information (such as inventories of incidents and
surveys of military families and area residents) could help officers formulate strategies to meet these challenges.

If problem-oriented policing is to help officers transcend their experience and respect data, it helps to start where the officers feel that their
experience falls short of guiding their actions. Such feelings spark a
desire for knowledge, which can be attained through research. Knowledge enhances understanding. It also guides action and makes it more
responsive and effective.

3

Participation and Work Enrichment

Police departments are paramilitary organizations. This means that police wear uniforms and are marched to and from classes during training. They receive orders that pass through chains of command. "In theory," write Eck and Spelman (1987a), "all the important policy decisions were made at the top. Line officers could legitimately make no decisions on their own, except perhaps the decision to quit the force" (pp. 22–23). Eck and Spelman (1987a) further point out that the tasks traditionally assigned to police were simple tasks, offering "limited opportunities for meaningful work, responsibility, and feedback" (p. 25).

The two attributes described in these quotes are not exclusive to the police, but have been the lot of most workers in most organizations since the advent of the industrial revolution. They are products of a philosophy that achieved its low point with an approach called "scientific management," which was the latest in management theory before World War I.

Scientific management was the brainchild of Frederick Winslow Taylor (1912, 1947a), a man who was obsessed with inefficiency, which he attributed to personal and group-supported laziness.[1] "The natural laziness of men is serious," wrote Taylor (1947a), "but by far the greatest evil from which both workmen and employers are suffering is systematic soldiering...which results from a careful study on the part of the workmen of what they think will promote their best interests" (p. 32). He charged that "so universal is soldiering for this purpose, that hardly a competent workman can be found in a large establishment...who does not devote a considerable part of his time to studying just how slowly he can work and still convince his employer that he is going at a good pace" (p. 33).

Taylor's solution to this insidious problem was twofold. First, he felt managers should ascertain the correct way of doing every job and write detailed instructions about how the work was to be done. Managers should realize, he said, "that *there is a best way in doing everything*, and that that best way can always be formulated into certain rules; that you can get your knowledge away from the old chaotic rule-of-thumb knowledge into organized behavior" (Taylor, 1912, p. 36, emphasis in the original). What Taylor meant by "rule-of-thumb" were the workers' own ideas about how to do their work, such as bringing their own shovels and shoveling coal in some favorite fashion.[2] He noted that time and motion studies had prescribed a standard shovel that holds 21 pounds, and that "the most efficient method of shovelling is to put your right arm down on your right hip, hold your shovel on your left leg, and when you shovel into the pile throw the weight of your body into the shovel" (p. 40).

Taylor called for the creation of a managerial class that would plan and direct the workers' activities in as detailed a fashion as possible. In his own factory, he wrote, "it meant the building of a large, elaborate labor office where three college men worked, besides their clerks and assistants, planning the work for each of these workmen at least one day in advance" (Taylor, 1947a, p. 39). The point that mattered to Taylor was that workers were not to think about their work, which was the prerogative of managers. In testimony before a congressional committee, he argued:

> it is next to impossible for the workman to develop a science. There are many workmen who are intellectually just as capable of developing a science, who have plenty of brains, and are just as capable of developing a science as those on the managing side. But the science of doing work of any kind cannot be developed by the workman. Why? Because he has neither the time nor the money to do it. The development of the science of doing any kind of work always required the work of two men, one man who actually does the work which is to be studied and another man who observes closely the first man while he works and studies the time problems and the motion problems connected with this work. No workman has either the time or the money to burn in making experiments of this sort. (Taylor, 1947b, p. 235)

THE HUMAN RELATIONS SCHOOL

Taylor was not only an autocrat but an industrial engineer for whom technology was the guts of production, with the human element subservient to it. Today he might be an expert on fast police response who would arrange for officers' deployment by incoming calls through an automated system. If this system made everyone unhappy, the expert would neither know nor care until the arrangement had been thoroughly sabotaged by alienated patrolmen.

The risks of such a technology-centered approach were recognized as early as the late 1920s, and the critique gave rise to a perspective called the "human relations school" of management. This school was first headquartered at Harvard and identified with a psychologist named Elton Mayo. The data on which the approach was based derived from a set of experiments referred to as the Hawthorne experiments, after the factory in which they took place. These experiments started with a study by engineers who sought to determine optimum illumination levels for fast output. Their findings did not make sense (production seemed to go up irrespective of lighting conditions) and a group of workers was assembled to explore the phenomenon. The workers experienced a variety of working arrangements, but seemed to find all of these irrelevant compared with their supervision (benevolent) and their fellow workers (congenial). The subjects in the experiment—which was known as the relay assembly test room—also made decisions about their work, but the importance of this fact was not discovered until decades later.

Many textbooks have discussed the experiment as showing what happens when beneficent attention is paid to subjects in social interventions. The argument goes that when one flatters persons who are accustomed to being part of a crowd by placing them on a stage (figuratively speaking), they will expend effort and show gratitude and high morale. This result—the so-called "Hawthorne effect"—is supposed to make any experiment work for a short period of time. Once the novelty wears off, however (the "honeymoon period" ends), impact on participants is expected to dissipate.

It can be argued on those grounds that problem-oriented pioneers performed well because they basked in the spotlight of their path-breaking status, but that commensurate results might not be obtained when problem-oriented policing becomes routinized and institutionalized (J. Fyfe, personal communication).[3]

The Hawthorne experiments included an observational study—the bank wiring room—in which observers observed workers sabotage efforts to make them work harder. The juxtaposition of contrasting experiences (relay assembly and bank wiring) suggested to the researchers (Roethlisberger and Dickson, 1961) that

> Much collaboration exists at an informal level, and it sometimes facilitates the functioning of the formal organization. On the other hand, sometimes the informal organization develops in opposition to the formal organization. The important consideration is, therefore, the relation that exists between formal and informal organizations. (p. 559)

There were groups of workers who seemed hell-bent on producing and others who followed Taylor's stereotype by limiting production, and it was hard to account for the difference. The experimenters concluded that engineers (like Taylor) did not hold the answer:

> From the Relay Assembly Test Room experiment they could argue that the company can do almost anything it wants in the nature of technical changes without any perceptible effect on the output of the workers. From the Bank Wiring Observation Room they could argue equally convincingly that the company can introduce hardly any changes without meeting a pronounced opposition to them from the workers. (p. 560)

To the experimenters, the answer seemed to lie in social arrangements involving workers and fellow workers and workers and supervisors. A group that felt respected, supported, and appreciated would in this view work hard. A group that felt affronted by demands of authoritarian managers and engineers—particularly if these demands disrupted group process—would retaliate by lowering production. Technological changes would be resisted because "they frequently result in the social dislocation of individuals and groups and disrupt the interpersonal relations which tend to give these individuals and groups their feelings of security and integrity" (p. 579).

Few episodes better illustrate this point than the rage that once surrounded the controversy (now being resuscitated) about the usage of one-person versus two-person patrol cars, after studies had suggested to police chiefs that two-person cars might be cost-ineffective and not appreciably safer than one-person cars. Whatever the merits of the studies, following their lead undersold the importance of riding partners to officers, which has been described as rivaling the intimacy of marriage.[4]

Police students—Reuss-Ianni, among others—contend that police chiefs have often ignored the social world of precincts, thereby earning the average officer's enmity. Reuss-Ianni (1983) writes that

> Management cop culture seeks to maximize the bureaucratic benefits of efficient organization, rational decision making, cost-effective procedures, and objective accountability at all levels of policing. As in all classical bureaucracies, the model proposed by management culture would do away with the organic and non-rational bounds among people as the basis for organization and decision making, substituting a consistent system of abstract rules and departmental operations and applying these rules to particular cases. (p. 6)

Reuss-Ianni sees the process as a vicious cycle in which interventions that violate the informal (street officer) culture produce further resistance to change. Speaking of police managers, Reuss-Ianni (1983) writes:

> Specifically, they have a "gut feeling" that informal social systems in the precinct are important, but have no clear understanding of what makes the informal social networks so critical to policing, nor how they operate. As administrators attempt to develop new programs aimed at reducing the discrepancy between "downtown" and the police officer's precinct subculture they seem compelled to somehow force these new programs into the existing formal structure of the department. That structure eventually corrupts the function, frustrates the administrator and usually increases the officers' alienation and cynicism. (p. 18)

Change resistance generalizes and can affect any intervention—however meritorious—that is presumed to originate from "above:"

> this conflict isolates the precinct functionally, if not structurally, from headquarters. The isolation produces disaffection, strong stress reactions, increasing attrition of personnel, and growing problems of integrity. This in turn reinforces street cop culture resistance to attempts by headquarters managers to introduce organizational change. (p. 4)

Early in the sequence of Hawthorne studies, personal interviews with workers were conducted for research and management training, and they were later continued as an end in themselves. Some 21,000 employees were interviewed, and these workers experienced the sessions as a testimonial to the company's interest in them, in contrast to the usual experience of anonymity, which they deplored. Workers expressed strong feelings about work-related conditions to the interviewers and talked about their personal problems, which seemingly benefited from being talked about.

The lessons that were derived from all this had to do with the need for a kinder, gentler work environment and for warm and considerate supervisors. The human relations school felt that workers must be decently paid, but that this was not enough. They concluded that workers need security, congenial fellow workers, and warm and understanding bosses who listen with empathy and care about workers as individuals.

CLIMBING MASLOW'S HIERARCHY

Human relations was an advance over Taylorism because it assumed that workers could be loyal to their employers and did not have to be bullied into working. In fact, a premise of human relationists was that directing production without considering the workers' perspective was counterproductive in that it invited resentment and resistance.

Human relations, however, less obviously agreed with some of Taylor's assumptions. It supported the view that people had to be seduced to produce and that production was the goal of managers and not

workers. Most modern developments in work and organizational reform—including problem-oriented police experiments—derive from the
demise of this long-standing assumption.

The key figure in the reframing of managerial perspectives—at least
in the United States—was a psychologist named Abraham Maslow. Maslow is known for a depiction of motivation as a stage-by-stage hierarchy
in which higher needs emerge as lower needs are satisfied. In Maslow's
words,

> Man is a wanting animal and rarely reaches a state of complete satisfaction
> except for a short time. As one desire is satisfied, another pops up to take its
> place. When this is satisfied, still another comes into the foreground, etc. It is
> a characteristic of the human being throughout his whole life that he is
> practically always desiring something. (Maslow, 1954, p. 69)

As work settings have progressed from Taylor to Mayo (with a little
help from labor unions), they successfully disposed of rock-bottom
physiological needs (by increasing pay), safety or security needs (by
affording retirement benefits), and social needs (human relations). This
meant that managers were now faced with the next higher set of needs,
which Maslow called esteem needs. These were needs that focused on
self-esteem or self-respect and on regard from others. The former needs,
according to Maslow (1954), include "the desire for achievement, for
adequacy, for mastery and competence, for confidence in the face of the
world, and for independence and freedom"; the latter comprise "the
desire for reputation or prestige (defining it as respect or esteem from
other people), status, dominance, recognition, attention, importance or
appreciation" (p. 90).

Once the two sets of esteem-related needs come to the fore, managers have the option of trying to satisfy these needs or of ignoring
them, which is tantamount to squelching them. Maslow (1954) writes
that

> Satisfaction of the self-esteem need leads to feelings of self-confidence,
> worth, strength, capability, and adequacy, of being useful and necessary in
> the world. But thwarting of these needs produces feelings of inferiority, of
> weakness, and of helplessness. These feelings in turn give rise to either basic
> discouragement or else compensatory or neurotic trends. (p. 91)

But this is not the end of the problem: If a manager could satisfy his
workers' esteem needs, he would find that many of the workers would
be happy, but some would not be. In Maslow's hierarchy, after esteem
needs are met, "we may still often (if not always) expect that a new
discontent and restlessness will soon develop, unless the individual is
doing what he is fitted for" (p. 91). The restlessness Maslow refers to has
to do with the highest human need (self-actualization), which is "the

desire to become more and more what one is, to become everything that one is capable of becoming" (p. 42).

Maslow's views about motivation were influential because they seemed to make sense. Less obviously, they raised questions many felt had to be raised about assumptions that had come down to us from Taylor in approaches that substituted carrots for Taylor's sticks. Incentives (whether positive or negative) were deemed necessary because we assume that work is a chore for most people, who want security, structure—and possibly congeniality—at work (McGregor, 1960). In Maslow's scheme this view describes workers who are motivated by lower-order needs. Higher needs (esteem, self-actualization), however, imply that a person needs work that gives him or her a sense of accomplishment or an opportunity to grow. Maslow told managers that if such needs (esteem, actualization) were not met, workers would become frustrated.

A more immediate implication related to styles of management. Security-centered workers were assumed to need direction, guidance, and structure, but persons governed by higher needs were deemed to prize autonomy and self-direction. Lower-need-motivated workers would have to be provided with rewards and higher-need-motivated workers would have to be afforded self-rewarding opportunities. They would have to be let loose to show what they could do, so that they could do their best. In the words of McGregor

> Management cannot provide a man with self-respect, or with the respect of his fellows, or with the satisfaction of needs for self-fulfillment. We can create conditions such that he is encouraged and enabled to seek such satisfactions for himself, or we can thwart him by failing to create those conditions. (McGregor, 1960, p. 92)

A different way of making the point about managerial style is to say that traditional management practices were congruent with needs of workers who were dependent children, or childlike adults. If we assume that workers are mature adults, this means that "formal organizations are willing to pay high wages and provide adequate seniority if mature adults will, for eight hours a day, behave in a less mature manner" (Argyris, 1957, p. 18).

The observation has a bearing on resentments such as those that one observes in locker rooms when The Chief is a subject of discussion. Chiefs are often oddly labeled (for instance, as "The Fifth Floor," "The Green-eyed Devil," "The Cardinal," etc.) and evoke ambivalence in officers. The depth of feelings that workers such as police have about managers has fascinated students of organizations, including Mayo and McGregor. McGregor (1944) has observed that adults who are treated like children can be expected to react childishly when they feel insecure. He has written that "the adult subordinate's dependence upon his superiors actually awakens certain emotions and attitudes which were part of his childhood relationship with his parents, and which apparently have long since been outgrown" (p. 56). Irrationality in work settings is invited by Taylorism, which treats adults as if they were children.

ENRICHING JOBS

Some implications of Maslow's perspective have been clarified by Herzberg, another well-known psychologist. Herzberg first asked engineers and accountants (and later, others) to recall memorable situations (critical incidents) that illustrated high points and low points of their work lives. In classifying the situations that were mentioned, Herzberg discovered that rewarding occasions invariably had to do with the work itself. By contrast, dissatisfying situations had to do with contextual factors, such as company policy and administration, supervision, salary, interpersonal relations, and working conditions (Herzberg, 1966).

Herzberg referred to this second set of conditions as "dissatisfiers." He also called them "hygiene factors," because he felt that their absence could spell an unhealthy work environment. In Herzberg's view, hygiene factors must be present in all work situations, but they can never inspire workers to work harder or better, except for short periods of time.

Satisfying experiences (motivators) pointed to factors that could make people work harder and better. These are five factors: opportunities for achievement, recognition, interesting or meaningful work, responsibility, and advancement. These commodities are of the kind that must be available in the job, and not in the context of the job, though recognition and advancement must be externally supplied. All motivators respond to higher needs, which implies that these needs are alive because lower needs (hygiene factors) have been met. Motivators also continue to engage higher needs, because they promote growth and stimulate further development.

The prescription in Herzberg's research is called "job enrichment," which simply means that jobs should be designed to enhance the sorts of motivators identified by Herzberg—a sense of achievement and recognition for one's achievement, work the person finds interesting and meaningful, greater responsibility, and the opportunity for personal growth and advancement. There are several other listings, but they are variations on Herzberg's themes. Hackman and Oldham (1976, 1980), for instance, suggest that jobs should offer skill variety, task identity (the chance to complete a whole piece of work), task significance (importance or impact on the lives of others), autonomy, and feedback (information about how well one has done). A diagnostic task identity question, for instance, is

> To what extent does the job involve doing a *"whole" and identifiable piece of work?* That is, is the job a complete piece of work that has an obvious beginning and end? Or is it only a small *part* of the overall piece of work, which is finished by other people or by automatic machines? (Hackman and Oldham, 1980, p. 298; emphasis in the original)

A parallel task significance question reads,

> In general, how significant or important is the job? That is, are the results of the person's work likely to significantly affect the lives or well-being of other people? (p. 299)

If one applies this prescription to policing, it is obvious that jobs in traditional police departments vary in the extent to which they supply these commodities. Task identity, for instance, is available to detectives, but not to patrolmen. Patrolmen may feed information they have gathered to detectives, who get credit for solving cases based on such information. Detectives tend to maximize task identity by concentrating on cases that can be solved. Task significance seems built into police work, almost by definition. But officers often feel that they are in fact accomplishing little, because citizens are indifferent and the criminal justice system undoes their work ("you take 'em in and they're back on the street the next day"). As for feedback, complaints such as "you are damned if you do and damned if you don't" suggest that officers get no sense that anyone knows when they do good work.

Enriched jobs are designed to inspire quality work efforts. Rewards derive from using skills to best effect, to accomplish something that matters. The excitement is in the doing, in seeing it done, and in knowing—and having other people acknowledge—that it is done well. None of this is possible if the criterion for assessing work is the number of widgets one produces, with no indication that widgets matter or that anyone uses them.

One cannot expect an organization to have much concern for quality production if it plays a numbers game in which numbers are ends in themselves, as are arrests or citations in some police agencies. If an officer is told to go forth and bring numbers, he must avoid situations that do not yield numbers and terminate "unproductive" encounters as quickly as he can. He must, of course, waste no time searching his soul about the validity, significance, or appropriateness of arrests that help meet his quota. Job redesigning requires that one reexamine Tayloristic criteria of productivity that leave no room for craftsmanship. This point has been made for the police by the National Advisory Commission on Criminal Justice Standards and Goals (1973), which has written that

> In evaluating performance, police departments rely heavily upon how many arrests officers make. Such a criterion, standing alone, is inappropriate as a measure of success in crime control unless factors such as the *quality of the arrest* or the *ultimate disposition of the case* are considered. Such a solitary standard may also distort measurement of the quality of policing on an individual level by ignoring such essential variables as an officer's use of discretion or his reputation for fairness and responsiveness to citizens. In no instance should the number of arrests be used as the only measure of an officer's productivity. Performance should be judged on the basis of criteria that reflect the necessary objectives, priorities, and overriding principles of police service. (p. 151, emphasis added)

Another prestigious group, the American Bar Association Project on Standards for Criminal Justice (1973) has pointed out that productivity must be differently assessed if the officer's job is to have meaning and purpose:

> Traditional criteria such as the number of arrests that are made are inappropriate measures of the quality of performance of individual officers. Instead, police officers should be rewarded, in terms of status, compensation, and promotion, on the basis of criteria...which directly relate to the objectives, priorities, and essential principles of police service. (p. 25)

What Maslow and Herzberg imply is that workers can thrive on meaningful work. This means that organizations such as police and workers such as policemen can have shared goals, such as quality policing. Workers (officers) can achieve their needs by taking pride in doing consequential things the organization (the police department) values. All it takes is for the organization to show that it approves of the skilled exercise of worker ingenuity and initiative.

THE WORK REFORM MOVEMENT

A Special Task Force to the Secretary of Health Education and Welfare concluded in 1973 that the needs of most American workers had changed to the point that job enrichment had now become a nonoptional reform. The Special Task Force (1973) wrote that

> Several events have occurred to make Taylorism anachronistic. Primarily, the workforce has changed considerably since his principles were instituted in the first quarter of this century. From a workforce with an average educational attainment of less than junior high school, containing a large contingent of immigrants of rural and peasant origin and resigned to cyclical

unemployment, the workforce is now largely native-born, with more than a high school education on the average, and affluence-minded. And, traditional values that depended on authoritarian assertion alone for their survival have been challenged.

Simplified tasks for those who are not simple-minded, close supervision by those whose legitimacy rests only on a hierarchical structure, and jobs that have nothing but money to offer in an affluent age are simply rejected. For many of the new workers, the monotony of work and scale of organization and their inability to control the pace and style of work are cause for a resentment which they, unlike older workers, do not repress. (p. 18)

The Task Force's case was buttressed by surveys that showed workers making new demands on jobs and on supervisors. One study covered a 25-year period (1950 to 1975) and 175,000 employees in a wide array of enterprises. The authors (Cooper, Morgan, Foley, and Kaplan, 1979) concluded that "all parts of the work force are beginning to overtly articulate their needs for achievement, recognition and job challenge" (p. 118). They traced this finding to the fact that "when these employees perceive their basic needs for adequate pay and job security are being fulfilled (as they are now), esteem-related factors...become more salient" (p. 123). The survey results showed that

The esteem-related items...are those that employees rate most critically. The decreases in favorable attitudes regarding equity, respect, companies' responsiveness to employees' problems, and advancement opportunities most clearly parallel the overall drops in ratings of job satisfaction....Thus the esteem-related items seem to account for the recent downturn in overall job satisfaction, while extrinsic items, such as satisfaction with pay, do not...The changes reported here are ubiquitous, pervasive, and nontransient. (p. 124)

One finding that is particularly relevant to the police is that young workers invariably show the greatest desire for work reform. Sheppard and Herrick (1972), for instance, report that

The labor force as a whole considered job content characteristics to be more important than the economic benefits derived from the job. The highest-ranked item among all age groups was interesting work.

Young workers placed even more importance than their elders on the nature of the work itself and far less on the comfort aspects of jobs. (p. 118)

The Special Task Force (1973), in its turn, concluded that

From our reading of what youth wants, it appears that under current policies, employers may not be able to motivate young workers at all. Instead, employers must create conditions in which the worker can motivate himself...The most rewarding race is probably one that one runs against oneself. (p. 50)

Another ominous finding for the police has to do with the fact that education increases the desire for esteem-related satisfactions and widens the gap between expectations and rewards. Police have come to prize educated officers, but have not made a commensurate effort to use education by taking it into account in work assignments or promotion. Overqualified workers tend to feel underutilized. Education also disposes them to chaff under do-as-you-are-told Tayloristic managers. In the words of a midwestern officer, "this was a smart breed of cats coming in, bright young college educated people who might not have a problem following the order, they're just asking why it is important" (*Grand Rapids Press*, August 10, 1981).

WHO DOES THE THINKING AND PLANNING?

Taylor held the intransigent view that while managers think and plan, workers must work and be subservient. He reinforced a time-honored caste system by hiring college graduates (middle-class men) to do his thinking and planning. This arrangement perpetuated a tradition of managers, such as in the military, where officers have always been upper-crust individuals, while those who must unquestioningly obey their orders are untutored sons of farmers and laborers. Police organizations are exceptions to a rule in which caste membership occurs through lateral entry and is correlated with class and educational backgrounds of managers and workers. While in some countries police managers are university graduates (lawyers, for example) who are laterally appointed, such is rarely the case in the United States. A chief may be imported by a police department, but will usually have started as a patrolman in some other department and worked his way through the ranks.

Since in the police managers are promoted rank-and-file workers, it is ironic that the precedent to which they subscribe is a "paramilitary" one, which sharpens the distinction between order givers and order takers. This fact has become doubly ironic because castelike organizations, such as factories, have taken a lead in democratizing decision making, while police organizations have remained undemocratic. Such has not only been the case in the United States, but also in Western Europe (where the participatory movement is called industrial democracy), in Communist Yugoslavia (where it is known as self-management), and in Japan (which is the country that has exported Theory Z and quality circles).

The American version of organizational democracy is known as quality of work life (QWL), defined as "direct participation of workers in day-to-day decision-making on the job" (Watts, 1983, p. 12). This definition is succinct and it is also important, because it was coined by the president of a labor union. Unions have historically been adversarial to management and their involvement in QWL represents a change in their perspective.

The QWL concept was born in the automobile industry, where it was first pioneered at the General Motors plant at Tarrytown (Guest, 1979) and at Harman International—an automotive supply factory—in Bolivar, Tennessee (Duckles, Duckles, and Maccoby, 1977). These pioneering ventures are different from each other, but both involve shop floor groups that meet and make proposals for innovations or reforms. These proposals are approved by labor-management committees and often require continued worker participation in their implementation.

Work democracy is an accepted practice in many assembly line operations, but has been slow to take hold in the public sector (with the exception of schools, where teacher empowerment has become somewhat fashionable, at least in theory). In policing, democratization was a notion introduced by the President's Commission on Law Enforcement and Criminal Justice (1967a, b), which favored the enactment of experiments in team policing (we shall return to these in Chapter 11). One of the goals of team policing—highlighted by Angell (1971)—was to promote "a flexible, participatory, science-based structure" for neighborhood police work (p. 194). Angell (one of the fathers of team policing) felt that a problem that faces most patrol officers is that they "tend to become nursemaids to the specialized officers such as investigators, and juvenile and traffic officers"; patrolmen also come to resent "their inability to affect their own working conditions (and the) continued utilization of classic autocratic managerial techniques by traditional managers" (pp. 192–193).

Angell's team is an autonomous group of officers that undertakes to police a localized community with input from citizens of the neighborhood. Angell's assumption was that "no procedural guidelines will be imposed on these teams by administrators in the organization" (p. 196). He also felt that officers must elect their leaders (coordinators) and rotate leadership among themselves. Goals are set in team meetings with citizen participation and officers would assess each other's performance. Teams could ask for technical assistance (for instance, from investigators), but they would not be obligated to do so.

Team policing has had a checkered history and has rarely lived up to Angell's prescription. Some experiments, however, have taken officer participation seriously, even at implementation. Sherman *et al.* (1973) describe the planning stage of one experiment (that of Holyoke, Massachusetts) in which 25 of 30 randomly selected officers volunteered for participation:

> In Holyoke, after the team members were selected, the outside consultants made it clear that the patrol officers, not the consultants, were responsible for developing the experiment. The consultants limited their own role to suggesting options and furnishing specific information. In this case, planning became training...Subcommittees of patrol officers were formed on such matters as uniforms, equipment, how to perform an investigation, and the rules and procedures for the team. Once the officers were convinced that the program was their own, they took the initiative. They made some quick decisions on equipment by contacting vendors directly. The decision to wear blazers was reached after the uniform subcommittee had arranged for fashion-show presentations. Another subcommittee developed a new team policy and procedures manual, which spelled out its policymaking process and the functions of the team chairman and various committees. (p. 64)

Another team experiment (in Los Angeles) started with a retreat at a location "selected for its atmosphere of calm and meditation" (Sherman et al., 1973, p. 47). Roommates were paired across ranks, and democracy prevailed in all deliberations:

> The most critical and uncomfortable session was the opening one. Captain Vernon...announced that during the seminar all ranks would be ignored and that any person who addressed another by rank would be fined ten cents. Dinner seating arrangements were changed at each meal to break up the old cliques (traffic, investigators, etc.) and to prevent new ones from forming. The officers were advised that each could interrupt any discussion by shouting "process" when he felt that the discussion was straying from the point. Everyone would then vote on whether the shouter's point was well taken and whether they should get back to fundamentals or continue in the same direction. Together the members of the new team decided that they would work three watches, with overlap; that they would have six marked police cars and four unmarked cars; that no team cars would be sent out of the area except in an emergency; that the traffic officers would continue to take a primary interest in traffic but would function more as generalists; and that investigators would be deployed by area. (p. 48)

Such beginnings are auspicious, but they are no guarantors of success. An individual taken out of an autocratic organization who is given a taste of democracy cannot be reinjected with expectations of having become a new man or new woman. The unlikelihood increases where power arrangements in the organization are left inviolate and where some persons are democratized and others are not. Sherman (1975) points out that police middle managers left out of team policing became skilled at sabotaging incipient experiments. For example,

> In Detroit the Beat Commander project was announced at roll calls with such prefatory remarks as "listen to this shit!"

> In Dayton such language was equally shrill and damaging. Shortly after the team policing program was announced, the captains circulated rumors that it was a communist conspiracy, manipulated via federal funding to get the police to cease law enforcement. Team patrolmen complained that the captains would tell the director of police what a great idea the team program was, then turn around and tell their men that the program would destroy the department. (p. 368)

The remedy used by some departments was to include all key players (even those not directly involved) in the thinking and planning:

> Kansas City, Missouri is one successful precedent for involving mid-managers, and all other levels, in a comprehensive planning process to improve the department. A task force of two patrolmen, two sergeants, two captains (there are no lieutenants there), and a major was established in each patrol division in order to identify community and organizational problems and develop programs to solve them. A constant effort was made to communicate with all other officers in the divisions, soliciting their suggestions and reactions to preliminary plans. (pp. 376–377)

Democracy is not a zero sum game, and Sherman (1975) notes that "it may be possible to expand the power of each level simultaneously with benefits to the entire organization" (p. 372). He also points out that power can *support* as well as *control* (a fact opponents of discretionary policing often ignore) and that persons in authority can be invoked to lend assistance rather than to give orders. One can find new roles for leaders, as a result of which "the followers (patrol officers) must do more leading of themselves, and the leaders must lead in new and different ways" (p. 373). Sherman concludes that "only if policemen at all levels can feel that this is 'our' way of doing things, rather than the boss's pet project, will democratization of any sort have a chance" (p. 377).

THE POLICE OFFICER AS A PROBLEM SOLVER

One of the most widely discussed facts in the police literature is that policemen exercise discretion in doing their jobs. Officers have power and make judgment calls in deciding what (if anything) to do in situations they encounter. They may arrest miscreants but are not obligated to arrest them, except in extreme cases. They can help people, but they can ignore claims to assistance. And while officers use discretion, the context in which they work deemphasizes it. The structure of police departments is military and training stresses limitations and constraints. New officers are enjoined to "play it by the book" and their "book"—a hefty departmental manual—is a compendium of mandates and prohibitions. The President's Commission on Law Enforcement (1967a) has pointed out that

> What such manuals almost never discuss are the hard choices policemen
> must make every day: whether or not to break up a sidewalk gathering,
> whether or not to intervene in a domestic dispute, whether or not to silence a
> street-corner speaker, whether or not to stop and frisk, whether or not to
> arrest. Yet these decisions are the heart of police work. How they are made
> determines to a large degree the safety of the community, the attitude of the
> public toward the police and the substance of court rulings on police pro-
> cedures. (p. 103)

The context of policing is a strange fiction in which enriched features of the job are shortchanged and the autonomy of officers is deem-
phasized. Nonetheless, there is talk that police are a "profession," a
claim that is undergirded by selective recruitment and training. But
recruitment and training for what? Selection and training are insufficiently tied to outcomes, which are judgments that benefit from selection and training. To ignore outcomes is tantamount to labeling a
surgeon a professional because he has gone to a good medical school—
never mind what he does in the operating room.

The emphasis on intuition and street sense is a reaction to such
fictions. It is a way for officers to say, "we exercise discretion, but we do
so on our own, very much as isolated individuals." And since officers do
not discuss why they do what they do (except when lubricated, or if they
write police novels), they substitute intuition for rationale. Theirs becomes a profession based on art rather than on systematic knowledge.

The paradox in all this is that it defeats the very point of the system.
"The book" is presumed to control the officers' behavior, and it is designed to make them obey legal, ethical, and organizational constraints.
But officers make hunch-based judgments, which are unconstrainable
because they are inaccessible. Rational judgments could deviate from
the text of "the book" but they can be surfaced, discussed, and guided—
in other words, controlled.

Rational judgments can be held to criteria such as congruence with
data or agreed upon facts. They can also be held to standards and can be
examined for premises on which they are based. Supervisors can influence rational exercises of discretion that are shared. They cannot affect
hunch-based discretion and do not do so—except for disastrous errors
in judgment—when it is usually too late.

Professional judgments can be institutionalized. The first requisite
is to welcome discretion, and the second is to assist officers to use their
heads. But how does one do that? One gambit is to draft a statement of
values that is supposed to guide officers (Wasserman and Moore, 1988).
But this is a top-down approach, since it is chiefs who write statements.
A statement also adds a second "book" by which the officers must "play
it." This book is typically abstract and hard to apply to concrete
situations.

To affect the exercise of discretion, one must deal with officers as discretion exercisers at the junctures where they exercise discretion. One juncture at which one can do this is at the point where officers become apprenticed, after they leave the academy. At this point they are most often assigned partners (field-training officers), who are presumed to be experienced and sound of judgment. The training officers usually see themselves as bridges from the abstractions of the classroom to the real world, which academy teachers have forgotten. They work with their charges in actual situations, exemplify "good police work," correct for naïveté, and explain the ropes. They have opportunities in this context to discuss why they do what they do when they do it, or dissect it after they have done it. If they are open, they can permit debate and admit mistakes of judgment. The premise would be that training officers are professionals, and that their professional judgments—like those of other professionals—have to do with effective problem solving, which can be shared and taught.

Problem solving is job enrichment because it has an outcome—the solution—and one can take pride in the skill one exercises to attain it. It can be rewarded with an emphasis on the ingenuity and intelligence that are deployed in achieving the outcome. It fosters growth and development because one can learn (from successes and failures) and improve one's capacity to solve problems. One can explore new ways of solving problems, which is self-actualizing, and one can move (if one is permitted to do so) from simpler to more complex problems.

Problem solving is participatory because it engages the worker as a thinking human being, who is left free—except in sharing his reasoning—to decide what to do. And problem solvers participate in setting policy because the output of the organization is the sum of problems that are solved. Such output can meet quality criteria (arrests that stick, citizens who are happy, new services provided), as well as production goals.

Dangers that are inherent in unfettered discretion can be reduced because problem solving is reviewable. Inappropriate definitions of problems and solutions can be independently addressed. One may thus decide that the problem-solving goal of discouraging prostitution in downtown Washington is appropriate, but that leading offenders on a forced march to the Virginia state line (*Washington Post*, July 25, 1989) is not a good solution. One can credit the ingenuity of the officers and encourage them to seek alternative solutions. One can make the logic (sundowning) explicit and achieve closer congruence between organizational and individual goals.

THE OFFICER AS "INTRAPRENEUR"

Problem-oriented policing goes beyond routine problem-solving approaches. While the latter rely on situations the officer encounters in his work, the former arranges more substantial arenas for problem solving. Officers use more data and resources in solving problems and are in a better position to affect organizational policy.

Problem-solving officers escape the constraints that Taylor placed on workers, while problem-oriented officers do a job Taylor reserved for managers. They study work-related situations and they make decisions based on scientific inquiry. What they do is applicable to future situations of the same kind. They set precedents, such as in initiating new services, which expand their organizations. Problem-solving officers learn from what they do, but problem-oriented officers can teach others. One reason they can do so is because they work with data, which enhances the generalizability of their inferences. They can also implement solutions (such as redesigned booking rooms and detoxification centers), which are institutionalized and emulated.

The distinction can assist departments in deploying problem-oriented efforts. Policy-relevant problems that are representative (or at least, not idiosyncratic) justify allocating resources that enhance the integrity of problem-oriented efforts, such as systematic data collection and technical assistance. They also justify giving officers a free hand to be creative.

In a foreword to a report about Baltimore County's COPE units (Taft, 1986), police Chief Behan wrote that "the COPE units answer the 'mean over ends' challenge by making police officers real 'intrapreneurs' — giving them wide latitude to go beyond the well-trod path of standard procedures, and to try innovative approaches they think will work" (p. 4). "Intrapreneur" is a term that has been used for privileged oases in which constraints that fetter members of an organization are suspended to encourage innovation and initiative. The favored intrapreneur is the creative person in an otherwise bureaucratic setting who is allowed to do what he wants. His is a situation that combines self-actualizing enrichment with complete autonomy. It is the apex and the culmination of work reform.

The model unfortunately has a downside because of the contrast it implies for the rest of the organization. The intrapreneur (typically, a slightly eccentric scientist who comes and goes as he pleases) is surrounded by nonintrapreneurs who cannot do what the intrapreneur can do. Police intrapreneurs may be surrounded by officers who are instructed to respond to assignments and do what "the book" (Taylor's legacy) tells them to do, while intrapreneurs do their thing. This is a situation that invites sibling rivalry (see Chapter 4) and other resistance.

If we take work reform experts seriously, we need to move on a broad front, knowing that problem-oriented reforms would fit best where jobs are otherwise enriched. This means that the average officers' intelligence is respected, their ingenuity valued, and their professional judgment trusted. A department where this happens would multiply opportunities, supports, and rewards for problem solving. It would do so across the board, while delegating a few officers now and then to pool their knowledge and thinking to address challenges that face the police collectively. A department that operates in this way would have harnessed its officers to subserve organizational goals while the officers pursued individual goals, which would have to do with being good cops. They would do this because they want to do it, which is what motivation means.

NOTES

1. Contemporaneous observers saw police as innately lazy and corruption-prone. Walker (1977) notes that "if one were to believe a 1915 investigation of the Chicago police, patrolmen spent *most* of their time in saloons" (p. 10).
2. Enemies of police discretion have similarly objected to the fact that rank and file officers can make policy, which should be a managerial responsibility. Davis (1975) writes that "the worst part of the answer to the question of who makes police policy is that professional people with specialized training seldom participate...if most policy is made by patrolmen, and if all higher officers are excluded, most policy is made by those with substantially less than 12.4 years in school" (pp. 43–44). Davis felt that the solution lies in well-formulated rules. He argued that where rules are instituted, "the quality of enforcement policy will improve because it will be made by top officers instead of patrolmen. The top officers obviously have skills and broad understanding that patrolmen typically lack. Under the present system the high officers seldom participate in making enforcement policy and are often uninformed of what it is (p. 113). Davis echoes Fred Taylor's concerns with the role of science. One of his arguments for rules is that "the quality of enforcement policy will be improved because the preparation of rules will lead to appropriate investigations and studies by qualified personnel, including specialists with suitable professional training. No longer will it be made primarily by the offhand guesswork of patrolmen" (Davis, 1975, p. 113).
3. Persons who draw attention to this possibility do not necessarily predict its occurrence.
4. The controversy predates the advent of the police car. Graper (1921) mentions that "when regular patrol service was first established it was customary to assign men to patrol in pairs. This policy was followed because it was deemed unsafe for one policeman to patrol alone" (p. 131). The one-man versus two-man patrol-car controversy was intensely waged following World War II. O.W. Wilson (1952) complained at the time that "in order to enjoy the companionship of a brother officer during routine patrol and the comfort of his presence in hazardous situations, some patrolmen are eager to prove that one-man patrol-car operation is unduly hazardous" (p. 85). Wilson saw sociability as

leading to inefficiency and corruption. He wrote that "the officer patrolling alone...is more likely to give his undivided attention to police duties. The presence of a second officer results in time spent in non-police activities; two officers are more likely than one officer to be involved in small delinquencies and infraction of the rules" (p. 83). The argument for one-person cars resurfaced in New York City in 1990. In an editorial (September 24, 1990) the *New York Times* complained that "the city's strong police union argues that one-officer cars are unsafe" in the face of evidence to the contrary. The editorial concluded that "because using one-officer cars is a sensible way to free up officers now for reassignment to foot patrol, it warrants the Commissioner's urgent attention."

4

Problems of Planned Change

The task of carrying out innovative changes in police departments is a formidable one. There are, however, encouraging leads that police executives could draw from reading about successful reforms in industry that apply prescriptions of current management theory. In police work itself, there are also indications here and there that it is possible for a progressive department to stay progressive, to integrate continual change and improvement into the way it operates. This continuity is particularly important for a department that seeks to create—as Eck and Spelman (1987a) have suggested is long overdue—a police science that is based on an epidemiological rather than symptom-treating approach to policing.

PROBLEMS AND OBSTACLES

There are near universal themes in reports of what can go wrong when one tries to bring about change in police departments. Among what can happen most frequently are

1. Change projects become "innovation ghettos" that isolate both the project and the people who carry it out. Project participants can become the butt of locker-room humor, reputed not to be real cops doing real police work, pets of the chief, and so on.
2. The initial commitment to the change effort "burns out" and early enthusiasms and visions give way to daily routines. Another way of putting this is to say that a Hawthorne effect occurs and runs its course for project participants.

65

3. The creativity that is needed for innovation and problem study turns out to be unattractive and/or more difficult for some officers than for others, particularly for those who see themselves as doers rather than talkers or academics. This is a specific instance of a more general problem that is becoming apparent in a wide range of organizations as jobs become more intellectual, as we become a more "high-tech," thinking person's world, and as the role of cooperation and conflict negotiation is advanced over aggressive action in problem resolution.

SOURCES OF RESISTANCE

A police department, like any other organization, functions both rationally and irrationally. Any organization may look surprisingly crazy if we expect it to look completely rational, like a machine, with inputs directed to the attainment of stated goals. We can come to a more realistic understanding if we regard the organization as an enterprise struggling to maintain equilibrium with the internal and external forces that impinge upon it, which tend to have goals other than those set forth by the organization. Reuss-Ianni (1983) illustrates this point. She conducted an analysis of an effort to install, from the top down, a system of management by objectives in the New York City Police Department and showed how "irrational" resistance turns out to be rational when we understand its origins. She documented the interplay of two police cultures, those of management cops and street cops. She points out that the two cultures have markedly different careers as well as operational values and objectives. What from a management perspective looks like irrational stubbornness makes sense when we understand it as a conflict of interest. It is the interplay between the two cultures that make the top-down mandated changes impossible to achieve.

As we have seen, Sherman (1975) makes a comparable point about the interests of middle management. He describes some of the problems that can be created by this middle group when its interests are ignored in efforts to introduce team policing. Sherman (1975) writes that:

> By fiat from the top, the bottom—patrol officers and sergeants—was given authority and discretion that had traditionally been reserved for, though rarely used by, the middle levels. In the perception of middle managers, team policing was a form of decentralization that gave them less control than any previous attempts at rigid centralization. The consequence was a multitude of attempts to block the proper implementation of team programs. (p. 364)

Beyond the problems that may result from internal jockeying for position, there are problems arising from external pressures, particularly, upsetting or disequilibrating events. In reporting on problem-oriented policing in Newport News, Eck and Spelman (1987a) thus speculate about the vulnerability of change efforts to developments in the political and management environment. They write that

> A series of celebrated crimes or a scandal involving police officers could have prompted the city council to demand a "back to basics" approach to law enforcement. The mayor could have appointed a city manager who took a "hands-on" role in managing the police department; such a manager would almost certainly have been unfamiliar with problem-oriented policing. Or a police chief who wanted to put his own stamp on the department could have been appointed from outside the agency. (p. 99)

One perennial limiting force is the budget process. A police department's existence depends upon negotiating the next year's budget, and this process is heavily skewed toward "more of the same." Many administrations have both an "A" and a "B" budget. "A" budgets are based on case and work load projections established from prior years and methods of operation; "B" budgets are proposals for innovations in operations. Generally, "B" budgets are only considered after "A" budgets have been negotiated, if funds are still available. Since it is inexcusable for an administrator to have "funds left over," it is not surprising that the best and brightest executives of a department concentrate on defending more of the same. This fact of life sounds inevitable, but it might well be possible to turn competent conservatives into exciting innovators by a simple shift in the budget process that gave "B" budgets priority over "A" budgets and considered funds for more of the same only after funds had been negotiated for doing things differently.

Besides political, community, and city administration forces, there are pressures that originate in the turf and policy concerns of other agencies—housing, welfare, the courts, and so forth—that interface with police operations, and in the turf and policy concerns of private groups, such as business, the ACLU, unions, churches, and criminals themselves, both the white collar and street kind. The role of crime as a factor in police operations is documented by Silberman (1980) in a report on a Cincinnati community team police experiment. One issue that was posed as a danger to this study was the risk of possible corruption among street officers if they were given the extra flexibility and autonomy that would be necessary for the team effort. As it turned out, no corruption was reported among the street officers. Shortly after the conclusion of the study, however, the police chief and six associates of his in the vice squad were accused of bribery, extortion, perjury, destroying evidence and stonewalling investigations of their activities; the six members of the vice squad were charged with helping the chief by inviting contributions from prostitutes in exchange for immunity from arrest. As a result of such well-publicized shenanigans, the chief was fired and was sentenced to time in jail (Silberman, 1980, p. 341). Several other police careers were also prematurely terminated.

FORCE FIELD ANALYSIS AS A REQUISITE FOR CHANGE

Since the operation of police departments is constrained by interactions with internal and external forces, it follows that any change effort mounted by a police organization must include a mapping of such forces and a strategy for coping with them.

Reuss-Ianni (1983) captures at least part of this issue in discussing how one could introduce MBO (management by objectives) in New York by pointing out that technological considerations are insufficient in mapping a strategy for producing change. She writes:

> Certainly, there are technological advances that can replace outmoded approaches to policing. Generally, however, we should assume that the major changes needed to produce more effective police work require attitudinal and behavioral changes both in the precinct and at higher administrative levels. This suggests changing the system rather than attempting to change individuals as the only effective means of institutionalizing changes. If relatively permanent (structural) changes are to be brought about, police officer perspectives on policing must also be changed, first to introduce appropriate change in attitudes as well as behavior, and then to maintain support for the changes once they are introduced. Often we speak of the need to achieve a certain climate of sentiment and opinion in order to produce change. Such changes in attitudes are essential but they will not be sustained unless the new ideas or techniques are incorporated in the value systems of the department, or become items on the agendas of both precinct and headquarters levels. (p. 122)

Planned change is much more complicated than discovering an effective innovation and getting a chief of police to order its implementation. Harry Truman is reported to have said about his successor's chances of making an impact on the country, "Just wait till Ike gives his first order." His point was that things may move on command, but the way they move may do little to bring about one's desired objective.

GARNERING COMMUNITY SUPPORT

Though there are serious obstacles to planned change in police departments, there are also resources available to cope with these obstacles. Many of these resources can be specified because they are similar to those available in the private sector. A police administrator may justi-fiably claim that his department is no General Motors, but public and private organizations face analogous demands for ongoing change and both struggle with change resistances inherent in their established bureaucracies.

In the private sector, the main driving force is competitive survival. In the service sector, it is the ratio of public (consumer) satisfaction versus dissatisfaction. When there is bureaucratic ossification and/or corruption, the public is apt, sooner or later, to become impatient and to demand reform. Public service organizations (and this includes the po-lice) may become pressured by community and political groups, as well as by research findings, to demonstrate not only effectiveness for tax dollars spent, but to show that their operation causes less trouble to consumers than the benefit it provides.

HARNESSING HUMAN RESOURCES

There are some operating principles that have evolved from an-alyses of successful corporations, interviews with reputable corporate leaders, study groups of executives, and reviews of current organization and management theory. The forms of the prescriptions vary, but there is general agreement on the need for the involvement of consumers and staff in self-management and regulation and the development of new kinds of leadership.

Vansina, Hoebeke, and Taillieu (1987) say that we now know that in arranging involvement one must move beyond the shop floor quality circles that were popularized by the Japanese (Ouichi, 1981) and one must involve all sorts of people who have a role in the organization's operation, letting them participate in the design of process and system changes. The experience and expertise of staff and consumers is re-garded as a resource for the management of an organization and an essential but not sufficient condition for organizational success.

A second condition that tends to be emphasized is leadership, but it is assumed that a new style of leader is required, one whose role can be described as that of orchestrator or facilitator. When successful execu-tives are asked to spell out what is necessary for this new type of leader, they tend to specify a consistent set of skills (Morgan, 1988). These skills define four attributes of effective leadership:

Providing employee support: being available as a resource; giving help as needed, without detailed supervision.

Fostering a climate of cooperation: promoting team building, networking, and the development of collaborative skills; remaining open to the
influence of others; promoting personal contact so that individuals will
develop commitment to joint efforts.

Facilitating decision making: being sensitive to all sides of an issue;
serving as an arbitrator between competing views; being open to intu-
itive approaches to problem solving; dealing quickly with uncertainty
and ambiguity; making decisions only when necessary; being willing to
serve as a hatchet man.

Providing vision and inspiration: developing an organization's identity and a vision of where it is going; inspiring others to identify with
this vision; communicating and building a commitment to the organization's values.

In this view, the top leader's role would have been changed from
providing top-down control to implementing and providing support for
bottom-up participation. But leaders, not managers, would be required
at all levels of the organization. According to Peters (1988), the world of
organizations would be heavily reshaped in terms of who provides what
sort of leadership. Bennis (1989), in summarizing Peter's work, says that
new leaders would need to take on risks "unimagined a generation ago,
but vital now." These tasks would include:

- Creating a flexible environment in which people are not only valued, but encouraged to develop to their full potential, and treated
  as equals rather than subordinates
- Reshaping the corporate culture so that creativity, autonomy, and
  continuous learning replace conformity, obedience, and rote, and
  long-term growth, not short-term profit, is the goal
- Transforming the organization from a rigid pyramid to a fluid
  circle, or an ever-evolving network of autonomous units
- Encouraging innovation, experimentation, and risk-taking
- Anticipating the future by reading the present
- Making new connections within the organization, and new rela-
  tionships within the work force
- Making new alliances outside the organization
- Constantly studying the organization from the outside as well as
  the inside
- Identifying weak links in the chain and repairing them
- Identifying and responding to new and unprecedented needs in
  the work force
- Being proactive rather than reactive, comfortable with ambiguity
  and uncertainty. (pp. 179–180)

SUPPORTIVE CONCEPTS

New organization and management developments are compatible with two areas of social science inquiry beyond the research on work motivation we have discussed in Chapter 3. One is that of research into the effects on behavior of choice, perceived control, and mindful decision making. Pearlmuter and Monty (1979) provide the following summary of the findings of these studies:

> It is now known that control and choice, however they are operationalized, almost invariably have good effects. Moreover, this has been shown to be the case for a wide variety of situations and manipulations. For example, both people and animals are happier, healthier, more active, solve problems better, and feel less stress when they are given choice and control...We are hard pressed to think of another area of psychology that has provided so many potential benefits for mankind in so short a time. The psychology of control and power has implications for cardiovascular functioning, retardation, IQ performance, job satisfaction, learning ability, child-rearing practices, therapy, psychopathology, poverty, and the lives of the elderly as well as the lives of college students. (p. 367–368)

Students of choice and control would argue that if building staff participation promotes organizational success, it is likely that it does so, at least in part, because it allows workers to have more active influence over the work aspect of their lives.

The second area of relevant research is that of cooperation and conflict negotiation, which is applicable to the advent of collaborative (as opposed to confrontational) relations between workers and managers. Deutsch (1985) notes, for example, that

> Few conflicts are intrinsically and inevitably win–lose conflicts. A common tendency is to misperceive conflicts of interest, as well as other conflicts in which the parties have become invested in their positions, as being win–lose in nature. A technology has been developing of how to help people maintain an awareness of their common interests even as they deal with their opposing interests...
>
> A full, open, honest, and mutually respectful communication process should be encouraged so that the parties can clearly express and understand each other's interests with empathetic understanding; such a process will discourage the misunderstandings that lead to defensive commitments and to a win–lose orientation...
>
> A creative development of a wide range of options for potentially solving the problem of the diverging interests of the conflicting parties should be fostered. In recent years, there has been a proliferation of techniques to help people broaden the variety, novelty, and range of alternative possibilities that are available to them as they attempt to solve problems—brainstorming and synectics are among the many procedures for stimulating creativity that have emerged in recent years. (pp. 72–73)

Principles such as these are particularly important in thinking about unions, who must be enlisted as partners in any consequential effort to develop a problem-oriented approach.

EVOLVING A PARADIGM

An organization's frontline personnel are grounded, necessarily, in the immediate, and someone has to deal with the larger question of where the organization is going. Addressing this question is one of the functions of top leadership: It is the chief in a police department who must develop and promote a shared vision (a paradigm) of his department's mission and how it is to be achieved.

Beyond this, there is the need for the chief to be sensitive to changes in the world beyond his organization. This means that his leadership visions may have to change to meet changing times. An effective chief must not only articulate a vision and promote participation in the service of this vision; he must also be aware that there will come a time when the old paradigm no longer works and new paradigms must be conceived and implemented.

Drucker (1985) argues that innovation must be a continuous activity, not only in private sector organizations and public service institutions, but in society as a whole. Change must become an ongoing process, an integral part of any organization's operation at all levels, grounded in the immediate yet going beyond the immediate. This requires a climate and an organizational structure that fosters innovation, that provides knowledge about how well innovations are helping the organization fulfill its mission, and that allows the organization to quickly correct its course.

In an organization that has institutionalized innovativeness, many of the problems that we have associated with abortive change will be minimized or disappear. There can be no innovation ghettos, for example, when a climate for change has been disseminated throughout the organization. Loneliness should lessen when one's innovation has been linked to an overall vision for which there is both leadership and staff support. Fears of being isolated or left behind by out-of-tune innovators (talkers and academics) should diminish when training and experience in self-management has been provided for all the organization's personnel.

STRATEGIES

Let us assume that a chief is committed to building a change-oriented organization based on notions of mindful decision making, cooperation, and visionary leadership. How would the chief approach his goal? Three contrasting strategies might occur to him as options:

1. The *kamikaze blitzkrieg* would be a desperate but quick and dirty strategy. It would be a choice of a top-down, essentially authoritarian approach that establishes a sweeping change before the forces that have resistance potential have time to mobilize. The advantage of this approach is that change does get implemented and sometimes even persists; the disadvantage is that this is often done at the cost of internal turmoil and that it may end the career of the administrator who carried it out. A dramatic example is the closing of juvenile correctional institutions in Massachusetts in the early 1970s (Baxal, 1973). Comparable strategies have been used to address problems of police corruption and violence, but the changes have seldom been long-lasting and a chief's tenure is usually abruptly shortened.

2. *Demonstration projects* are a classic approach to change. The point of these strategies is for the effectiveness of an innovation to be first demonstrated on a small scale and then, if it proves to work, to have the innovations extended throughout the organization. But many successful innovations do not work when they are later transplanted and many demonstration projects do not get this far. Experiments tend to get isolated and to become unpopular, inspiring jealousy or sibling rivalry among staff. They foster rumor and suspicion, making it unlikely that their benefits could be deployed on a larger scale. Aborted demonstration projects contribute only to knowledge development (which should not be undervalued), but do not contribute to effective action.

3. *Adaptation* calls for a gradual strategy, which draws on the experience and input of concerned parties as they take place, turning potential grass roots resistance into support for the change process. A question an adaptation strategy must always face is whether it can retain a larger vision of where the organization is going and how it is to adapt to changes in the outside world. For effective adaptation to occur, there must be a role not only for supportive consumers and staff but for intellectual and managerial leadership.

When leadership and participation are linked, we approach strategies that use the procedures advocated by current organization and management theory. Such strategies bring together staff at all levels and diverse functions of the organization in shared problem-solving exercises that redefine the organization's mission. What emerges if one keeps doing this is a new organizational paradigm oriented toward continual change and problem solving.

TOWARD AN EPIDEMIOLOGICAL SCIENCE OF PROBLEM-ORIENTED POLICING

Eck and Spelman (1987a) tell us that policing, like medicine, must be concerned not only with handling emergencies (incidents in policing, sickness and injury in medicine) but with the common problems that underlie them. Eck and Spelman conclude their report of problem-oriented policing in Newport News with this seminal statement:

> Police will never be able to make an improvement in public safety until they start to investigate underlying conditions. Problem-oriented policing holds out the hope that law enforcement agencies will be able to do this. But this will take a long time. The efforts of officers in Newport News represent a modest beginning. As more agencies experiment with this approach, learn how to do it better, and share this information with other police professionals and the public, policing may, in the long-run, be as effective as epidemiology. It is with this hope that we advocate the continued study and development of problem-oriented policing. (p. 113)

Eck and Spelman contend that the problem-oriented thrust in Newport News illustrates the need for total organizational reform. Another example of this strategy is represented by the attempt of the Houston Police Department to bring about step-by-step change (Oettmeier and Bieck, 1987, 1989). Houston began with initial demonstration projects in neighborhoods and worked toward linkage of patrol and investigation operations. They expected then to move on to building linkages between these and other departmental operations.

Leadership for the change effort came from the chief and from staff of the Field Operations Command. With Police Foundation support, a group of operationally experienced personnel were brought together in a series of executive session meetings to design a model for "transforming the concept of NOP [neighborhood-oriented policing] into a sustainable, reality-based policing style" (Oettmeier and Bieck, 1987, p. i). Having laid out an overall model (a vision), the group moved to the redesign of local operations through widespread officer participation.

Such a combining of a problem-oriented approach to neighborhood policing with a problem-oriented approach to the police agency's operation offers the opportunity to develop knowledge about the problems that underlie police incidents and to improve responses to these problems through modifications of police operation. Ongoing evaluation is an essential part of this process. It creates new knowledge (it is as important to know what does not work as it is to know what does), and thus allows continual improvement of the operation.

Eck and Spelman (1987a) speak of building links from police departments to other police departments as a way of sharing experiences with change efforts. Such networking is done by the Police Executive Research Forum and offers a way of assuaging loneliness and disseminating knowledge. And as problem-oriented experimentation expands, so can networking that links experiments so that they do not feel lonely or reinvent the wheel. With or without the use of computers, electronic mail, and fax machines, one can envision an expanding network that first would link precincts and teams within a department, then police departments with each other, and eventually police departments with other human service organizations. Such an effort would allow police to build knowledge about kinds of incidents, by kinds of problems related to incidents, by kinds of political, community, and organization forces that impinge on problems, and by kinds of strategies to deal with problems, including ways of evaluating the effectiveness of these strategies.

To be useful, cumulating knowledge would need to be organized and cross-referenced so that anyone could retrieve problem-oriented information applicable to their specific local problem, whether it be incident related (increases in auto theft, muggings, or drug sales, for example) or organizational (officer resistance, jurisdictional conflicts, budget cutbacks, and so forth). A department that was faced with a sudden increase in crack sales would be able to have immediate access to the relevant experiences of other network users. These would include what others found to be plausible underlying causes of the problem's proliferation, external forces to consider in strategies for solution, and procedures for evaluating each of the strategies. The department's own efforts to deal with drug-dealing incidents, whether it decided to follow approaches tried by others or defined new problems and newly designed strategies, could then be built into the knowledge base to be used by the next agency down the line.

We are obviously here envisaging an ongoing system for collecting and organizing problem-oriented information in which network users can receive knowledge and feed new knowledge into the system. Such an expanding reservoir of knowledge could be made available not only to police departments but to allied human service and government agencies and to scholars in the social sciences. It is conceivable that the ongoing analysis of problem-oriented information could lead to new concepts and new principles about the behavior of police clients and to new models (paradigms) for the operation of police agencies.

Any large police department can begin this kind of process. It can share information across teams, precincts, and headquarters. But as the effectiveness of the network is developed and demonstrated, other departments and other groups may want to participate, thus building support for the network's maintenance and expansion. Each new network member could be encouraged to contribute new information, to ensure that the network would not replace local participation in local problem solving. It could serve instead as a resource that would give outside leads to local decision makers and allow them to address the formulation and solution of their specific problem in a more cosmopolitan way.

The kind of knowledge system we are describing is not simply an information system that directs its users to a book or a computer screen. Nor is it the kind of knowledge that develops from an accumulating body of academic research. The knowledge at issue is gathered from the bottom up. It comes from the collective experience of people who are trying to solve pressing problems, and its primary function is to provide support to people who need to make action decisions. People must create knowledge through their own experiences and feed it back into the system, thus contributing to the ongoing updating and expansion of the knowledge base.

A problem-oriented information system would have uses beyond those of local problem solving. It would provide a constantly updated body of knowledge that would allow its users (either local problem solvers or others) to develop generalizations across kinds of problems and kinds of solutions, to develop general concepts, and to contribute to the development of social science and organization theory.

5

The Oakland Project

Once a problem-oriented experiment has its foot in the door, how does it work? How are problem definitions arrived at? How do policemen ask scientific questions? How do they collect data and mesh these (if they can) with experience? How do they face tedious chores of analysis and inference? How do they deal with conflict, such as challenge to habits and to norms of their groups? How do they work through ideas for change? How do they sell such ideas to superiors? peers? bureaucrats? targets of programs?

In answering these sorts of questions, nuances matter. Thoughts and feelings must be captured to convey a sense of process as it unfolds for participants. It helps to know how it feels to sit down the first day and ask oneself, "Why are we here?" And it helps to know how one lives with—as one officer put it—the "dim light at the end of a long, long tunnel." There are also transitions such as between the end of one process (a solution that makes sense) and the beginning of another (a program that works). The problem-oriented experience is rich and it helps to have it available in the words of those who have lived it.

The chapters that follow present an account of problem-oriented activity that preserves details, flavor, and authenticity. It helps that the police agreed to have the process memorialized. They recorded high points of sessions, summaries of achievements, and reactions to experiences as they unfolded. The officers also taped conversations with key players in settings in which they worked. Such process research shows respect for science and faith in lessons one can convey to those who follow in one's footsteps.

THE OAKLAND POLICE DEPARTMENT

The story we shall convey took place in an agency (the Oakland police) that had a tradition of hospitality to research. This fact was a mixed blessing because there had been "hit-and-run" exercises that had left officer participants feeling exploited. The experiment we detail is therefore an example of trust where officers risked new disillusionment. They did so because they wanted to make a contribution to policing, though the odds seemed discouraging.

The Oakland (California) police covers a metropolitan area of 75 square miles and in the 1960s deployed close to 700 uniformed personnel and a patrol force of 400. The city of Oakland had some 360,000 inhabitants, and was "a city of contrasts and a variety of cultures" (Muir, 1977, p. 7).

Oakland is a study in contrasts and the hills overshadowing its deteriorated core contain many affluent homes. But Oakland is poor: Most of the streets the officers patrol are slums—some teem with life and others present shells of buildings and seedy, ugly commercial sites. Minority enclaves are concentrated in sterile housing developments and small, crowded homes. They range across the spectrum, from black and Hispanic to Asian, American Indian, and Eskimo.

Many of the city's problems are fruits of poverty, discrimination, urban decay, and political turbulence. Antiwar activists in 1967 had held massive demonstrations against army induction. A riot had ensued and the police had intervened, "formed a wedge and moved into the demonstrators, swinging billy clubs" (Wilson, 1968, p. 199). Many young persons were hospitalized as a result, and the police department was blamed. Other criticisms followed bloody battles with the Black Panthers, in which fatalities occurred on both sides.[1] The Panthers had made Oakland their headquarters and centered their efforts for years on a war against the police. They served food to children, then taught them to sing "There is a pig upon the hill. If you don't kill him, the Panthers will." They distributed a free coloring book to children. Kids could color "a black man shooting a pig-faced policeman as a young girl looks on. The caption: 'Black Brothers Protect Black Children' " (*Time*, 1969). The Panthers shadowed police offers and taunted the officers mercilessly as they conducted their business. Their rallies (monitored by the police) threatened extermination of Oakland officers.

Such developments had ramificationss beyond escalating the hatreds they engendered. Wilson (1968) estimated that over 38% of black citizens had "formal involvement" with the police in a typical year. Every black person interviewed in a survey conducted by Wilson charged that he or she had been harassed by the police (p. 191). The police department had responded to the problem by inviting minority group involvement. It had encouraged complaints against officers (including anonymous complaints) and processed these quickly and punctiliously under supervision of the chief. The strategy discomfited officers, but did not reassure citizens. Wilson (1968) reports that

> in Oakland almost every patrolman interviewed was bitter about the fact that the internal affairs section "harassed" them, investigated them, and disciplined them, often, they claimed, unfairly and over minor issues. But also in Oakland, the Negroes refused to believe that internal affairs was doing anything at all. (p. 187)

Monitoring of officer behavior was routine in the Oakland department, which was noted for its straightlaced integrity and lack of penny-ante corruption. Officers took pains to observe rules and kept close records of their actions. The officers' adherence to rules is illustrated by Wilson (1968), who tells the following story:

> In Oakland, the police parking lot is across the street from headquarters. The direct route to take to and from the building is to cross in the middle of the block. Routinely, interviewers watching the shifts change saw officers leave the building, walk to the corner, wait for the light, cross, and walk back to their cars. "Once or twice, maybe, I'll dash across the street," a patrolman told an interviewer, "but you get used to not jaywalking, and that's the way it is all the time." (p. 180)

In Oakland, officers were nationally recruited, generously compensated, and rigorously trained. Their training included emphasis on minority group relations, but was also heavily legalistic, because the Oakland philosophy was one that highlighted full and fair enforcement of law, emphasizing formal dispositions, including arrests. Oakland since 1950 had been an arrest-driven police department, and the productivity of officers was defined in terms of the number of arrests they made. Arrests and citations were seen as responses to crime and ways of preventing crime. "The more traffic tickets you issue," writes Wilson (1968), "the better the chance of catching a real criminal; if you catch a real criminal, you make yourself look good; thus rewarded, you have even greater incentive to make more car stops" (p. 182). Most officers in Oakland prided themselves on being tough and enforcement-oriented. Muir (1977) writes that

> history was handed down within the department. For example, in the scuttlebutt of the locker room, incoming rookies would be regaled with the stories of the free-for-alls between the department and the (Hells Angels), a notorious motorcycle gang. This gang of hoodlums, virulently anti-black and defiant of civilized standards, profited by narcotics traffic and partook of the

violence inevitably connected with the business. Those stories abounded with powerful images and homilies; thus, the realities of history transformed themselves into lessons for today. (p. 9)

The Oakland chief of police is a central figure in our story. He had been reared in the department's tradition, but came to question its premises. Muir (1977) describes the chief's perspective and the way his troops stereotyped him in the locker room. Muir's account is perceptive and worth quoting in full. He writes:

a constant topic of conversation in the ranks was the chief. His policies and his personality aroused strong feelings. He evoked hatred and respect, and often from the same men. Whenever the officers spoke well of him, they admired the undoubted clarity of his mind. They referred to his philosophy as "progressive." He tolerated no brutality, no illegality, and no graft among his men. He imposed the strictest controls on the use of firearms. He publicly applauded the due process revolution effected by the United States Supreme Court, and he took steps to explain to all his men how to adhere to the new restrictions on interrogations and searches and why adherence was a good thing.

When his men spoke bitterly of him, as a general rule they referred to his personal quirks and particularly to the unnecessary humiliations he inflicted on them, in his public disparagements and private scoldings of them. Because of his personality, he was not a popular chief. Under his tutelage, his men were often sullen, full of animosity, and increasingly resentful of his brittle, acerbic, and denigrative style.

But no man among the officers I met doubted that he had turned the philosophy of the department upside down, from a legalistic, arrest-prone, evenhandedly repressive department in which a policeman's arrests (as quantified on his weekly "activity sheet") were the unchallenged measure of his worth, to a service-oriented one, where too many arrests were treated as a signal of police ineptitude and where anything novel was assumed to be better than the old police methods. (p. 10)

The last paragraph provides the context for our story. Muir notes that the chief's personality was unfairly characterized by officers, who resented the fact that the chief ran a tight ship, and that he disapproved of the cherished specialized, enforcement—oriented culture of the Oakland police. The chief—Charles Gain—himself has written:

...there is a growing awareness of the need to improve our abilities in coping with people problems....We have, then, discovered that a series of order maintenance activities which have grudgingly been performed in the past are important to our mission and that they should receive new recognition. They should be, and in some cases are now, given equal importance with crime prevention and control because of their frequency and significance to our clientele—the citizens we serve. (Gain, 1972, pp. 5–6)

The goals of his administration included:

1. Stress on the observance of suspect rights.
2. Increased attention to police–community relations.
3. Deemphasis of public-order crimes.
4. Introduction of new and improved service modalities.
5. Stress on "quality enforcement."
6. Reduction of police–citizen violence and conflict.

The chief accepted legalism (Wilson, 1968), but preferred legality; he valued evenhandedness, but not in the sense of evenhandedly arresting offenders in borderline crime situations, which invited resentment and promoted conflict with citizens. It is with respect to this area of concern that the chief encouraged research. He also promoted a problem-oriented experiment, which we shall describe in the chapters that follow.

FROM RESEARCH TO REFORM

Our association with Oakland began after the chief learned of a study we were conducting of violent offenders. At this time (the mid 1960s) the Oakland planning and research unit was reviewing police–citizen confrontations, which were proliferating. Suspects were being conveyed to emergency wards and then arrested for resisting arrest or assaulting officers. There were many complaints from citizens, and the department's reputation—which had never been good—was declining.

The planning unit's research suggested—as did studies else-where—that specific officers get the lion's share of problems. Though these officers are productive, other officers are similarly productive without inviting conflicts. Obvious questions arise about who the officers are and how they incur difficulties. A study seemed in order, and the chief asked us if we would undertake it as part of our research.

We interviewed Oakland officers with high rates of PC 148 (resisting arrest) and PC 243 (assault on officer) arrest rates and incorporated our impressions in a book entitled *Violent Men* (Toch, 1969). In this book we described patterns of violent behavior, which consisted of common-alities among violent incidents. Violent encounters were classified across persons and for individuals—viewing persons as composites of violent involvements. This approach led us to a typology of violence-prone persons based on themes that seemed to characterize their violence. We also looked at encounters that involved two violence-prone persons, such as a problem police officer and a violent offender.

In interviewing Oakland officers, we found our subjects eloquent and forthcoming. We also heard insights in the side comments the officers made while they told us about their experiences. Some of the officers were concerned about their involvements, which had led to unfriendly inquiries and had endangered their careers.

We discussed our interviews with the chief, who shared our impressions of the officers. The chief thought it would be desirable to save the officers, if an intervention might make this possible. The chief also wanted a vehicle that could address the larger organizational problem, which had to do with high rates of police–citizen conflicts. His assumption (which we shared) was that this problem included our subjects, but transcended their conflict-inducing activities.

The idea we evolved was in some ways unprecedented. We envisaged a parttime unit of patrolmen, called the Violence Prevention Unit. This group would be charged with studying police–citizen violence and devising interventions that could address the problem. To start off, such a unit could be created with our involvement, if we obtained the needed government sponsorship.

The next step carried risk: We proposed to man the unit with violence-experienced officers, including former subjects of our study. We would begin with seven officers, most of whom would have histories of involvements. Later, these officers would work with other officers, who would all be violence-experienced. Matched persons would make up a comparison group whose behavior we would study.

The officers in the unit would have a free hand in setting their own agenda, with the understanding that they would do some research. This would hold most particularly for the first group, which would define the problem with which the second generation (three groups) would have to deal. The first group would be entitled to make proposals, but the other groups would be obligated to make them. This was premised on the assumption that the first seven officers would have their hands full preparing to run the second phase of the project, which would relegate us to the sidelines.

The Oakland project is a problem-oriented intervention in that groups of officers were charged with studying a problem and reducing it. But the project was different from other problem-oriented projects because many of our officers had a hand in producing the problem they were charged with addressing. The hope was that as the officers dealt with the department's problems, they might mitigate their own, given that their overall goal could benefit from changes in their behavior. We also hoped that knowledge the officers would acquire in doing their work might inspire them to change their perspectives.

Every problem-oriented effort aims at products—ideas that can solve problems, or at least ameliorate problems. To varying degrees, one must also care about the process and what it can do for participants. In Oakland, in particular, we hoped that our problem-oriented groups would become learning experiences and vehicles of personal change. We hoped that officers could satisfy esteem needs by contributing to organizational reform and that their approach to policing might become commensurately enlightened.

Oakland, at the time of our intervention, was a notorious enclave of arrest-driven legalism. It was touted in textbooks as espousing the control-centered philosophy that problem-oriented policing was invented (10 years later) to address. The department had suffered undesired consquences of its approach (such as conflicts and complaints), which confirmed, for the chief, the need for planned change. He was ready to experiment with change, including initiating it through the officer culture and its less progressive members.

No one expected that this approach would be easy. If it succeeded, however, it might make a convincing case. At the least, we could not be accused of having stacked the decks to document the potential of rank-and-file involvement in police reform and the possibility of turning a police department around.

INCEPTION OF THE PROGRAM

Our last conversation with the Oakland chief of police had taken place early in 1968, and 12 months later we had National Institute of Mental Health financial support (a training grant) to set up the project.

In late June of 1969, three of us conducted group interviews designed to select the first seven members of our Violence Prevention Unit. Some 80 officers were interviewed. These were drawn from four sources: (1) officers who had been included in our own violence study in 1966–67; (2) officers drawn from high-incidence lists of "resisting arrest"; (3) officers recommended by their superiors as "good officers"; and (4) officers suggested by peers as promising group members.

What we wanted was to locate men with violence-related experience, who were held in high regard by other officers. The latter attribute was essential to us. Candidates were chosen by rating the quantity and quality of their contribution to the interview situation. Those who were listened to with respect were invited to participate. All agreed to join.[2]

The seven officers who were included in this first group ranged in age from 26 to 41, with a mean age of 31. Their time with the department varied from 1½ to 18 years, with mean service of 6 years. Three had been subjects in our study (one took up a whole chapter of our book); four were secured through other sources.

The arrangements that we had worked out meant that each officer remained on his beat three days a week and worked on the project two consecutive working days. During these two days the group met from 4 P.M. to midnight. The last half hour of each meeting was reserved for tape-recorded statements.

During the summer of 1969, the group met for 11 weeks—a total of 176 hours of meeting time. The group continued on a less ambitious schedule between mid-September and June of 1970. Generally, the group put in 8 hours every two weeks, except for more intensive planning sessions in December and April. In the summer of 1970, the seven officers conducted the second phase of the project, which we shall sample in Chapters 7 and 8.

We shall first describe (in Chapter 6) the 1969 summer session. We can then turn to the 1970 generation—two of the three groups—and their proposals (Chapters 7 and 8). Two proposals are worth further attention: one addresses officers' behavior, which we track individually and in the aggregate (Chapter 9); the second calls for interorganizational links to be forged (Chapter 10).

Our review will take us from the inception of ideas to some results of implementation. The reader may get some sense of our officers as persons, and their progress in the groups. As for the officers' impact, it lasted for some years.[3] This is not forever, but change, as we have noted, means continued renewal.

NOTES

1. J. Edgar Hoover called the Black Panthers "the most violence-prone of all the extremist groups." With regard to police violence, Bobby Seale has reminisced that "they (the police) wounded 60-odd of us, we wounded 32 of them. I think the reason we killed less and wounded less was because they had...more equipment" (Barclay, 1989). Huey Newton has said that the Panthers' stance toward the police was influenced by Malcolm X. The derivative view "that blacks ought to defend themselves with arms when attacked by the police became one of the original points in the program of the Black Panthers" (Hevesy, 1989). Newton was involved in the killing of Oakland police officer John Frey on October 28, 1967, in one of several gun battles.
2. The second-generation members of the project (Chapters 7 and 8) were randomly selected—through multiple coin tossing—from officers who had accumulated high violent incident rates. The men were neither self-selected nor picked because they had special skills and interests. Moreover, it is difficult to argue that the project benefited from an evanescent Hawthorne effect, given that officers remained involved over a period of years.
3. Discontinuance of the innovation was a painful step for the department to take, and one that it took reluctantly. Skolnick and Bayley (1986) point out that

As the department had to cut manpower by more than 100 between 1972 and 1979, virtually all of Gain's innovative programs were cut from the departmental budget. Gain's successor, George Hart, says that the "critical incidents" program [sic] was perhaps the most valuable of those cut. "But," he explains, "we couldn't afford it. The peer review panels usually occurred on days off, and the union required that we pay each panel member time and a half. I figured that each panel cost about $3,000. We simply couldn't afford to continue this worthwhile program.". . . "It's true," he says somewhat ruefully, "we don't have a lot of programs. But it's tough to have innovative programs during a period of economic austerity." (pp. 151–152)

The Oakland police began to experience violence problems almost as soon as the interventions were discontinued. Skolnick and Bayley (1986) note that "the worst year for the department, the absolute low, was 1979, when nine black males, including a fifteen-year old, were gunned down and killed by Oakland police" (p. 155). A large assembly was held in the wake of this incident, and "the Mayor wisely recessed the meeting as the anger and resentment reached a really frightening pitch" (p. 155).

The problem to which our intervention was addressed had now again resurfaced. The department's administration, according to Skolnick and Bayley (1986), "would like nothing better than to develop a predictive device to ferret out problem cops, potential users of excessive force" (p. 156). Such was one of the issues, two decades previously, that inspired Chief Gain to create the Violence Prevention Unit and to institute the peer review panel.

6
Defining a Problem
First-Generation Change Agents

Two groups of relative strangers—seven officers and three civilians—convened at 4 P.M. on an early summer Wednesday in the imposing Oakland police headquarters building. One of us civilians gave a rousing welcoming speech outlining the violence reduction project. We promised the officers that we would not tell them what to do, but that we would provide resources and help. We acknowledged that the group could face some tough assignments, some tense moments, and understandable problems of trust, but we assured the officers that if they stuck with it, they might learn a great deal from their involvement.

After this statement, the group began to consider entry points into its subject. As a start, the men listed types of encounters and incidents likely to produce conflict. They then selected one category—the family dispute—for closer examination. As a first exercise, they considered "cues" available to the officers as they entered a family fight, which could warn them of impending trouble. The officers also speculated about ways their department could affect their response to such cues. Among the contexts they listed as making a possible difference were recruit training, dispatching, and communication—in particular, communication between patrolmen and their supervisors.

During the course of the first session, several officers took a lead in urging more systematic inquiry. One of the officers, for example, requested statistics on the relative prevalence of arrests for resisting arrest[1]:

> Of the list of calls we had, I think we should know almost percentage-wise what amount of 148s occur in family beefs, when they occur in car stops, walking stops. Do young-looking policemen have more? Do recruits just out

of the academy have more? What type of policeman has the most 148s? And then, if we can put our finger right on a specific problem, maybe come up with some reason as to why they're happening, and maybe a solution.

Another officer called for more concern for reliability in the content analysis of street incidents:

> When we went through a couple of incidents, we went immediately to an analysis; I would have preferred to have more incidents on the floor so you could draw them together rather than trying to do an individual analysis. We didn't want to move to the analysis of the incidents as quickly as we did. We would have preferred to have the information out and then do the analysis so you have more possibilities to draw from.

One group member advanced a suggestion for a concrete research project; someone mentioned role-playing, and he asked whether one could tape-record calls, to permit a step-by-step review by the group:

OFFICER: You mentioned the actor-type thing where you go through these emotions of the typical family scene. Why couldn't we go to these things and have the officer tape it, rather than try to act the thing out?

STAFF: That might be extremely useful.

STAFF: Are you suggesting a hidden tape?

OFFICER: Hidden, naturally, from the people involved. And it would give us that point of view. I'll admit the officer will perhaps not present it in the same light he would without this. But by the same token, it would give you an idea of the things that do present themselves and develop a pattern.

OFFICER 2: We certainly would get the citizen's side of it.

STAFF: We've got seven officers at this table some of whom will be responding to that kind of call.

OFFICER 3: We'd look kind of obvious carrying a tape...

OFFICER: No, just like small things. Just like your transceiver. It wouldn't make any difference, and then you could see how each different officer handles....

This idea was not pursued during the session, but was revived, discussed, and implemented at a later date. This also held true of other ideas raised during the first sessions.

Trust problems did arise, but on a low key, and usually with overtones of humor. The following exchange is fairly typical:

OFFICER: Well, I'd like to be called Sam from now on. Because every time he refers to Mills he's using my first name, and I'm the one that's going to get the ax.

STAFF: May we have it for the record that Joe is Sam.

OFFICER: One thing that I heard several times tonight, and I'd like, of course, to express my opinion, was I think there's some doubt on the part of you gentlemen, not the officers, but the gentlemen who are conducting this program, as to our honesty, because of the trust we might place in whatever's going on. And I think that you're going to have as complete cooperation as possible. I don't think there's going to be any problems withholding information, not wanting to say something because you're afraid of what could happen. Going on to one of the points that Hiram made....

OFFICER: The name is Genevieve.

A staff member who handled the first group summary paraphrased several spirited remarks made by the officers during the session. One of these quotes sparked the following interchange:

OFFICER: The summarizer mentioned, "If violence was to occur, hit first," which was kind of general. And I'll clarify that very briefly, because it doesn't sound good on the tape, first of all. Secondly, we were speaking of a specific incident at the time, and the general conversation, at this particular time in the conference, was that if you happen on an individual that was outwardly going to become violent, we were in fact in position where it would not behoove us to lose. And that if this were to occur, if in fact violence were to occur, and were to be leveled on us, that it would be much to our advantage to level it first in coping with the situation. So I'll leave that.

OFFICER 2: How are you going to put it, "the officer should be in the position to take appropriate action"?

OFFICER 3: I thought what you were saying was that the best defense is a good offense?

Group members did show some reserve in relation to other officers—often producing an illusion of harmony and unanimity. One of the men noted in the summary that

> I think there was some reticence on the part of the group to challenge each other. I saw people who obviously didn't agree with the other guy sort of let it go, and I don't think there's anything wrong with challenging each other. I mean, we're all trying to find areas here. I think if we test each other, we'll move a little bit forward and have a little better possibility of getting to these points...if somebody doesn't agree with somebody, that's fine.

In addition to the indirectly raised issue of trust, there was resistance on the part of one group member to the emphasis on officer violence. The argument raised by this man (which he renewed in several other sessions) contained two themes: (1) police officers tend to respond to civilian contacts in standard ways; and (2) civilians are responsible for any resulting violence:

OFFICER: The officers here are all experienced; they've been on these calls. I think it behooves us to think about that we are all one nature, that even though there are certain small things that we would tend to differ with, that we are police officers, and we are of a state of mind as police officers. We should, perhaps, get into a different plane, perhaps interviewing people who are the victims of family disturbances.

STAFF: Participants?

OFFICER: Participants of family disturbances to find out what is going through their mind, what response, what state of mind they were in when the officer arrived on the scene. At the point where they settled down and discontinued their violent nature, what caused the discontinuation of their violent nature. And this is just scratching the surface of family disturbances here. There are many other conditions. We only discussed ten; I'm sure there are many others.

In connection with the tape-recording idea, the same officer proposed that the tapes would demonstrate that

> The officer goes in and uses all these ideal responses, and still gets the militant-type response from the people; it may show that it's not entirely at the officer's discretion to prevent these things from happening.

Beyond this objection, the group voiced little concern or reluctance. They stipulated their mission, accepted the staff, and launched into their assigned subject. If they harbored resistances, these remained latent. Testimonials ranged from "I enjoyed the session. I feel like I'm much better for it," to "I'm going to learn a lot up here," and "a lot of what was said up here will keep coming back to me." The program had achieved—it seemed—qualified acceptance.

EVOLVING A JOINT FRAME OF REFERENCE

The second session continued and amplified the exercises that were initiated the previous evening. The group moved to a second category of violence-prone incidents, involving crowds of juveniles. Again, personal experiences were used as a basis for discussion and there were some disagreements among group members about the handling of calls. The analysis proved systematic, compared with that of the first session. The group produced a detailed inventory of situational cues to violence and discussed the consequences of behavioral options facing the responding officer. There was discussion of "games" played by officers and suspects and of component "strategies" and "moves."

It had become obvious, late in the session, that the group had accepted a common language, which it used easily and comfortably. As a staff member put it:

> I think when we speak of "games" from now on in, we all will be pretty much talking about the same thing. When we speak of "cues" and "moves," we'll be talking about the same thing. It isn't just a matter of anybody using this language just to do somebody else a favor.

Several members of the group voiced their surprise as they discovered systematic differences in police conduct, including their own. One officer stated that

> I was under the impression that these are all the results of incidents, and everybody that's involved here, that is, all the policemen that are involved, have always been the same. I've had a tendency of not having any insight into how I did anything. It was revealing to me to lay it out and just to compare it with the rest of the fellows just to see where the differences were, in regard to what was suggested for me, and the differences in my attitude. Perhaps I'm all wet in my attitude, I don't know. But I never had given it any thought before, and it has been enlightening looking at myself.

The dissenting voice was that of the previous night's holdout, who reiterated that

> We have a sameness of mind and a sameness of thought; it does exist, I believe. And I don't think that it should be forcefully changed to please the staff. Not that you're inferring this, but I just thought I would bring it out that we have the same sameness of mind and thought that *you* do.

These views were ventilated in the context of a no-holds-barred debate, featuring open but friendly disagreements. One officer noted proudly that "tonight we exposed our souls possibly a little more, and we're willing to talk about things and take variance with each other more than we did last night." Others concurred with this assessment of the evening's climate. As another officer put it:

> I have something to say about last night, and that is that I'm very pleased with last night because it got us to where we are tonight, and I find myself somewhat disappointed that tomorrow night's not going to come until next Wednesday. The ball's rolling, and you just kind of hate to see it stop.

Coming after a 16-hour marathon, such tributes confirmed the existence of a surprisingly high level of group morale.

FACING LARGER IMPLICATIONS

During the third session, the group received a visit from their chief, Charles Gain. The chief endorsed the violence prevention program, and emphasized the uniqueness and importance of the group's work. He said, in part:

I'd like to impress upon you the significance this project has to me and to the Oakland Police Department and policing in general. We find in policing today that so many things are occurring, and sometimes we don't know why, and too much the tendency is to do nothing about it. So that when we can identify that there are problems, and this is a problem area as you well know, to me it is absolutely essential that we explore and that we find out what is going on, why it's going on, and what can be done about it; hence the emphasis on this problem in my judgment. It's highly important; it's not something I can do at all. And there are many areas, of course, where this is true. It's something where we have to have people who are involved in the nitty-gritty, gut level, if you will, of police work. So it's highly significant to me. I think it's going to be a landmark thing for policing if it turns out the way it should; and, of course, that's totally unknown now, I suppose, to any of us. But it will be a classic-type study, one that will surely benefit this police department and individuals in an area where day by day we are finding there are problems on that street. And there will be a spin-off and a trade-off for policing throughout the country, so it would benefit officers as regards safety of their persons, and also citizens. I think most importantly, it's something that you have to do. Again to emphasize that I can't do it. It's something that no number of experts could do from the outside. It's something that individuals who are involved in the work process themselves have to engage in, and that is a highly important part of it.

Pleased with this endorsement, and bolstered by the Chief's expression of confidence, the group set to work. It proceeded to randomly review arrest reports of high-incidence officers. The result was an animated but unsystematic discussion, with little closure. One officer complained:

When we get down to going over these reports, which I thought was a waste of time—it's my opinion, of course, maybe everybody doesn't agree, and I want to hear about it. But I don't believe that we had any objective or purpose in mind when we started going through these things. We didn't know really what we were looking for. I'm speaking of myself; I should say "I"—I didn't know what I was looking for; I didn't know what to look for, and I think, in my opinion, we kind of went off on a tangent of nonrelevant analysis of the whole thing that didn't really...when I think about all the discussion about all these different reports, I don't think we came up with anything that was worth a damn as far as furthering our real objective in this thing. And it's because of the lack of objectivity, because of lack of purpose on my part, that I wasn't able to come up with anything. Had I known what the staff, who, I might add, has been very patient in letting us run on these things,...had I known what really to look for, it could have well been that I would have come up with something. But I didn't think that I had any cue at all as to what to look for, and so consequently I just ran through these things and listed things that really didn't move me at all. I don't think I've gotten anywhere with this report reading.

Another officer took issue with this negative assessment; he complained of a tendency among some group members to defend every action of the men who had filed the reports:

In going over the reports, I don't think it was a total loss for me, because there are a couple in this stack right here where I would not have done what the officers in this particular case had done. It wouldn't have been that important to me. I can't go against Joe's analysis that it wasn't good police work. I just don't think that the end result at this point in my career—I'll put it that way—would have made the damned thing worth while to me. Everybody looks at it differently, probably everybody in this room does—the officers anyway. I just feel that it isn't worth the hassle at this stage. Ten years ago it might have been different.

The same subject also brought a personal reaction by one of the staff:

I must confess that I have trouble with visualizing an officer standing there watching a person who is handcuffed being beaten up. I have trouble coping with this thing, and I have a hunch that here's an area for me to work through; I don't know which way I want to go. I just have an unresolved problem here which I find myself worrying about at this stage.

This statement elicited solicitous concern from several members of the group:

OFFICER: [You object] from a humanitarian point of view?

STAFF: Yah, I guess so. The problem is I really want to be with you guys. On the other hand, I can't reconcile myself to that kind of business.

OFFICER 2: I could have a solution for you after it's all over.

STAFF: O.K.

OFFICER 2: You've got 32 hours a week you can ride next to me in a patrol car.

STAFF: All right, I will take you up on that.

This interchange produced an arrangement whereby one of the staff sometimes accompanied group members on patrol. This not only furnished feedback opportunities, but also helped cement rapport between staff and officers.

Third-session morale was again high and discussions uninhibited. A spectrum of views (with "right-wing" and "left-wing" advocates) had begun to appear. The group had also begun to form identity and in-group loyalty. In discussing possible interviews with high-incidence officers, for example, there was much concern about locker-room reaction:

When we talked about the possibility of bringing officers up here and possibly showing them some report and asking them what they though about it, and hoping that they would give some idea as to some of their problems, there are going to be officers in this department, and probably some of those that we choose, that are going to be very resentful of the fact that we've picked them out to partake in this study, or whatever you want to call it. And I'm just wondering is there some way that we can contain this resentment and prevent it from going downstairs amongst the ranks to where it would be harmful to our program? All it takes is one officer to go downstairs and say "these guys are a group of finks," or "this study is no good," and it could spread around this department like wildfire, and we'd have a real problem.

The group had coalesced despite differences, and felt that it had a distinct function. In the weeks ahead, the group was destined to struggle with the definition and scope of its aims.

THE INADEQUACIES OF THE ACADEMIC APPROACH

At its fourth meeting, our group had reached the juncture of discontent with talk. In the session summary, one of the staff diagnosed the condition as follows:

I think if we don't (get to work through the details of our projects) the group is going to get an increasing feeling that we aren't getting anywhere, that this is too vague and sort of bull-sessionish, and it's going to be very hard to conquer this, because sort of saying that there is some vague sense of something that we are carrying away, which is knowledge, ain't going to satisfy us. There's just so long that we can say "Gee, I'm getting a new look at this," without this getting a little unconvincing in our own minds.

This statement provided the stimulus for a frank explosion among the officers. One group member, who had previously declined to comment on the sessions, proclaimed:

OFFICER: I'm at a point of really wondering just what the hell we're up here talking about. I think a good example is our discussion with the sergeant in the lounge before we came up today. The only thing that we could relate to this man about what we're doing, the only thing I could say was, "well, our purpose is to see if there was some way, through research, that assaults that occur on the street, directed against police officers, can be proportionately cut down. I realize they can't be completely obliterated; it's impossible. But our purpose is to find some way, if any, of how to proportionately cut them down." Now, great, you know!

OFFICER 2: The next question is "How?"

OFFICER: Well, honest to God, I just sit here right now; I'm tired, I was argumentative tonight...I'm almost at a point of frustration, because I don't think we're getting anywhere. I don't know what to say. I don't know what we're trying to do, still!...I think what the staff is doing is sitting back on their laurels, and waiting for us to come up with what they want us to come up with anyhow. Now, wouldn't it be a shortcut if you just tell us what the hell you want, so we can get into it and maybe find out something! That's all I have to say.

Despite feelings of this kind, which were shared by other officers, the group had made progress on several fronts. For one, they had experienced an opportunity to test and revise a formal hypothesis. In reviewing incidents volunteered by one of the group, the officers had guessed that one of the suspects was violence-prone. The "rap sheet" was secured, and the hunch confirmed. Later, in another incident, the civilian proved to have a record clear of assaults. This finding produced an interest among the group in further investigation of police assaulters.

The session had also yielded a volunteer among the group for a trial interview, who was furnished the opportunity to explore alternatives to his actions. The officer, who had struggled with the temptation to defend his behavior, commented:

> I feel that one thing that's got to be destroyed in part of us—in all of us to a great extent—is our automatic attitude of defending the officer's action. We identify very quickly with the officer; and I think we're going to have a tendency, to a great extent, to try to find reasons why the guy was right. I really don't want this totally destroyed in me, but nevertheless, I'd like to be able to have enough of it broken down so I can at least look at the problem objectively and say "well, damn it, the guy did make a mistake."

The staff tried throughout the session to deflect the group from the habit of evaluating (and therefore, defending) officer actions. In the context of this struggle to arrive at a nonevaluative level of discourse, the idea for a critical-incident questionnaire was born:

> I'm not going to argue with Officer Mills there about everything is good police practice, but I think George and I can agree that it would be kind of nice to find out what other officers think about what's good police practice. And I think we can do this; I think we have the imagination here among us, the way we talk, to build the instrument, to put down the incidents and the questions that relate to the incidents, so that we can find out what people think.

PRELUDE TO ACTION

Early in the fifth meeting, a member of the staff listed the research possibilities that had originated with the group. The group set to work. It initiated four projects: (1) it collected all arrest reports by one officer, and studied these for patterns; (2) it discussed a trial run with live recordings on the street; (3) it resolved to administer a critical-incident questionnaire on police interventions; and (4) it resolved to interview the civilians (Hell's Angels) involved in a recent conflict with police.

The group expressed satisfaction with its progress, and with the staff feedback that initiated it. Bill, the officer who had exploded in the previous session, asserted:

BILL: We had a guide to follow tonight when we came to work, and I think as a result we got a few more things done, and we had a little more direction than we've had in the past.

OFFICER 2: We can thank the staff for that.

STAFF: Excuse me, but I think we can thank Bill and the comments when we left off Thursday; we had a mandate to be well organized.

A number of practical difficulties were discussed. The group resolved to notify other officers involved in taped incidents beforehand, to obtain their consent. In the case of the critical-incident survey, the group discussed implications of the findings. As noted by a staff member,

> I think we have laid what one could over-fancily call a conceptual base for this critical-incident survey. I'm not quite sure that we are all convinced of this being terribly worthwhile, but I think we have enough consensus here so that we can proceed. And it will be our first really formal research effort, in that this will call for the development of items, for the design of some kind of sampling procedure, for formal analysis in which we will be engaged; those of us in the group that have not done formal research before will be engaged in the kind of thing that is usually reserved for Ph.Ds.

The pattern analysis of the officer's reports yielded a number of hypotheses, which the officers thought plausible. One of the group commented:

> I think that we got a lot out of the reports tonight, at least I did. In studying a lot of reports from one particular officer, I think that you can see a pattern as to why he might be having some of the trouble that he's having out on the street. I think that it was a much better way to go about it than studying a lot of different officers' reports, and trying to get something from that. Just sticking to one man you get a much better view of it.

For the first time the officers analyzed incidents in terms of patterns, as opposed to merits or demerits of action. One officer argued:

> Maybe we ought to be getting off the kick of justifying every action that a police officer makes just because he is a police officer. We seem to be heading in that direction an awful lot. We spend an awful lot of time justifying what is done, rather than finding some of the reasons for it.

The group was pleased with progress, but the labor of the session had none of the "honeymoon" flavor of the first meetings. A staff member summarized the phenomenon and extrapolated it by telling the group:

> It seems to me, we worked pretty hard. This session was probably a little less fun than some. On the other hand, I think we are off the kind of note of unhappiness we were on at the end of last session. In order to get off it, we had to sacrifice some entertainment, and I had to sacrifice some correct procedure and do a lot of pushing that I don't like to see myself do. But from here on in, I think we are working, and next time we will be forced to

immediately go into the business of working out our interview if we discover that we have people available. And from 8:00 on, this group is going to turn into a research group, in the sense that it will actually be out there asking questions, getting answers; then we can think about them. The next day, Thursday, we can revise our procedure and our thinking in terms of what we've found the previous day, and again we'll be busy getting information and thinking about it.

THE TRAVAILS OF PLANNING

The next session brought another stage in a cycle that repeated itself, with variations, throughout our project. The joys of untrammeled debate had been followed by a call for action that resulted in working sessions. The latter usually proved taxing. Restless interludes were followed (as we shall see) with elation over achievement; this led to doubt over impact.

The sixth session was one that required detailed planning, and the group showed apprehension and boredom. A staff member summarized the sequence of events:

> We started the session by going over the tape recorder and its use, and there was a lot of joking about erasing and the procedures for erasing, and a lot of reluctance to talk into the tape recorder. There was a reiteration of the doubts in reference to the recording of other officers and even of recording incidents which we got yesterday in the last session.... From the tape recorder we moved into the instrument, into the design of the critical-incident instrument. The group went right to work on it. They produced a whole series of incidents, although at one or two junctures they got off into collateral discussions.... During that discussion two of the members of the group went down to the patrol division to make their contacts, and upon their return they reported that there had been some joking about the unit's role as a fink group.... When that discussion of fink-type joking was initiated, the whole range of public relations problems for the unit was broached. Some members of the group made the very sensible suggestion that the members ought to make themselves available for questioning at lineups about the function of the unit. They also expressed some anxiety and interest relating to an Information Bulletin about the unit which was to be released soon.

The staff member analyzed the situation, as he saw it, for the group:

> By and large, I think we can regard today's session as being 90% a working session. It's about the first time we've actually sat down and worked—other than, say, what happened yesterday when we looked over these reports. I was a little afraid, because by and large I know how boring this can be. I warned you about this last time; I warned you about this when we started. It's, on the one hand, obviously a little frustrating to just sit around and have a bull session, because you get the feeling you aren't getting anywhere, and we had this out last week. On the other hand, when you really move to

respond to this, and you start saying, "well, let's not talk at all, and let's start working," this brings in another set of frustrations, and you have to face those. It's going to pan out, because as soon as we go on to the next step, we'll get information back, and when you get information back and you look at it, and it makes sense, and you have questions that are answered, that's where all this frustration looks less frustrating. But at the moment, when we're just kind of sitting around, worrying about thinking up incidents and how to word them, and so on, there is no immediate payoff.

The "payoff," as it happened, was relatively close at hand. In fact, it emerged during the next session.

THE FRUITS OF LABOR

In its seventh session, the group conducted (and analyzed) an interview with officers involved in the incident with the Hell's Angels. The group also reviewed the first version of its critical-incident questionnaire.

The group emerged from the evening with the feeling that their mission had integrity, and that they could easily defend it. As one officer put it:

There is a closer support of the staff and confidence in this new experiment or process. (We feel) that we are in fact moving forward toward an end product that we, I think, find mutually agreeable. The enthusiasm we had tonight was comparable to the first couple of times we were here. I think this enthusiasm brought us back to the realization that we haven't severed ourselves from the other officers, a feeling that was kind of...allayed tonight.

The cooperativeness of interviewees left the officers with a feeling of potency. One group member commented:

I don't know that my enthusiasm ever did reach a terrible low point in this project. I guess I always hoped that something was going to come out of it. But after tonight I find that, although I may not be able to express it, that somehow I've got a renewed enthusiasm that there can be some good come out of this group and that there probably will be. I'm beginning to understand more why the staff have been so cagey with us, in perhaps letting us see this for ourselves, rather than telling us maybe what we can accomplish. No question in my mind that they had a lot that they hoped we could accomplish up here, and that they could have told us what they hoped we could accomplish. If they wouldn't have an idea what could be accomplished out of this, there would have been no need for the project. After talking with these guys up here tonight, I think that maybe we all saw in that one incident, the Hell's Angels incident, that there was perhaps a very big alternative. And it renews my enthusiasm that something meaningful can come out of this.

The session also produced a research idea that was to occupy much attention at a later date. This idea arose during discussion with one of the interviewees, Officer Beam. As noted by the summarizer:

> One thing that we thought about and Beam brought it out himself was the
> influence that the older officer has on the new officer, the training officer on
> the rookie officer. And I think we should and will take a long look into this
> aspect. Do we need to be more selective in placing new officers?

The group tried hard to "sell" itself to its guests. In this effort, it
met with partial success. The interviewees did "buy" the group's credibility, but not its concern with violence. The group, in turn (to maintain
credibility), showed no inclination to argue the violence case, once the
interviewees forcefully made their point:

> During the interview, the group took the opportunity to try to sell the four
> officers on the merits of the Violence Prevention Unit. They tried to sell it on
> the basis of it being an avenue to reach the chief—and incidentally, the
> interviewees voiced all kinds of strong feelings about the administration. So
> one of the ways the group justified its existence was by characterizing itself
> as an effective avenue for the expression of grievances. There was also some
> talk of reducing violence, but the interviewees seemed to cut this short by
> voicing very strongly their views that violence was a function of the situation,
> and that the only way to deal with violence was to have adequate weapons
> and physical force and competent physical specimens—and that further-
> more, violence isn't really necessarily bad. I mean, "why all this concern,"
> was the question, "with riots"? The implication being that maybe a good riot
> isn't so bad after all.

The informal leader of the visiting team, Officer Beam, availed himself of the group forum to make a strong pro-violence statement. According to the summarizer, he

> talked almost continuously, and very volubly, and not only related two inci-
> dents in response to questions about them, but expressed himself at great
> length about his own philosophy with regard to interpersonal interactions,
> police work, and responses to violence. There was a strong pitch about the
> necessity to meet force with force, to instill respect, to show power, to set
> precedents by moving into situations forcibly—the merits of direct physical
> action, the merits of hardware, the need for some kind of tactical force, and
> so on.

Members of our group listened to this statement with seeming rev-
erence. A staff member later confessed his trepidation, wondering
whether

> Beam's pitch was so convincing that it could set us a month back. And as I
> was sitting here watching everybody nod their heads and say, "Isn't that
> true. Shit, isn't that exactly what it's like! Isn't it really true that we gotta go
> out there and display force in order to get them to respect us? And isn't it true
> that we gotta mount a machine gun on the rear fender? Ain't it a fact that the
> only thing these guys understand is a show of force?" There was a kind of
> nagging doubt in my mind about, gee, you know, we lost everything!

Although in its analysis of the interview the group returned to previous form, the lesson remained. The pull of the locker room had been felt. In the months to come, we would experience it repeatedly. We could build a subculture, but we could not, with equal ease, insulate and defend it. Contagion runs both ways. Change agents are subject to change and to impact.

REVIEW OF AIMS

The principal activity in the eighth session was identical to that of the previous day: the group interviewed officers involved in the Hell's Angels incident. This time the question of interview objectives was raised and cast a pall of gloom over the group.

The issue was posed by a staff member, who embarked on a talk about interviewing procedure early in the session:

> I picked precisely the wrong moment to feed in some technical information about interviewing. The reasoning behind it was, "well, we're now in the process of interviewing; this is the time it would make most sense—while we're doing it." In fact, it backfired because what it very plausibly sounded like was a kind of critique of what happened yesterday.

The technical information was lost on the group (in the words of one officer, "most of it went over my head"), but the discussion did pose the question of aims and accomplishments. The group had rushed to embark on research. The aim (comparing police and suspect versions of an incident) had receded in favor of divergent, unverbalized ends. One of these was to "sell" the group; another to explore the philosophy of special-duty officers; a third, fact-finding, and a fourth, group thinking. Once this became obvious, the success of the previous evening's venture was less evident. As the staff summarizer noted:

> We did emerge, by virtue of this ambiguity of our objectives, into a kind of unhappy state where we were shouting at each other about what went wrong when in effect that is a question you can't really answer because you can't talk about what went wrong when you don't know what's going right.

Group morale was low. Interview participants felt attacked and deprived of credit. Others demanded structure. One officer stated:

> I think it's about time we start getting down to the nitty-gritty of what we're doing, go back a little ways, bring up what we have done, and perhaps this will give us some sense of what direction we're going to go. Now we've been here two months, and we've rambled on and on and on, and we've brought up a lot of problems, and we've brought up a lot of different areas that possibly will be applicable to this survey, but it's been two months, and we need something solid and concise to go on. We've been here eight times; I'm sorry, one month, and I think now we need to get things set down in concise terms as to where we have been, and where we're going to go.

The interview again went smoothly. It was lively, with much give and take. The exploration centered on "special-duty" philosophy and stimulated considerable discussion among the group. One of the officers volunteered to prepare a summary of interview content and conclusions. Another group member brought up the critical-incident survey, and the group spelled out sampling and distribution procedures.

TWO STEPS FORWARD

The next session saw a rebirth of morale. The group witnessed a significant victory in the form of a good tape. A cassette recorder had been borrowed for experimental use, and one of the officers, Bill, had produced a powerful, pointed incident. Bill supplied explanatory comments and the group added to them. Several officers suggested that the discussion, added to the tape, could make a useful, self-contained training tool.

The group spent several hours with the commander of the special-duty unit whose members had been the previous week's guests. The officer had requested the interview under the impression that the group was interested in his unit. Although the time was tangentially invested, it proved satisfying. The interview went well, and the group was flattered by the opportunity of talking with a supervising officer:

> There's no question that everybody was very much with it. Again the group gave a number of testimonials to a guest about their own conversion and insight, and so on. And even when he sort of misunderstood and side-tracked, they returned to it to make sure he got the point. I think the group was also reinforced in that they saw that they were perceived as powerful outside. The questioning today was nowhere near as irrelevant as it was last week, in the sense that most of the questions that were asked were fairly incisive and to the point, and there wasn't any of the spurious agreeing with. It could have been extremely inviting. After all, the man who was here was a lieutenant.

The group also discussed definitions of the police mission (a subject reopened by the interviews) and the chief's problems in implementing his definition. The officers resolved to take up this question with the chief at an early date.

A HAPPENING

The next session proved to be a high point in the group's development. In line with previous plans, the suspects' version of the Hell's

Angels incident was obtained, together with information about the motorcyclists' view of police, life, and each other.

The officers felt that the interview was eye-opening, and that their guests (in particular, the Oakland chieftain of the Angels) were impressive spokesmen for their camp. One officer exclaimed, in the wake of the experience:

> I'm really at kind of a loss of words, because I'm so damned impressed with that Sonny! I can see why those guys look up to him, because, it seems to me that whatever in hell he decided to do in life, he would have been "A-1" at it. The guy makes a lot of sense. I'm very impressed with him. I'm not saying that I'm so sympathetic with the Hell's Angels that I'm seeing their side, and not the police side; that's not the case at all. The guy put forward a very frank and forthright presentation; his answers were very concise, very clear. Undoubtedly the guy lives and believes what he represents. I was very impressed with it. You know the full impact of it, I really haven't had time to think about it, and I'm sure that I will be giving a lot of thought to exactly what took place in this exchange of words in this interview.

Another group member confessed:

> You know our orientation as to what the Hell's Angels are. Before coming on the police department I heard about their big rape raids across small towns in the United States. When you first come into the department, going through rookie school, you hear various officers talk about them; nothing good is ever said. I was so surprised that a guy could sit there who is an outcast as far as society is concerned, that the guy could sit there and just speak so frankly and in such a way that everything he said, you could just hang on the word; the guy's got a hell of a way of expressing himself, and I guess the reason it is, is because it's so damned simple.

Some members of the group proposed a Hell's Angels session with recruits in the academy. One suggested a videotaped discussion. Another officer argued that veteran officers, like himself, could most benefit from group contact:

> I think it's too bad that more people couldn't have heard it besides us seven. I'm wondering if maybe the fact that it was so spontaneous in such a unique situation, if maybe this wasn't.... I'm wondering if they went before a class of recruits or something I think something would be lost in it. Maybe not, but that's my opinion. I think something might be lost, and right this minute I think the most important thing isn't impressing a class of recruits, it's impressing the officer that's working the street now, like I was impressed.

The interview had gone extremely well as a technical effort. The men had spent the afternoon with a nonpolice group, and had created an atmosphere of cordial openness, in which much information was obtained. A staff member characterized the session as an "impressive exercise in communication and seeing the other guy's point of view." He added:

> Except for one little tense moment involving a little notice on the board, which was not meant for our guests, depicting police officers confronting eight motorcyclists with a legend such as "It's pretty lonely out there—" except for that, which they took with pretty good humor, there was really very little tension about this. An extremely free exchange. And I might say I was extremely impressed with the way we were able to question these people without being patronizing, hypocritical, or hostile. There were some questions asked that were quite sharp; the answers were frank. What we told them seemed to me to be quite frank.

A point noted by the summarizer was that, viewed as a subculture, the Hell's Angels had orientations and problems similar to some police officers, and particularly to the "special-duty" officers with whom they had clashed:

> One point that we certainly got out of this, most of us got out of this, is that there are some parallels between Hell's Angel problems and police problems. That came through quite striking with points such as young Hell's Angels, young police officers; the code of brotherhood. And also we sensed, I think, that in some of the things they were describing, they could have been talking about one of the units in this department very aptly.

One officer said that in managing group problems, the Hell's Angels might, in some ways, be better socializers than their police counterparts:

> He mentioned something to me that impressed me that is diametrically opposed to how we think, how we act, and what we, in fact, do on the street. And that's when he brought up the fact that "when we see a guy out of line, we stop him, man, and kind of let him know that he's out of line." This is diametrically opposed to anything I've learned in six years, and it's opposed to what Sam has learned in all the time he's been on the force. I'm wondering if it might not be a good idea. I think that it could be done in such a way, that Bill brought up plenty of times up here, or a few times up here, that he's maybe saved somebody's ass, or maybe saved some policeman from getting the grease by very tactfully and unnoticed grabbing some guy and getting him the hell away from there. We make mistakes; I've made mistakes; everybody here has. Just like Sonny Barger said, the whole Hell's Angels group has to suffer because of one man's mistake. We have to suffer because if I get in the shit, and Sam and Bill have to come in and bail me out, they're not going to be happy if I'm wrong; then they have to ride my heat too. We brought it up, but it's something to think about.

The success of the experiment did not blind the group to the need for planning further activity. They scheduled interviews to document their case for more systematic assignment of training officers. They discussed recruit-training innovations to improve the sophistication of young officers in the human relations area. They also talked about questionnaires.

A REBIRTH OF ANXIETY

In their next session, the group prepared itself to meet the chief the following night. In the context of worry about the chief's reaction, the group became concerned about its effectiveness to date. Once again, Bill was the catalyst of discontent. It was noted in the summary that

> When we were talking about our discussion with the chief tomorrow night, Bill made a statement that kind of kicked off a good deal of discussion and kind of brought us back to that third or fourth session when we started saying, "Where in the heck are we going?" It seems kind of surprising that it would pop up at this time, but Bill said that if the chief asked him what we've accomplished down here, he says he wouldn't know what to tell him, and I think it probably made us all start thinking, "well, what the heck would we tell him what we've accomplished down here?" Then it kind of gave us the idea and a little bit of worry that, "son of a gun, have we really accomplished anything?" I know I think it kind of affected me that way to a certain extent, and I find myself wanting to charge ahead and act on a lot of proposals that have been made, a lot of ideas that I thought were kind of held in the balance.

It seemed plausible that such worries were inspired by awe of the chief, but they took the form of complaints about progress. The staff faced these complaints by reviewing the group's work and its plans:

> With his (staff) summary of the things that we do have in the fire that have not really been pushed to the wayside, I think perhaps it kind of made us feel like, feel better about what we had accomplished up here, of what we may accomplish.

The men spent part of the session interviewing an officer who had a high incidence of conflict experiences. The interview was a model of self-study. The interviewee—a young man with some graduate school—was articulate in thinking about himself. He produced a number of observations, one of which related to the impact of training on his own development. The officer's testimonial renewed the group's enthusiasm for its study of training-officer assignments:

> It seemed to be in Joe's mind that the training officer will cause many lasting impressions in the new officer's method of operation on the street. Joe can see a lot of merit in properly selected and properly trained training officers. He seemed to indicate to me that he changed after four years, or during the four-year span of time, kind of by the trial and error method.

Group morale was raised by the interview and by the discussion it inspired. But the men remained concerned throughout by their impending talk with the chief.

An Identity Crisis

The summer was at its midpoint, and the group had progressed far in its development. It had identified with program goals and had isolated relevant parameters. It had come to view its context in terms of critical junctures for impact and change. It had asked questions and obtained data.

Throughout, the group had struggled with its role. It felt itself powerful, but saw no impact; it viewed itself as productive, but saw no products. It felt itself needed, but had no praise. In the context of this crisis, the chief's presence was propitious and ominous. Too much was at stake, and too little was possible. The hidden agenda of the session made demands that were unreasonable and inchoate.

The chief encountered hunches rather than data; he faced crude ideas and hopes for change. He saw a group in search of a mission. His role was that of a creditor whose clients had prospects, but little collateral. Given this fact, the chief did the best he could. He urged the group to proceed; he shared thoughts about the department and its fate; he testified to faith, and he expressed hope.

The group felt deflated without knowing why. One of the staff observed that

> The chief responded, it seemed to me, perfectly frankly, in terms of what went on in his mind, from the vantage point of his desk, to some general questions we raised. The fact that he was doing so here, and the fact that he was putting so much effort into it, could conceivably have been seen as a positive feature; instead I think it sort of made us increasingly depressed. I don't quite understand why.

The session was contaminated by the group's depression. The group interviewed the sergeant of a special-duty unit, without knowing, or caring, why. While waiting for their guest, they listened to tapes that had been recorded under unsatisfactory acoustical conditions. One incident had been recorded over and the rest was static. The experience was described as a "waste" or "minor tragedy."

The sergeant, who had requested the session, appeared in a friendly and expectant mood. The group had no questions, and the sergeant made a statement, throughout which the men sat preoccupied. There was a long silence, which one officer broke by inquiring about the Hell's Angels incident, which had been reviewed on four previous occasions. While the sergeant covered the ground once again, the men doodled. At length an officer inquired, pointedly, about the prevalence of violence among the sergeant's men. The interview ended and the sergeant left.

Bill, who had been one of the most obviously depressed members of the group, reviewed his role and came close to an apology:

BILL: I don't know if I've been a disruptive influence on this group for the last couple of days. I think I have, for some reason, fiddley-fucking around with a piece of paper while Jack's trying to summarize, which isn't really very cute for a grown man.

JACK: It's all right—it's all right.

BILL: No, but I'll tell you what. Maybe I've let a few personal problems I happen to have lately in to sort of push this thing out of my mind, and I've lost a hell of a lot of enthusiasm for some reason, I don't know why. I don't want to. But maybe like Waterman says, if we can get down and start producing something concrete, it'll come back. And that was a real boring, shitty night, as far as I'm concerned, and practically a complete waste of time. And like I say, I don't know why.

Other members of the group were equally puzzled, but saw some hope. They called for project-related work, and resolved once more to move ahead.

TASK FORCE ACTIVITY

Officer Waterman, the group's conscience, had called for small task-related work groups. He had proposed that

I'd like to spend some of this time instead of talking and interviewing, I'd like to go to smaller groups and sit down and get some of this stuff down on paper. I'm a paper man when it comes to projects. I would really like to pursue this training-officer thing.... And we've all bitched about this radio room for as long as we've been on the street; we've told our sergeant about it, sometimes we've bitched about it on the air; we've called him up on the telephone so mad and told him, the dispatcher, off over the phone because we couldn't do it over the air. Here's a chance maybe to do something about it, and I'd like to get down to the nitty-gritty. I really would.

In line with this proposal, the group divided into subgroups, and worked on the training-officer study, the idea of a radio room survey, the technical problems of tape recording, and the analysis of the questionnaire pretest.

Progress was made on each front. The critical-incident group diagnosed a communication gap within the department on the basis of supervisor–subordinate differences. They discussed special uses for the instrument, involving a number of target groups:

It was brought out that it could be sort of found where the communication gap lies, if any, between the DC and the chief, the deputy chief to the captain to the lieutenants down to the sergeants and the patrolmen; whether or not the patrolman was reacting in a way that the sergeant wanted him to react, or in other words, differences of opinion; if these differences between particular sergeants exist and influence subordinates that work under them. And the patrolmen, just giving it to them in a straight way, and then giving it to them and having it filled out on the premise of "What do you think the chief would want you to do?" to find out if there's a lack of knowledge as far as the chief's policies are concerned. It sounds kind of garbled. Then we brought out that it could be given to special groups, rookies that are just on the street, and Sam came up with the idea, or somebody did, that it'd be kind of interesting to find out what they'd put down on this thing. Then, of course, time on the job would have something to do with it, and the high 148s, guys that we've talked to, especially those that do have a high rate of 243 and 148, to see if their answers are a little different.

The live-taping group explored ways of editing material and devised a "sound-on-sound" technique for the processing of incidents. Waterman, whose avocation is electronics, became director of the project:

We talked a little bit about the ways of transcribing these tapes and dubbing information into them to make the critical points in the incident more meaningful. We talked about whether to do this by a stop-and-go process; in other words, play a part of the incident, then when we reach a critical point in the incident, where maybe it turns to violence, or where violence was averted, stopping the incident tape and dubbing it by voice sort of as explanation of what occurred there from, say, from what we've learned up here about the way people react. This is one way we talked about it; another way that might be meaningful was discussed as to whether or not to try the sound-on-sound technique of bringing the incident in kind of full bore, so that the whole incident can be heard, not the whole incident, but the critical points of the incident, and then kind of fading the incident into the background and bringing the narrator's voice in till it's in the foreground; in other words, when the narrator's being heard, the listener will still have the psychological effect of hearing the incident going on in the background, much like these narrative shows in TV do. I feel personally that it wouldn't be too hard to do with sound-on-sound–type equipment, and I brought up the point that I have some rather nice recorders at home where this type of thing can be carried out, and I'm perfectly willing to make a few experiments at home, not only by myself, but anybody else who wants to come over and kind of tinker around; we may try this technique. It may be more entertaining to the rookie sitting in the classroom listening to it in this manner.

The total group felt encouraged (with one caveat):

OFFICER: Well, I think overall for tonight, we've gotten more done just from the standpoint of deciding what we're going to do, and then getting right down to the nitty-gritty of planning it out. I saw a renewed enthusiasm from this standpoint, that we were getting down to doing something of what we're here for.

SAM: Well, I'd like to go on record as saying that I can't stand that word "NITTY-GRITTY"!

OFFICER: Strike "nitty-gritty."

Officer Waterman, the organizer of the subgroup procedure, predicted continued progress:

> Seriously speaking, last Thursday I thought was a catastrophe. I think everybody here thought it was a catastrophe. Today I came in very sleepy, you know? I wasn't really looking forward to.... Now I feel we've got something that we're all going to be sinking into from here on out; at least for a couple days, the enthusiasm is going to be renewed.

But not all was auspicious. The Oakland police were facing strike possibilities, and several of the men were worried. The officers were also in an oddly humorous mood: Bill talked of mass resignations, and someone mentioned firing the staff. In a more serious vein, the issue of locker-room reputation had again risen:

> Joe brought in an incident which I think is worth mentioning. He was present in a situation in which an officer had become a little impatient with a suspect, and Joe found himself forced to exercise a little calming action. Then it developed that another officer present at the scene took it upon himself to misrepresent Joe's participation in a way which could conceivably partly reflect on Joe's membership here. Now I guess that we decided that there probably was no immediate connection between the repercussions of the incident and Joe's membership in this unit. We decided, I think, that this was probably the backwash of an interpersonal difficulty, a personality conflict. But on the other hand, it gave rise to a series of comments that have to do with the reason why Joe brought this up here; namely, that there is a question of what does our role here imply in terms of how we are seen, and what does it imply in terms of the strategy we have to follow in order to be able to do what we feel we ought to do? But I think, at an even more significant level, what it implies is that some of us, at least—and I think many of us here feel that in some way—if we haven't changed our thinking, at least we have articulated it a little more, so that what we have to cope with is not what people think of us as members of this unit, but what we have to do in order to cope with what we feel is new and different about the way we think.

Despite these ambivalences, the next session (the fourteenth) went smoothly. Members of two subgroups embarked on individual research assignments. One officer interviewed the commanding official of the training division, while his subgroup drew up criteria for training officers. The radio room task force embarked on interviews with dispatchers and on observations of the radio room (including the monitoring of calls). The group also began to prepare a flowchart of the dispatching process.

The questionnaire group, temporarily unemployed, spent its time reviewing the design of the entire project. In response to inquiry from one of the officers, a staff member shared the project proposal with the group and delineated the men's role as trainers in the next stage of the study. The subgroup began to discuss the procedure for selecting trainees and control groups:

> One of the biggest things that we discussed in my opinion was how are we going to get these people up here, the second group which will be 17 people that are violence prone? And then we have another group that we are going to watch, that we aren't going to do anything with that are also violence-prone, for comparison. We discussed how we are going to get them up.

The entire group met briefly for status reports, declared itself satisfied, and disbanded.

Diminishing Returns

The fifteenth session was reserved for subgroup reports to the total group. It went badly. The bulk of the discussion turned on the need to revise some of the questionnaire items. Several hours were invested in rewording four questions, and the task was boring. An effort to add one question to the instrument, which consumed 30 minutes, proved fruitless. Bill, a member of the questionnaire task force, felt particularly despondent, in part over the redundancy involved in the group's review of subgroup work:

> But then again I feel that when we sat in here for five hours and went over these things, that we were much more aware of what we were doing and what we wanted to do and that it was just as impossible for the others to come in here and to jump right in and understand the whole picture as it would have been impossible for us to jump right in and understand their study of the radio dispatcher or the training officer, because we just didn't spend that much time talking about it.

Staff expressed some worry about group morale:

> But I do think in general the fact of the matter is that we need to think of some way of enlivening the situation here with some variety. I mean, we have responded to the call for complete tasks. That gets us into a lot of routine. I think maybe it's about time we swung the pendulum back pretty soon and got into something which is a little more interesting, and then got back to our tasks.

The officers had not reached a complete "low," but made it obvious that they were bored. During the last hour, which called for the summary, the men abstained:

> The group was most blatant tonight in a growing tendency to shut off the shared discussing and summarizing during the last hour of the day's session.

> It reached a point tonight where it was made blatantly clear around the table that none of the officers were to contribute anything, and indeed that was almost 100% the way it worked out. The staff made the main statements that were made and only upon being called upon directly did Bill add anything to the discussion.

The session ended early, on a restless note.

THE FEEL OF SUCCESS

The next session (the sixteenth) was a stormy one, but suffused with enthusiasm. Closure had been reached on several projects, and the men were happy with their achievements. The questionnaire group had a draft of their instrument and a design for its administration. The tape group had produced an incident that inspired a stimulating analysis session. The dispatcher group presented an impressive draft report.

Controversy arose with respect to the training-officer project. Several objections were raised to the criterion list, including a demand by staff for more emphasis on human relations skill. Waterman, as spokesman for the task force, replied very heatedly. Another officer (Bill) played a conciliatory role:

> I got kind of hot last night about somebody talking about or criticizing what we had done in here on this questionnaire thing when we had spent four hours. I didn't think it was right for anyone to come in here and in five minutes kind of rip me apart. So I've got a lot of sympathy for Hank, because you guys have really worked your tails off in there apparently and really thought this thing over. You've done a lot of hard work on it and I'm appreciative of it. I think it'll work out and we certainly don't expect you to come in here and everyone to agree with everyone else.

Waterman, who had agreed to review the criterion list again, stressed the group-product aspect of the projects:

> I was somewhat offended by what occurred after I finished reading these criteria. I don't feel I could—I guess I was in a way. Like Bill said, this was my baby, but in a way this whole thing is my baby, too, everything that's happened in this unit. It was a response that I didn't expect. I by any means didn't expect staff's response, and I don't think he expected mine. Anyway, I just wanted to point out that this whole field-training-officer thing is a group effort of the whole subcommittee, both phases of it so far, as the additional phases will be.

Both the negative and positive reactions showed ego involvement of officers in the projects with which they had been concerned. Each subgroup member became an advocate of his group's effort. A staff member recalled that

When we started the tape-recorded incident today, there was a lot of restlessness and a lot of kind of sighing and sitting back with a pained expression on their faces. But when they heard the results, they became quite sold, and of course it is significant that Young, whose incident it was and who was the main participant, was especially sold. He was quite anxious after the session to inquire how do we incorporate this into group training and so on. The same thing happened with these other projects. For instance, Bill, who is by no means gullible, has become extremely sold in the critical-incident study to the point of seeing all kinds of applications of it that are even vague to me. Both he and Sam have been trying to sell this instrument to the rest of the group, where at least Bill, before he became involved in tabulating the responses, was asking questions like "what the hell good is this?"

The men were generally pleased, and looked forward with vociferous anticipation to early tangible products.

The Group Has a Guest

The seventeenth session was spent with a visiting expert, Chief Fred Ferguson of the Covina (California) police. The staff had invited the chief because of his role as innovator, particularly as the originator of ingenious training techniques. The chief's men had participated in role-playing on the street, including a stint as jail inmates and a night as make-believe skidrow alcoholics. Chief Ferguson related these experiments, and the group listened with interest and enthusiasm. In turn, the men broached their own activities to the chief.

The group's reaction to Chief Ferguson is illustrated by comments such as:

Quite possibly we should have had Chief Ferguson in here when we first started, because he is quite dynamic. He does something new and different every day, or I get that idea. We started on a project here that's never been tried before and I think it would have been helpful to us to have gotten his views early in the game.

I feel that this man has an awful lot to offer law enforcement. Apparently, I don't know how many people around here have even heard of him. I never had until he came here. That's probably my fault. It was really a pleasure to listen to him, and it was also a pleasure to be associated with somebody of his caliber, and I'd like to thank the staff again for bringing this man here. If you've got any more like him we'd sure like to see them.

The techniques discussed by Chief Ferguson proved of considerable interest. Bill—a natural mimic—became especially taken by role playing as a training technique:

I can see a lot more use in this role-playing as a training method now that I've talked to him and I really would like to go and see it. I think it would be an asset to the group; and like I was telling Joe—he couldn't believe it—I'd go

> down there on my own time and pay my own way down. I really would. I'm
> that interested in it.

Chief Ferguson, in turn, was impressed with the group's work and with their enthusiasm. The officers talked about specific projects, each emphasizing the work with which he was most closely associated. One officer stated:

> The interesting thing to me about this last hour, for instance, is that if we had
> this guy here two weeks ago, and if we had gone around the table and we
> had described the group to him, we would have said all kinds of things about
> what we were doing here, none of which was said. And it wasn't only that we
> have the most recent experiences in mind when we think about what we do
> here, but also that we seem to be very involved in the projects that we are
> associated with. And each one of us, I think, is most strongly attached to the
> project that he is immediately involved in.

Chief Ferguson had planned to stay for half the session, but was sufficiently impressed to spend 7 hours with the men. He left with parting remarks concerning the "power" of the group.

AN UNSUCCESSFUL EXERCISE

The second session began with a review by staff of the outline for the second phase of the project. The group was almost exclusively concerned with the manner in which they would introduce the project to the stage-two trainees:

> Step one would be to introduce the program to these people, to put out a
> sales pitch to them, to let them know that violent experiences are an asset as
> well as a liability, I would suppose, and that we're neither condemning nor
> condoning these violent-type situations. Also, that we don't want anyone
> fired. It was kind of agreed that this would be a very good pitch, that we felt
> anyone who is having these problems, if he's a good officer, he's worth sav-
> ing. He's worth helping him keep his job.

One interesting sidelight evolved as a result of the previous session. Sam had declared himself incapable of role-playing, and was goaded by Bill into a display of short but unplanned anger. He confessed that

> in what Bill was doing—this role-playing on a small scale—he did raise me
> up. For a second there he got me going a little bit, which was spontaneous.
> He did a very good job of it. I think there's a lot of merit in what he did and
> the way he did it.

Another positive event in an otherwise dreary session emerged from a tape played by one of the officers. This tape provided an excellent recording of excerpts from a session in which the officer had dissuaded a motel guest from committing suicide:

> We played Joe Young's recording at the Thunderbird, where he helped this fellow with the solution to his money problems and turned a real sympathetic ear to the guy, perhaps helping him to work out his emotional problems as well. At one point staff stopped the recorder and asked Joe if this is police work. I think we all agreed that it is police work. My own thoughts on this is that we go out and catch a burglar for instance, and we take two or three hours sometimes to write up the reports and tie up the loose ends and get the evidence. I think the possibility of a man losing his life, or the fact of possibly saving a man's life is possibly worth the two hours that Joe stated he spent on this particular call.

The remainder of the session was perceived as relatively unproductive, and was terminated early.

INTENSIVE WORK

The next two sessions were spent in project-related activity, partly in task forces. The group's concern in the first session was mainly the tape project and in the second the questionnaire results. The taping discussion was initiated by Officer Waterman, who had prepared an impressively edited incident:

> I showed up a little late for work with some tapes that I'd been working on until about 4:30—a tape I was working on. During the past couple of days I've been working on this sound-on-sound technique. Actually, what I wanted to do was to make a tape that would demonstrate the process of using sound-on-sound and keeping the incident phased down in the background so you could still hear the incident at the same time you were hearing the explanation. Much to my surprise, it came out better than I'd really expected. I came up with an almost finished product. Perhaps it needs a little bit of editing, but it turned out very well. What I did was I took two incidents that I recorded over the weekend from our little Sony portable recorder, and from that recording I made a tape in one track of one of my stereo recorders. I used the other stereo recorder; I jacked the incident from one recorder into the first track of the recorder that I was doing the composite tape on and hooked the microphone into the other track. As I went along recording the incident, at certain points I would just use the volume control on the track that had the recorded incident in it and phase it down to a low level and just speak into the microphone some explanations of what was going on at that time, some descriptive explanation.

The results were impressive. As Bill describes them,

> Although it was quite some time after the incident happened, you still got the feeling that he's like a newsman standing out where Rome is burning or some goddam thing and he's telling you all about it.

The taping group discovered, as the evening wore on, that it had the beginning of a respectable library:

> We spent the whole evening listening, first of all to this composite tape that I'd put together, and then after that we went through three cassettes that were recorded by Bill and our two Joes. We found that we had a good variety of incidents—much more than we expected from our previous experiences.

The subgroup made a determined effort to communicate its enthusiasm to the other officers, and to promote more tapes. Bill argued:

> It's probably hard for the guys that are in the other room to get real enthused with this, because you haven't done anything with it. You've been working with training officers and radio room projects and you've been real involved in these things where we've been involved here, and it's hard in turn for us to get enthused about what you're doing. But we've really got something in these tape recordings, in these critical incidents that we're putting down on tape. It's going to be something that's going to really be a fantastic first. It's going to be a hell of a training tool. But we're going to have to have everybody's cooperation. Now I've been guilty of leaving that thing in the locker myself. But with this sound-on-sound we've got something that's really going to be good, it's really going to be worthwhile.

Bill also reasoned that the dramatic impact of the edited tapes should be a motivator among second-generation trainees:

> Another thing that just crossed my mind is that it's not only a training tool, but if we can work these things up interestingly enough, this is going to be a real good thing for involvement next summer, when we get these guys up here. Because if the tapes sound good enough and wild enough and interesting enough, they're going to want to take that goddam recorder out and do the same thing. I would.

On a more low-key note, the subgroups concerned with the dispatchers and the training-officer study reviewed outlines for their reports. They anticipated having completed drafts ready for editing at the next meeting.

During the next session the reports were written, despite the fact that some time was required for coding of the questionnaire. At the end of the session, the studies were ready for editing and presentation to the chief. The critical-incident data had been coded. The tabulations showing intradepartmental differences were summarized by the subgroup.

STAGE FRIGHT

The group began its penultimate session by scheduling task-force presentations for the next afternoon. According to the staff summarizer,

> We started off with going over our schedule with Chief Gain tomorrow and outlined a program that we'll present to him. Chronologically we'll begin at 2:30 in his conference room. The field-training study will be gone into. It's

printed up in a nice form, I was really impressed with it and from what I've read of it, I think you did a real good job on it, for what that's worth. At three o'clock the training tapes will be presented to him. And at 3:30 we'll go into the questionnaire results. At four o'clock the dispatcher study will be presented. At 4:30, the chief will be down here and we're going to have a group discussion with him. We might even get into what we're going to do next summer with the chief, if we can and if he's interested.

Planning was following by a discussion, led by the staff, of eight principles of group dynamics, as summarized by Cartwright. The group considered each principle in relation to its own activities and those of prospective second-phase trainees. The discussion went well until dinnertime, but was then discontinued. Instead, the group wallowed in cynicism, pessimism, and doubt. As one officer put it:

> I can think of very little — nothing right now — that has been acted upon that came out of the patrolman's lineup. I will be very happy if anything comes out of this, but like I say, I'm not going to jump into this thing 100% and bust my ass on it and get all worked up about it until I see that there is going to be some good that comes out of it. I really don't understand how anybody could be that optimistic and how they could throw themselves into a project 100% without knowing that it was going to be acted upon. It's been very hard for me to get with this program, as you probably know.

The men took turns making statements in which they emphasized the need for the chief to accept their recommendations:

OFFICER 1: Now when you ask these guys to change in the streets and you just sit there and say "if you don't change you're going to get punished," it just means that they'll figure out another way to do it. That's all. But if you show them at the same time you're asking them to make these changes that Chief Gain is going to make some changes in the department that are favorable to patrolmen, to make it nice, to make it a little bit better, that he's coming around and he's going to listen to patrolmen, this is going to be very important. And I believe it's very relevant to what's going on here. You're interested in violence; I'm interested in departmental change, too. I think the two go hand in hand. If you have a department that's changing and it's because of patrolmen — like if you bring these guys up here with the idea that they're here because they are the reason for the necessary changes, it's not going to work. If you bring them up here and you tell them, "we're bringing you up here to help us make the changes" it's going to work. . . . And then it's going to be much easier next year to get these guys up here. Because they're going to see it not only as a group that's studying violence. They're going to see us as a group that's doing something within the department. And they're going to see themselves when they walk in as being in a position of being able to do something also, which is important, something constructive, something directly related to what they're doing down there.

OFFICER 2: Now if we can show that we're successful in having some recommendations accepted by the chief, that we as a group are successful, then it will lead these other people to believe that they can be successful. If we fail, they're going to believe that they're going to fail. Therefore, they're not going to work on these projects, and why should they work on them? Now if they're not working on these projects, what are they going to do up here? They're not going to work on projects unless we show them that we're successful. If we tell them about five projects that we worked on here and we had a lot of fun and we documented a lot of stuff here...

The group was concerned about impact. The men had labored hard, invested much, and were hopeful and afraid. They needed acceptance, but could not risk assuming it. Unable to express hope, they instead voiced their fears.

A FULL MEASURE OF SUCCESS

The subgroups met with the chief all afternoon, and the chief met with the total group, briefly. The chief's reaction throughout was unambiguously positive, and the men were stunned.

One surprise stemmed from the fact that wherever written material had been available, the chief had studied it. As one of the men put it:

Jack and I met with the chief on the field-training-officer study. He had a copy of the study beforehand and as he indicated later, he read it in some detail. I don't know about Jack, but I was totally surprised at his first reaction. He indicated to us that he thought we had a heck of a good thing here and that we'd researched it and we'd come up with some real good ideas, which right off the bat gave us the impression that he'd bought the program in totality—and in effect, at this point he has.

The men also discovered that the chief was determined to give them a role in implementing their proposals:

He threw the ball right back to us: "You guys have got it started, now we're going to go into—you can follow it through by doing the staff study routine."..I think what he's saying to us in effect, you know, "you've come up with a good thing here, and you're familiar with what you want, and if we just hand this paper to somebody else and have them working on it, that a lot of your ideas are going to be lost. Since you are familiar with it, it's more or less your responsibility to go into the staff studies and learn that these things are feasible or not feasible and keep as many of the points in your original proposal as possible, in the end product." Although he's thrown the ball to us to get this thing going, I think...we've impressed him with this thing to the point that he's willing to give us the responsibility of carrying this thing on through.

The chief had thought of possible extensions of the project, and had proposed these as further group activities:

Another ball he kind of threw to us just in passing, which I don't really think I got the impact of until later, although I think I turned to Jack and thought "Oh my God, now what are we getting into," was the fact that he was talking about what the course content should be for this field training officer training class. There were some little words passed there to give me the impression that we may be involved in writing the program, what's going to be taught the field training officers.

The chief's reaction to the survey data the officers showed him was similar to his thoughts about the proposals:

He thought of all these things that this could be used for, which I thought was very good. And he said he's very interested to see further analysis of this thing by putting out more of these. I did mention we were going to do it. In critiquing, for instance, feedback-wise in the recruit academy. He said he would be very interested to know just what point they were at in the academy when they fill out the questionnaire and the study material that had been covered when this questionnaire was given to them, because there was an obvious ignorance of the particular laws that were involved in some of these incidents.

The chief stressed that some of the material presented to him was new information:

I feel that the chief was very surprised at the results of the questionnaire. It was pointed out to him—I got in kind of late on this thing, but it was pointed out in the analysis that we had done and Bill presented to him that there was a very great difference in a lot of his thinking and policies and what was going on in the department. His indication was more or less amazement, I guess, that so many people had made arrests in some areas that he could see no legal basis for. We both pointed out to him that this was happening all the time and it was more or less accepted in some areas.

The chief also appeared pleased with the competence demonstrated by the officers. A staff member who had observed the chief's reaction commented:

I think all of the studies, all of the presentations, did convince the chief—something he may have thought of or not—but convinced the chief of the ability of patrolmen given time and inclination to do staff studies and make recommendations within this department. And this came up very strongly and it sort of bubbled to the top in regard to his comments, in regard to "well, maybe I ought to detach all you people and put you to work on specific projects."

The group, following their meeting, expressed themselves relieved, stunned, and elated. The session had the air of a victory celebration. It had drawn the group closer and had made it aware of its mission and its responsibilities for the future. In the words of Bill:

I don't know whether it's been a real pleasure or not. I think we said before, it's a hell of a lot easier to go out on the street for 16 hours and kind of do our thing on calls in a relaxed, nice atmosphere. Because this has been a lot of work. It's been a good experience for me, because I'm lacking in formal education and I probably got something here that I would never have gotten otherwise. And I am appreciative of everybody here, especially of the staff members. It's been a good association. There's been a lot of name-calling and a lot of kidding, and I think most of it has really been in jest on my part. My sardonic, morose attitude isn't bad all of the time. Generally I feel very close to you assholes, and I'm looking forward to seeing you again next summer.

A PROFILE OF MORALE

We had attempted no formal measurement of group process and morale. To trace progress through the summer, we resorted to a rough content analysis of session summaries. Figure 1 depicts the profile resulting from this review. (See Appendix for the form used for systematic monitoring of subsequent sessions.)

Figure 1 shows much variability. It shows a fever curve alternating between "high" and "low." We see a possible "Thursday Slump" syndrome: three of four "low" days fall on Thursdays, as do the majority of combined "very highs" and "highs." On the other hand, "very high" Thursdays outnumber "very high" Wednesdays.

More significant may be the nature of the task (or absence of task or anticipated task) facing the group. High profile points seem to involve (1) substantial group efforts yielding immediate new information, and (2) products of long-term group activity. Group morale hinges on documented group achievement.

Conversely, low morale appears related to (1) difficulties in seeing a purpose in group activities, (2) worry about the place of group products in a larger context, (3) unsuccessful effort, and (4) work in which the product was not as yet available. Low morale seems tied to the unsatisfied need for documented achievement.

The cycle of group development appears to comprise (1) elation over learning from a new activity, (2) doubts over the significance of new learning, (3) evolution of redefined new tasks, (4) involvement and contentment, (5) restlessness over the lack of tangible product, (6) elation over a product, and (7) worry about the significance of product.

Several personal roles had evolved in the group. There was a "group barometer" (Bill) whose moods anticipated and stimulated feelings; there was a "group superego" (Waterman) whose responses to nondirectionality catalyzed activity; there was an "agent of reassurance' (Sam) who promoted faith through optimism. The group also contained a "group skeptic" (Mills) and a "group amuser" (Young), although such functions were exercised by all group members. A final stabilizing ele-

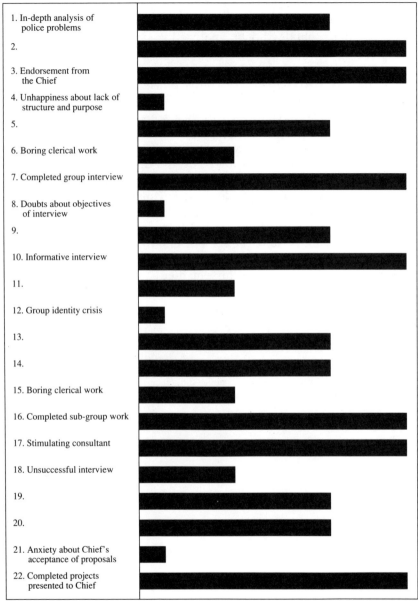

FIGURE 1. Profile of the group's rating of its own morale during the first summer.

ment was the "group editor" (Jack) whose tolerance for paper work overrode the restlessness of his peers.

The officers had acted as a problem-oriented group and progressed in logical sequence. They had engaged in problem definition, formulated questions, obtained data, analyzed it, drawn inferences, and initiated implementation. The change process was thus mobilized and the stage set.

In the next two chapters we sample phase 2 of the project, in which the phase-1 officers had become group leaders and catalysts. The phase-2 groups were composed of violence-experienced officers who were given the job of reducing Oakland's violence problems. They did so in several ways, but we shall concentrate on two of their projects. These differ from each other in that they address different types of violence problems. One involved the police primarily and could be studied and addressed without going outside the department. The second problem was one that was encountered in the community, and the officers felt that to solve it they needed assistance from community organizations.

Chapters 7 and 8 describe the officers' thinking leading to the inception of their proposals. Chapters 9 and 10 follows up the officers' interventions after they were implemented, to find out how well they had worked.

NOTES

1. The focus on arrests for resisting arrest (PC 148) confirms that the officers regarded such arrests as a plausible measure of police-citizen confrontations. In other words, the officers assumed that the charge (resisting arrest) would be lodged if a physical conflict had occurred.

7

Addressing the Problem
Inventing the Peer Review Panel

Few ideas are as much of a challenge to Taylorism (see Chapter 3) as the notion of worker peer review.[1] The group that applied this startling concept to the police began as a free-floating late-evening seminar. There was bemused talk of the possibility that unhappy experiences at home could affect a man's equanimity on the street. There was talk of the dangers of being seduced into "mob psychology" in a crowd situation. There was talk of "thresholds" of explosiveness or emotionality. The bulk of the talk, however, focused on the likelihood that young officers could enter the arena of police work with undesirable psychological dispositions, insufficiently corrected by training and experience.

After its A.M. lunch, the group listened to a tape that had been made the previous week by one of its members while out on a call. The production of the taped incident was a gesture of goodwill and an expression of willingness to play ball. What was accomplished, however, was that the fate of the group was ordained. The group was being treated, during its first meeting, to an exercise in systematic analysis of a behavior sequence. It is this analysis that culminated, several sessions later, in the peer interview project.

THE INTERVIEW EXPERIENCE

The incident taped by the officer was a violent encounter that started with an effort to examine a suspect's eyes with a flashlight. Our officer was the first person to have contacted the subject, but his subsequent role was that of supporting cast to the officer who arrived later.

The tape of the incident suffered from relatively poor fidelity. Our officer—who we are calling Jones—was able to fill in from recent memory. He played the tape, supplemented it with narration, and answered questions that were posed by the group. The group leader (who was very good at systematic interviewing) began a more detailed reconstruction of the incident; a participating staff member involved himself in a further analytic reconstruction, which in turn led to a general discussion by the group.

As it happens, Jones had proposed that the discussion of his incident be taped. We thus have the discussion on record, and we can draw excerpts. These excerpts may show how our group witnessed, during its first session, the results of a diagnostic process on which they subsequently capitalized.

The reconstruction of the incident starts with Officer Jones arriving on the scene, where he encounters the suspect (in the vicinity of a reported burglary) working under the hood of his car. The analysis starts with this encounter:

JONES: I arrived first, and I talked to him and got his driver's license. And he was trying to tell me about the car, but he wasn't making any sense at all.

AN OFFICER: Was he cooperative with you?

JONES: Yeah.

STAFF: So he didn't seem to be alarmed at your presence at all at that point, huh? In fact, he was sort of viewing you as a source of help and advice with his mechanical difficulties?

JONES: No, I don't think he was doing that. He appeared that he had this problem and he was going to do it himself.

STAFF: But he was telling you about it. He wasn't viewing you as a menace?

JONES: I don't think so.

STAFF: And you asked him for information and he at least gave you that.

JONES: Yeah.

STAFF: And then what did he seem to be expecting?

JONES: He went right back to his car. He said he wasn't going to drive it, though. I got his license and he said the car had rolled down the hill and on the sidewalk. And he said "I don't care if I ever drive it again." And then he went back under the hood and started playing with these wires. He had a real concoction of thin electric wires rigged up under there for some reason.

AN OFFICER: Maybe he was practicing putting a bomb in it.

JONES: He mentioned that. He said "There's a secret bomb under here."

STAFF: So he was sort of joshing you.

JONES: Well, maybe joshing at that point, but with everything else he seemed to be serious.

STAFF: Did he seem to be scared of you at all? Did he seem to think that you'd do anything next?

JONES: No.

STAFF: So as far as he was concerned the interview was over and he was going to go back to work on the car.

JONES: Yeah.

The degeneration of the incident is explained by Jones as resulting from the suspect's drug intoxication. Jones indicates that he had become apprehensive about the suspect almost at the point of meeting him. The group was intrigued by this fact, and probed further:

AN OFFICER: And then what? Did he show any type of belligerence to you before your cover got there?

JONES: No.

AN OFFICER: Well, then, why were you apprehensive? That's what I can't understand.

AN OFFICER: Because of his physical condition? Was there any difference in your sizes?

JONES: Yeah, he was bigger than me. Everybody's bigger than me.

STAFF: But when you say "high" now, that means he was nervous, incoherent, sort of happy. It does not necessarily mean that he's aggressive or nasty, does it?

JONES: No.

Jones explains his apprehensiveness on the basis of his "experience." His fear grows as the suspect drops a piece of tinfoil on the sidewalk (subsequently the foil proved empty) and the apprehension reaches its high point as Jones' partner, Dave, arrives on the scene. Jones tries to communicate his impressions to Dave, without success.

Dave meanwhile independently decides to verify the suspect's condition by shining a flashlight in his eyes. The man has no prior warning of this contingency. Jones, for his part, expects trouble:

AN OFFICER: Did you or Dave, one of you guys, tell him what you were going to do with the flashlight, or did you just come out and put it in his face?

JONES: We just stuck it in his face. Dave said, "Let me see your eyeballs."

AN OFFICER: Nobody explained, "I want to see your eyeballs. I think you're under the influence and I want to give you a sobriety test," or something like that?

JONES: No.

LEADER: You said that you anticipated him making a move, you expected that he might move. When did you first get the feeling that he was going to make a move against you? Did you have the feeling before the other guy got there?

JONES: I had the feeling from prior experience that if I tried to take him to my car, he would probably resist.

LEADER: This is before the other guy got there.

JONES: Yeah.

Jones reveals that the suspect—up to this point—has given no indication of apprehensiveness or concern about the presence of two officers. As he is suddenly faced with the flashlight in his eyes, the man strikes out at Dave's arm; Jones at once grabs the suspect around the neck in a choke hold, and Dave uses his Mace on the man's face:

CO-LEADER: What was his first resistance? You said something about shining the light in his eyes and he shoved it away or something?

JONES: Yeah, Dave said something like, "Let's see your eyeballs." And he stuck the light up in his face. And he pushed the light away from Dave, and then I grabbed him around the neck and started choking him out. He wiggled out of that, and that's when Dave said, "If you keep it up you're going to get hurt." And he poked the light in the guy's stomach a little—he didn't jab him, he just kind of pushed it. And he started coming back at Dave again, so I grabbed him again and Dave pulled his Mace out and maced him and me.

LEADER: Were you close enough to see when Dave wanted to look at his eyes— apparently you were, because you grabbed him, right?

JONES: Yeah, I was right next to him.

LEADER: How did he do it?

JONES: You mean how did he push the light away?

LEADER: Yeah. Stand up. You're the suspect. _____ is Dave. How did Dave shine the flashlight on the guy? Did Dave have ahold of him?

JONES: No. He was standing right next to the car, his back was to the car, and we were standing in front of him.

LEADER: Show us how to get it. Now how did the suspect do it—he went like that? That easy?

JONES: No, he hit it hard. He didn't have a chance to do anything, because I grabbed him around the neck then.

LEADER: Why did you grab him?

JONES: To control him.

LEADER: What were you thinking about then?

JONES: We were in such close proximity, he could have just taken a step and started in on Dave. Because we were just inches apart. So I grabbed him so that he wouldn't.

LEADER: What did you think the guy was doing when he made his move?

JONES: Well, the first thing, getting the light out of his eyes?

LEADER: Is that what he thought?

JONES: Yeah, because I had the feeling that he was high and he didn't want this light in his eyes, and I knew he was going to go to jail eventually.

STAFF: But if all he wanted to accomplish was to get the light out of his eyes, and he had gotten the light out of his eyes, what made you start assuming that he would then go and do other things?

JONES: Well, the way he did it, he hit, you know, hard at the flashlight. It wasn't just like a swatting away. It was a good hard jab at that light.

The group analyzed the sequence of events in several different ways. Their first concern was with breaking the incident down into steps and exploring the assumptions of the officers at each juncture:

LEADER: I think what we're interested in is the sequence of events, and Joe was trying to sort of draw a diagram of what was happening between you and this guy when you were alone with him; of him ignoring you, a feeling that you would have that would control your next move which is, one, you're apprehensive about him because you've arrested people that have used drugs before, and they have always resisted. Or you've always had a problem with them. So, this guy is going to give you a problem. Two, you were expecting him to make a move toward you although we brought out that there were really no signs or cues that gave you that reason, merely because this has happened before. So these two cues that you have, rather unconsciously on your part, are going to govern what you do next. Officer Two drives up. You try and tell him the guy is high, but he doesn't catch it. He doesn't talk to you, so there's no consultation. You haven't gotten rid of your uptight feeling about this thing, you know, in talking to the other guy about it. You kind of feel like you might have to handle this whole thing yourself, because the other guy isn't aware of how dangerous this man is. This is probably what you were thinking.

JONES: Yeah.

LEADER: When he shines the light to check his eyes and the guy says, "Keep the light out of my eyes," maybe he moved the flashlight away and all your expectations have at last been fulfilled. This guy moved and showed that he's done what you expected him to do. That would cover your maybe hasty move in grabbing him around the neck...

JONES: Yeah.

The group proceeded, in a positive and sympathetic fashion, to guess at Jones' motives and premises, and to illustrate their plausibility by citing experiences in which other officers had been involved:

LEADER: Like this guy really wasn't playing your game until you shined the light in his eyes, because you kind of anticipated all kinds of things to happen, and none of them were happening. The fucking guy's cooperating, talking kind of slow, fumbling around like he's high, sort of clumsy and nonchalant about the whole thing, and that's not really what you want to play right then.

You've got a real dangerous dope fiend on your hands, and you know he's going to make a move at you, but the cocksucker won't do it.

AN OFFICER: How many of you have gone to the door of a live party? I hate that call more than anything else. I hear that report on the radio and I'm ready to fucking quit, you know. I worked six Saturday and Sunday nights and there was always parties I'd have to take. You'd go to the door, and there'd be 100 people inside this little apartment and they're gassed and having a fucking ball. The stereo's blaring out, and they're all dancing and drinking and having a great time, and you go up and you bang on the fucking door, and usually a couple of them saw you come in, and they go and say "he's coming." A lot of times you're by yourself, and somebody will swing the door open and say, "well, come on in" and they'll just leave you. They swing the door open and tell you to come in and then just go back to dancing and drinking and having a great time and just leave you standing there with your thumb up your ass. Nobody comes forward or nothing. Maybe you can latch on to someone and talk to him and then they'll shuffle off and ignore you and you're really frustrated as hell. And then once in a while you'll manage to get a hold of the host, and then somebody in the background will say "Let's barbecue that motherfucker," or "Let's throw his ass out the window. . ." I know when that feeling gets to me the most, where I'd love to get a bunch of goddamn guys and wipe the place out, just because I'd been treated so rude when I was there.

LEADER: I haven't had that happen to me, but I find that when you try to stop a car for a traffic violation, a lot of times they just stop where they wanted to go in the first place. And they get out of the car and you get out, and they just sort of walk away, and there you are with your headlight going—like if you ignore the guy, he'll go away. He's not real. I say, "Where the fuck are you going? You know, I haven't got that light on for my health!" And they'll say, "Oh, yeah, I didn't see you." But could that be what was happening? You've got the other guy's strategy all figured out in this game, and he wasn't doing that?. . . I guess if I was standing behind the guy and he made a swift, very forceful jab I'd lose control somewhat.

This "but-by-the-grace-of-god-it-could-have-been-me" approach to the officer's motives made it possible for Jones to seriously consider other possibilities, and to admit to them:

AN OFFICER: Is that the way you felt?

JONES: Well, I think the gun was maybe in the process of going off, but this might have been the situation. Or I thought it was going off and maybe it really wasn't.

The group not only attempted to reconstruct Jones' perceptions and concerns, but also those of the suspect. This type of analysis enabled the posing of questions about the interaction of motives and about the transactional genesis of violence:

LEADER: Maybe you wouldn't have to say he was scared so much as he's surprised. He's making what he thinks is an innocuous move—hitting the flashlight out of his eyes—when he's attacked from the rear. And he finds himself being choked. Trying to look at it from his point of view—he sees a light in his face and all he wants is to get it out. So he makes a move and then he's being choked. That's what he sees happening. I'll bet you ten to one if you talked to him, that's what he'd say. "Shit, I wasn't doing anything, and the next thing you know a light was in my eyes. It hurt my eyes and I wanted to get it out." He would probably add, "I said please, and I didn't slap it—I just reached up to move it, when all of a sudden this fucking maniac is grabbing me around the neck and trying to choke me to death!" That's what he would say. And maybe that's how he really saw it. Because there were some things that he drummed up in his head about you maybe, because of a contact with another policeman.

Jones also became involved in the analysis of the suspect's motives, and began to see the other side to the interaction:

STAFF: Now this guy is panicky because he has been grabbed about the neck, right?

JONES: I would say he was, yeah.

STAFF: And the rest from there on in is more and more panic.

JONES: Yeah.

STAFF: So he's really getting scareder and scareder and scareder until he's sitting in back of the car screaming.

JONES: Well, he's screaming because he hurts.

With the evolution of a group-shared frame of reference, it becomes possible to explore new courses of action and to discuss these with Jones:

CO-LEADER: You don't think there was any way you could have talked to him, just talking, talking until he was in the car? I'm not talking about a "you're under arrest, you're going to get into the car one way or the other" approach. Don't you think you could have talked him over to your car? Like you could say, "Well, we got a call about a burglar. I'm going to check into this. You want to come over and..." and you're walking while you're talking, and you open the door for him just like you might open the door for your wife, and the first thing you know you're sitting in the car talking.

JONES: It didn't even enter my mind, I don't think.

At this juncture, Jones can view his incident in terms of options, including some that were clearly destructive or represented errors in judgment:

AN OFFICER: Do you think macing this guy was necessary?

JONES: I wouldn't have maced him, myself. . . I was surprised when Dave came out with it. . .

STAFF: At that point he was really pretty effectively restrained?

JONES: I thought he was. I thought I was doing a pretty good job. He was starting to gag a little bit. He was just starting to feel the lost air, I think. In fact, after he was maced, I kept the hold.

STAFF: What do you think gave your partner the impression that he required Mace?

JONES: That's a good question. I didn't expect it.

LEADER: Why do you think he thought he needed macing?

JONES: Well, like he said later, the guy didn't have his shirt on, so he didn't have any clothing to control him with. Or he thought that was the best way to control him at that point, to mace him and let him worry about himself.

Finally, Jones could cite contributing errors, including problems inherent in his customary mode of operations:

AN OFFICER: If he was being cooperative, totally, when your cover arrived, how come you didn't, still observing this man, take time to relate the situation to Dave?

JONES: Because he's the senior man, and I usually let the senior man do what he's going to do.

STAFF: Could he have assumed that you had already gone into all the explanations necessary, because he didn't know what conversation you had with the guy? So he might have thought the man had been briefed.

LEADER: Could he have also assumed that you had already talked to a complainant and this in fact was the guy that she felt was a burglary suspect?

JONES: He could have, yeah.

Still missing at this point is the working out (in the group context) of alternative solutions. This last stage, however, was soon to be supplied.

FOUNDATION BUILDING

The second 8-hour session of the group can be described as a period of exploration, leading to the building of trust and group purpose. The conversation ranged widely, as is illustrated by the following summary excerpt:

> We discussed police states, crowds that gather at scenes of arrest, and how sometimes it would be beneficial if you could get across to the people that gather why you have taken the action—why the guy's all bruised and sitting in the back of the police car and bleeding. Why it takes an ambulance so long

to get to a scene. Why they can't talk to a prisoner in the back of a police car, or maybe that they can talk to him, maybe they can give him cigarettes, things like this. A ___ brought out an example of a call that he'd been on that was very touchy where he assisted a person that had been shot by a policeman and gained the sympathy of the crowd. And then we discussed the using of a person in the crowd to assist us in our work so that the people that gather can get some kind of identification with us, that we're there to help. That we have one of their group sold on whatever it is that we're doing, and therefore they should be sold on it. We discussed the locker-room talk, the locker-room atmosphere, and how it could possibly influence new policemen in their actions out on the street. How locker-room talk can be used by different officers in a kind of status-seeking thing. Then we got off on a discussion of marijuana, alcohol, and the justifications for making it legal or illegal.

The officers uniformly described the session as "rambling"; several characterized the topics as "tangents," and called for the initiation of project-related work. On the other hand, the group noted with pride and pleasure that ideas were presented openly and freely. Several members stressed that the session was "honest." As the following statements illustrate, they became pleasantly aware of a developing propensity to speak without constraints.

> B ___ mentioned to me at a break that he felt that it was very good that we were getting down to talking to each other and being fairly honest about it, and that the ice is sort of being broken, and this is going to be very good for the unit. I think that the first four hours that we spent here, although it did seem rather rambling and blah blah blah, was very valuable for group development.
>
> People today opened up and said things, even though they may not be directly, right then, relevant to violence, they might not directly be relevant to a project that we could study, they are honest opinions that maybe we're a little surprised to hear. Things were justified, feelings were rationalized, other people opened up and admitted a few things that they probably wouldn't have said if this hadn't happened. So although we didn't get any work done, I think we reached a level of a high degree of honesty and openness with each other which will be beneficial in future discussions.
>
> On the whole the one thing that's come out of this that strikes me, that stands out very much in my mind, was that we found out tonight that although we're all policemen, we don't all think alike in any particular instances out on the street. And I think we'll see as time goes on in here that we'll all have a little bit different ideas of what our roles are out there on the street as police officers.
>
> I believe this is a beginning to break down our own feelings to each other and strip to the bare truth what our own feelings about issues are in the process of becoming honest with each other.

The lack of project-related effort led to the request by one group member for guidance from staff. This request provided an opportunity to reiterate the rule that project ideas had to originate in the group. A staff member indicated that

Part of the problem with this sort of a project, and one of the problems that came up very often last year was the questioning of "what do you want us to do?" And while you didn't say it quite that way, you were talking about what are the directions of the unit, and the aims and the objectives. And we can't answer that. We can say what we want to do generally. The title of the unit implies that. But in terms of telling you what to do, or what projects, that would destroy the intent of the project. It simply would, because if we tell you what to do, then it isn't a group of officers deciding what should be done. And while there are ground rules, we can't teach molotov cocktail making or anything like that I suppose, the ground rules are very limited in that regard. And that's my reply generally. Now, it's not a cop-out. It's really and actually true.

The group leader confirmed the point, and recalled that in the previous summer, "we went through that crap for hours and hours and weeks and weeks," until the group became convinced that it would not receive substantive guidance from staff. He concluded that

we're going to have to come up with it. And it's a son of a bitch when somebody says, "We're all sitting down now. Think of something good." There's no harder task in the world than to think of an original idea. It's an utterly unbelievable, frustrating, bastard experience. And it is. And this ain't all gravy. I hope I made the point strong enough that this is true.

Another trust theme that emerged in the session related to the question of impact. Here, also, the group received reassurance, but the result was inconclusive:

It's a little hard to believe after four years of having people tell you, "Well, when you want to make a change, wait till you become a captain," it's hard to believe that anyone around here will say to 25 patrolmen, "You come up with some ideas and we'll make the changes." It's still a hard thing to accept that whatever ideas we come up with, even if they're really good, it's still right now hard for me to believe that they would be implemented even if they meant saving the lives of five policemen next year. It's still hard for me to believe that these organizational changes would be implemented.

STAFF: The only reply I would have to that is test it.

OFFICER: Well, I'm willing to give it a chance. It's just that right now I'm still skeptical.

GERMINATION

The next session was the fifth project meeting and the third group session. It was during this meeting that our principal project—the Action Review Panel—was born.

The session started with Smith (later categorized as the "group filibusterer") bringing up a television show that had impressed him. The discussion quickly branched out, became increasingly germane, and grew quite spirited:

> Smith somehow brought up the fact that he saw two New York policemen on television, and they had long hair and long sideburns and is this a good thing? Do policemen have certain rights that are taken away from them that might help them on the street to identify with certain groups of people? We got into talking about conformity to sets of rules and do the police have to conform to a certain degree. And this of course led into the ideas of rules and regulations, general orders. Are we given too many general orders and rules and regulations to the point where maybe the men on the line level don't even know what the rules and regulations that we have are? That we just sort of know that they're a vague set of laws in a Great Big Book. And that even if we know the rules, that a lot of times we will violate them to do the job out on the street. Knowing that possibly nothing's going to happen unless we get caught and unless the administration has a big thing about the rule that we do violate. This then led into the idea of the militarism of the police department, or is there militarism in the police department and are we a quasi-military organization, and is it in fact necessary to be this in order to accomplish the "police mission?" And then C. ＿＿ [asked whether] in the realm of rules and regulations, can line patrolmen come up with guidelines that would be followed by other members of the department?

At this point Officer Jones, who had been thinking about his experience in the first session, initiated the topic that led to the project idea:

> About this time Jones came up with the point that the attitude of a particular officer, if he's an old-timer or if he's been on just a little while, greatly affects a new patrolman out on the street. And that maybe when he's been working with the old-timer and he gets out and he works with a little more aggressive police officer, that he's suddenly finding himself in the midst of a large conflict in how to accomplish his police mission, because of the diversity between the two approaches.

It was this posing of the problem that set off Officer Kent—the author of the panel idea—in search of remedies. Officer Kent (not his real name) has remarkable facilities: he is not only equipped with a strong theoretical bent, but has the capacity for working ideas out on paper, in detail, in the midst of noise, distraction, and sometimes chaos. He himself summarized the birth of his idea, and describes it as follows:

> And about here I started scribbling.... And I started making little notes about maybe coming up with trying to work up some sort of system where we can have line patrolmen or the peer group meet in some sort of order review or some sort of review unit where you can analyze the problems that the specific officer might be having on the street when it becomes apparent: Recommendations from superior officers, numerous trips up to Internal Affairs, just numerous violent incidents on the street. This would not be a disciplinary unit or anything like this and it wouldn't really come up with any particular finding pro or con about the officer's actions.

The idea was immediately praised by a staff member, by the leader, and by Officer Jones:

> Jones mentioned that he certainly could have used (such a) unit and would have come up here willingly had a unit offering this type of service been available, because he did have a judgment problem. But that the problem wasn't prevalent enough, although he was aware of it and felt it, he didn't feel that it made sense to go to anybody else in the department. I would imagine for a number of reasons—that they would have thought him this incompetent guy, or he doesn't have self-confidence, or what the hell's the matter with him? Which is a problem all of us have—if we have something that doesn't go right on the street, it's very hard to go to somebody and say, "Hey, Joe, I need a little help." Most of us just don't do that.

The group leader not only noted the importance of Kent's idea, but spelled out the need for the development of skills necessary to implement it. He pointed out that the acquisition of such skills involved continued experiences with systematic interviewing and pattern analysis:

> The idea Kent came up with about perhaps offering the VPU [the Violence Prevention Unit] as a service to guys in the department kind of showed me that after 400 hours seven of us couldn't come up with everything, and it encourages the hell out of me, because this is only the fifth session and bango, we've got something that we can work on and look into. And as an offshoot of that suggestion we're going to have to be able to somehow learn to skillfully extract information from a particular officer who is in need of aid from the unit. We're going to have to get that information out before we can really get down to the crux of anybody's problem.

The group immediately implemented this advice by proceeding to interview Officer Graham, one of its members. The interview was mainly conducted by the leader and proved incisive but inconclusive. Graham (a previous skeptic) participated in the summary by expressing surprise and satisfaction with his experience as a subject:

> The first time we brought out someone's reports I was very disappointed in it, in comparison to listening to the tapes, in comparison to some of the more interesting topics that we got into. But now after going over my reports, I think that I now feel that it can be good. But the person who gets the most good out of it is that one individual, not everyone in the group...I may have forgotten a lot of the incident, but I still remember well enough that I remember getting the call and most of the general appearance of everything, from the house to people who were there, emotional flare-ups, little things that I remember about these things but don't go into length to describe and that aren't reflected in the report.... I didn't think too much of going over reports before. But for the individual who is having his report on the chopping block, it is beneficial and little things can be conceived as a possibility that may be applicable to that case. And in the future I think maybe you'll be looking for maybe a couple of those little conclusions...whereas I didn't think much of this before, I do see a lot of benefit now, for the individual who's getting his report reviewed.

The leader disagreed with Graham's point about the restricted benefits of the interview, and pointed to the possibility that patterns might be generalizable:

> But I have to disagree that it's not profitable to everyone else...I'm sure that it will increase and pretty soon you'll kind of get to the point where you can have a lot of fun with these things and sort of laugh at each other and laugh at yourself. And I know damn well that I saw myself a few years ago in every one of your incidents, as a matter of fact. In fact, I had a couple of little analogies here that matched mine so much that I'm not going to go into it now because every one of you will hate my guts.

Graham, however, was validated in one respect: although the group rated the session enjoyable and moderately productive, their participation ratings proved low. The group was beginning to see the point of Kent's scheme, but had not yet moved to share in its implementation.

A SIDE TRIP

In the first half of the next session the group continued to explore the pattern analytic theme; in the second half, a different concern took temporary precedence.

The men concentrated for a time on the premise that had inspired the panel idea—the fact that an officer who had developed destructive patterns could perpetuate these through contagion.

The group also conducted a short, relatively impromptu interview of one of its members. This interview developed in fairly circuitous fashion through exploration of tangential topics:

> And then we discussed how members of the community would react to this incident, and how the police react. And then we discussed whether or not police should be more sensitive to cultures. Whether or not they should be aware of the individual culture of the people that live in the area in which they work. We stressed more positive ways to stop people on the street, and we got into Al Cole's approach to stopping people. And Al was more or less criticized by the other participants because he at least said that he was rather impatient and he didn't go to any length to tell the people exactly why he had stopped them and what the reason was, what the crime was in the area that may have precipitated that stop.

During the discussion following the interview, the group's co-leader stressed the generalizability of patterns, and the fact that interviewers could infer behavior rules from the analysis of incidents:

> In reference to Al's walking stops and things that we discussed, it ought to be remembered that when we're bringing things out and discussing them that although you might be on the hot spot at one particular moment, every-

body in the room is kind of listening to the discussion going back and forth. And sometimes an impression comes out that maybe you do this all the time: in your case I don't think this is true. But the rest of us as we're sitting here listening to the discussion going back and forth on your methods of stopping people on the street, we're taking all of this in. A lot of us do things at times that aren't correct also, and when you're discussing your case with someone else, all of us are learning something at the same time. Whether or not it's actually true that you do this, it's important this discussion did go on. A lot of us picked up tips on walking stops at the same time you two were discussing it.

The remainder of the day was spent in session with the sergeant of the internal affairs unit, exploring questions related to discipline. The group felt that this interview was "informative," but not focused. More positively, the willingness of an outsider to meet with the group was encouraging for the men, even though hasty planning and unclear objectives deprived the experience of more concrete benefit.

DEFINING THE MISSION

The fifth session was probably the most constructive and fateful in the life of the group. Paradoxically, the meeting started with a free-floating, rambling exploration of tangents. The summarizer notes that

When this meeting started off, I actually thought nothing was going to get done tonight at all. It was the most rambling start—from Internal Affairs back to the shooting—the most idle conversation that we've had so far. It went just on and on without even talking about anything at all.

Other men made similar observations. One member noted (on the back of his reaction form) that "the meeting started slow and rambling— not staying on the same topic, but going back and forth." As the group adjourned to an early (2 A.M.) lunch, prospects for constructive work appeared slim.

Directly after lunch Officer Kent pulled out a thick stack of notes, and began to expound the details of his panel idea. He proposed "some sort of review unit made up of patrolmen. When another patrolman gets into a behavioral pattern (such that) he is having violent incidents on the street—and it becomes apparent that he is...help him out, help find where he's going wrong, before he has to go up to Internal Affairs, before he gets hurt on the street."

Kent stressed the necessary informality of the procedure, the desirability of an "off the record" approach, the need for a positive, constructive emphasis. The sessions of the panel, he indicated,

Would be conducted more as an interview rather than an interrogation. And what you're going to try to do then is review the behavioral patterns of the person and analyze what he's doing and somehow make him, in this process, come up with some self-critique, like we do here. You know, after he reads the report somebody asks questions. "There's some questions in some of your reports that you'd probably want to go over" — "why did I do this this way?" And you'd have to stop and think, "Do I do that very often?" I think this type of review is going to be helpful. In other words, just sort of as an assist unit for the individual patrolman.

The group quickly took up the discussion. One point it made was the desirability of having relevant insights originate with the officer being interviewed, rather than with the panel:

OFFICER 1: Wouldn't it be good if we could sort of switch it around that he bring out his own problem?

OFFICER 2: I think that's the only way.

OFFICER 3: You bring out his problem and you're another Internal Affairs.

OFFICER 2: That's why I said we've got to have a system or technique in order to bring it out. It would be a self-awareness on his part. In the interviewing and talking to him all of a sudden the bell would go off.

In connection with the need to have the interviewee arrive at his own inferences, two points were made: First, that prejudgments of the problem resembled traditional supervisory technique, and second, that this method could produce retreat into inactivity. A person who did not spell out his own difficulties in specific terms was apt to equate a diagnosis of poor quality with a mandate to lie low:

OFFICER: You're never going to get to the crux of the problem by pointing to the problem. Because this is the M.O. [modus operandi] that this department has always used. When there was a big purge in patrol division, all these guys were called into the DC's office and told if they have any more 148s they're going to be fired. That's what happened. "Killer" Baridon went to (a neighboring department) and "Killer" was a pretty sharp guy. He could have worked out a lot of his hang-ups on the street — he has. But my point is this. The M.O. has always been, "Look, Louie, you've got a problem. And you'd better stop whatever you're doing, although you don't know what it is, or you're going to be fired." And the guy walks out of the room saying "son of a bitch." I did when I was called in by a captain several years ago. I really thought that I was doing a good job. I'm a hell of a cop. I get involved, I get out there and I fight crime, and I'm running into nothing but assholes — bad luck. You know, right, we all do good police work and it's the citizen's fault. Resistances. And I thought, "Fuck them. I'm not going to do nothing."

Probably in an effort to convince itself of its integrity, the group became concerned with the need to "sell" its panel to the interviewee, while remaining completely honest with him. Both the ethical implications and the pragmatic aspects of approaches to the interviewee were ventilated:

OFFICER 1: You could destroy a good tool by being completely honest. Why don't you tell your wife about all your extramarital love affairs and say, "But, baby, I love you!" I did that, and it's going to cost me $4,000 a year for the rest of my life. I was completely honest with her.

OFFICER 2: I think you were a dumb shit.

OFFICER 1: Right. That's exactly the point. Now, would we be dumb shits?

OFFICER 3: Are you going to tell that guy that's 6 feet 9 inches, 250 pounds as you walk up to him and you know he's a burglar and you walk up to him and your cover ain't there, "You're going to jail." I wouldn't do that. I'd walk up to him and say, "What's your name," as I look over my shoulder, "Where the fuck is that cover?"

OFFICER 4: Jack, what you say does make a lot of sense. I guess this is it—these could be some guidelines to think about. If the guy says, "Why am I up here?" we tell him, "Your supervisor recommended that you come up." If he doesn't say, "Why am I up here" I guess you don't have to say it.

KENT: In your initial interview, state the purposes of the VPU as a whole. Very, very basically state it as a whole. "Lower the violent confrontations, fewer cops get hurt, and in order to do this, this program has to come up with new changes. In other words, this is a program of change." Get that across there somewhere. Then tell them, "You've been recommended by your supervisor. Now the reason you've been recommended is because apparently you've been getting involved in the street. So since you're getting involved in the street and you seem to be concerned with what's going on, two things can happen from it. One, you can help us and then we can help you."

There was general agreement that the panel had to be introduced to the interviewee by stressing its benefits to the police in general, and to endangered officers in particular:

OFFICER 1: Maybe we could say we don't want to emphasize that, because he's going to be aware of it, and I guess that would sort of be adding insult to injury, you know, to emphasize it. "You know why you're up here, Charley, you vicious bastard you!"

KENT: You've got to get across to them that the purpose is twofold. One, to prevent the violent confrontation, and because you're doing this you're going to help policemen (1) not get fired, (2) not get hurt. Whichever order of preference you want to make it.

OFFICER 2: We could say we want you to help us to prevent people from getting fired, screwed up. Not you necessarily, but everybody.

OFFICER 3: What you are able to offer us may help some other guy coming up next.

A number of procedural alternatives were explored by the group, and their advantages and disadvantages were considered. One such alternative was that of "embedding" the interviewee in a discussion group or involving him with other officers who also had demonstrated difficulties:

OFFICER 2: There's just a slight hazard to doing it that way...Let's put it this way. If we had three people up here at one time who were recommended or were having problems and needed a little consultation, it wouldn't be too smart to give them even odds. You know what I mean? It's kind of hard to talk to a guy and bring out an incident when you have two other guys sitting there saying, "Bullshit, he did the right thing. I think we ought to kick the shit out of all of them sons a bitches, you know, mow them down." You could have too many guys.

STAFF: Of course there is another complication to this which one ought to consider, and that is that unless you pick three guys awfully carefully—your problems are different enough from mine so that we can get awfully confused if we start trying to discuss them all at the same time and the same place.

OFFICER 3: You've got to break down to the fact that a lot of confidence is supposed to be here. If a man comes to a psychologist, he wants to tell him his problems. Say he's a businessman and he's got a lot of hang-ups. Well, he doesn't want two other businessmen sitting there listening.

A related possibility was that of involving the interviewee indirectly, by dissecting the patterns of other subjects with his participation:

OFFICER 1: Or we could do it this way. We're going to have to do the homework on the guy before he comes up here, right?...We all know who we are. If we see his reports and hit on some where we have that same type of pattern that got us into shit, start talking about that pattern as related to ourselves first—criticizing ourselves, and then as the discussion goes around the table to him, maybe by that time he's reading his own report, he can more or less see that same pattern, but never referring directly to his reports. Do you see what I mean? In other words, if you're always having trouble with women, like the one guy did as an example, pick out our reports where we had trouble with the broads, and then maybe in the discussion, while we're talking about, "Well, this is what I did," you say something like, "Son of a bitch, I have a lot of trouble with women." And maybe this guy will look at his report and say, "So do I."

OFFICER 2: He's probably going to say, "Do you assholes really think I don't know what you're trying to do?"

The group moved from discussing procedural variations to the planning of sessions in which techniques and strategies of interviewing could be tried out. It proposed to start with members of the unit and subsequently to branch out to volunteers secured elsewhere:

KENT: I think initially (we ought) to continue what we're doing now. From within our own group here. Within the three groups that we have. To see if we could work out some kind of interview system here, since we are as close-knit groups as we are now, the guy being interviewed would say, "Now look, you're beginning to piss me off" or "I'm beginning to feel in a corner. I don't like the way you're doing this. Let's forget that line of approach in questioning me regarding these particular incidents." Things like this. Because really, as you look through the three groups, it's a pretty good cross section of patrol.

This discussion led to an unexpected testimonial from Officer Graham, who revealed that in a postinterview session in the cafeteria he had arrived at unexpected insights into his difficulties and now saw a pattern in his involvements:

KENT: As an example, and this struck me very much, what you and Graham went through the other day would have been a tremendous thing. . .

GRAHAM: Can I say it, because I went over it?. . .I had a problem and didn't even know it—wasn't aware of it. Me and Bill (the leader) were really having a lot of laughs on my reports, and I walked out the door and still didn't have any awareness or conclusions. It was a lot of talk. But then we started bullshitting out there and he related a couple of incidents and then I remembered the Angels and I pointed out the one about the Angels and then Bill pointed out something. And I found that I was, without even being aware of it, anytime there were insurmountable odds against me I was tearing-ass into it. Three Angels in the ____ and no cover. "Outside, all three of you, let's go. Take you on." No cover. I could have waited. Two men inside 647f already slammed the door in my face made a statement they're going to kill the motherfucking pig. I didn't care—I went right on through anyway. "Here comes supercop." Without even realizing it.

STAFF: With a slingshot.

GRAHAM: Yeah, that's what he said—David and Goliath. And I never realized I was doing that. I'm surprised I haven't got my back busted or my neck broken. I don't really know whether I was trying to prove anything, because I wasn't expecting anyone else really necessarily there.

Graham himself indicated his satisfaction with the interview as a procedure and so did other group members. The session was universally characterized as "constructive"; it was rated extremely high in productivity and morale. The group leader summed up the spirit of the occasion by exclaiming that

> I never cease to be amazed at how you people are getting through these eight hours as compared to how we did. It's unbelievable. Everything I've got on this session rating form tonight is very high. I can't think of anything bad about it. I think we've come a hell of a long ways in coming up with this idea. And it's going to take more work, but it's going to be worth it. And I just want to say that I feel real good about it.

The session ended with a collective determination to expend whatever time and energy it took to get the review panel idea firmed up, so that it could be proposed to the chief as a strategy worthy of adoption.

CONSTRUCTIVE CONFLICT

The sixth session represents a forced departure from group project development. The leader of the group had been scheduled to instruct the recruit academy in "violence prevention," and requested help in the preparation of his class outline. Collective drafting exercises somehow proved painful to our groups, and this one was no exception. The period was enlivened, however, by spirited conflicts of views relating to training concepts and techniques.

One of these conflicts related to the word "game," which had become a staple in the working vocabulary of our first-generation officers. To us, the term was synonymous with interpersonal interaction and denoted moves and countermoves with latent purposes and assumptions. The new group had bypassed the conceptual exercises leading to the development of vocabulary and thus was unfamiliar with "in-group" language. One of the officers objected to references to violence-prone "games"—arguing that the word was unnecessarily flippant. A lively discussion—initiated by the group's co-leader—followed the objection. Interestingly enough the new members joined the "old-timers" in defending the word, and the dissenter declared himself eventually satisfied.

The second argument was not similarly resolved. Again, it stemmed from a prevalent first-generation assumption, relating to the value of role-playing as a training tool. One of the new officers (Graham) objected to the technique, classifying it as artificial and unconvincing. (The point was a carryover from a "retreat" session, where the same subject had come up.) The group spent considerable time on the pros and cons of various forms of role-playing and even staged an impromptu demonstration. The debate terminated in a proposed subcommittee on role-playing, which was never constituted.

Probably of more interest than the subjects of these conflicts was the form they took. A staff member noted in the summary that

> Part of what we ought to be looking at is what happens here other than the content of what we are talking about, just in terms of, for instance, how we get along. It would seem that from that point of view it was rather interesting that what we had after what Jim calls lunch was a complicated kind of thing. We had a lot of fun. We were all chuckling pretty well, but along the line we also did quite a little solid fighting which we wouldn't have done if we didn't

> trust each other enough to say all kinds of pretty forthright things; in the process I think we discovered how we really feel about a subject in terms of where we all stand with respect to it, and now we can all start working on it constructively.

The relaxed group atmosphere could be viewed as indicative of the development of trust. Another such index arose when two group members reported that they had been adversely received in the coffee room by three officers to whom they broached the subject of the unit. They discussed the incident as follows:

OFFICER 1: There were two patrol officers and one from traffic and (we) were sitting there talking to them, and they were entirely negative to the VPU idea, period. If their thinking is contagious...

OFFICER 2: Were they negative because of their lack of knowledge of it, or because of what they had heard by rumor, or what?

OFFICER 1: We tried to talk to them a little about it, and it was like talking to the wall, wouldn't you say?

OFFICER 3: Well, I said, "I like you and everything, but I can't help it if you're not progressive and have a very narrow mind."

OFFICER 4: That was a very forceful, diplomatic way of putting it.

OFFICER 1: Well, if you had seen how negative he was!

OFFICER 4: Did you feel like getting violent with him?

OFFICER 1: Yeah, like reaching over and knocking his head in.

One of the officers who complained about this encounter suggested that the reaction might be more general and pervasive. He recalled that he had been previously subject to negative feedback:

> Well, you know what I think: A lot of them...really think that we are a peace and flowers organization, "turn the other cheek, run up and kiss them." You know what I mean?
>
> "Blazers with flowers on them" — what else did he mention? "Take your gun off." Those two points they both mentioned.
>
> And I think that a lot of them feel that way. Because I went all the way up around Clairmont or somewhere to cover somebody on a 10 or 11 for two hippies who went up behind a building and ran up in a middle of a block of apartments behind some stairs. One officer comes in this way and is blocked by a fence and yells, "There he is," and another officer literally flew over a fence and came down on the guys, put them right down to the ground, a wrestling match out to the car. And one of them in his frustration, who is a good friend of mine, looks at me and says, "How would you prevent that?" And I never even thought anything! You know, this was a guy who just splits and all they did was take him. And he looks up and he said, "How would you prevent that?" And I said, "I thought you did pretty good police work." But part of this was that we are supposed to be sitting here saying, "Oh, you pushed him down. Did you scratch his elbow?"

The group leader was reassuring. He characterized adverse views as unrepresentative expressions of uninformed envy:

> I guess it's kind of like the guy who has a Cadillac. If you can't afford one or you can't get one, the normal thing to say is, "I don't want one anyway, and I wouldn't have it." My conclusion is that that's about it. You know, there's kind of a fear of it—something new. You're a little envious in a lot of respects. For instance, I wouldn't take very seriously what either one of those two individuals said. I think we both know them.

He also, somewhat indirectly, counseled patience and forbearance:

> Last summer we tried to ride with the punches and not create any more animosity than was necessary. But I also got to the point where I was bugged so bad one night, for instance at the Public House, by a guy who I went along with for about an hour, and I finally got him in a corner and said, "Look, Joe Blow, you've had an awful lot of fun at my expense. And I would suggest very strongly that you change your line of conversation, or I'm going to knock the shit out of you." But I rolled with him for a long time. I'm not suggesting that you'll have fistfights. I've never done that in my life, and I hope I never do. But I think we can play the game with them, talk to them about it, maybe sell it. But it ain't going to be easy.

On a more serious note, the leader suggested that sobering experiences were the price one had to pay for commitment to change:

> Getting back to what Bob said about he was kind of discouraged, I'm glad. Because if you weren't discouraged a little bit I wouldn't feel too good, because I went through an awful lot of that and I guess maybe it's just because we've got a few hundred hours under our belt and a lot of digging remarks that you sort of get used to it after a while. It's sort of like being called dirty names on the street. If you weren't discouraged, I would be discouraged. You know, I mean, if you really didn't give a shit, I'd feel bad about it.

Despite this reassuring conclusion, the men felt that the session was anticlimactic. There were many ratings of "average," and words like "exasperating" and "inconclusive" cropped up among the (largely favorable) characterization of the meeting.

TOOLING UP

Much of the next session was taken up by the first effort of the group to prepare itself systematically for a panel interview through analysis of background information.

The prospective interviewee (slated for the following evening) was a member of the project consensually regarded as violence-prone and impervious to influence. This characterization was not only shared by the group, but was part of the officer's general reputation in the locker room.

The group agreed on the point that, "If we can make impact on this guy, we can change anyone." However, they were not hopeful. As one of the men put it:

> I'm a bit pessimistic insofar as he's concerned, because I don't really think he's the type of individual we're going to make much headway with. He obviously knows what the attitudes of his fellows are here and he's obviously uninfluenced by this attitude; and I think he'll be similarly uninfluenced by our attitude toward him or by anything we say to him.

But others noted that the interviewee's anticipated obduracy made him an ideal "test case" for the interview procedure:

> While we're all probably pretty pessimistic about this particular individual, especially those of us who have had an occasion to work with him even if it's only one time, that if this particular individual who had such strong convictions can be made aware of the fact that he does in fact have a problem — because I don't know that he's really aware of it — there shouldn't really be anybody else that we would have as much of a problem with as I think we're going to have with this one.

The first approach to the background analysis was a qualitative one. Members of the group read reports aloud, and hypotheses were formulated about general themes. The group also solidified its impression of the magnitude of the interviewee's problems:

> It was a bit thought-provoking to think that such an individual actually goes out there among the citizens. I'm a little staggered by it. I'd heard all the stories, but it's another thing to see the man put it in his own words and tell it the way he sees it!

In digging deeper, a system was devised for tabulating salient features of the report. This innovation again originated with Kent, who recalls that

> While we were all sitting here talking, everybody had a report or a series of reports in front of him, and we were all just generally making comments. And it began to hit me that there were certain areas or patterns that were developing just from the casual conversation that we were having before we were even really going to analyze these reports. So I just took a little piece of paper and drew a bunch of white squares on it in order to pick out some of these things.

The group thoroughly enjoyed the classification exercise that followed. Almost all session ratings were "high," and the adjectives most frequently used in descriptions were "constructive," "relevant," and "purposeful."

THE OPENING NIGHT

The group arrived the following night full of anticipation and curiosity. The interviewee (whom we can call John Spark) appeared on time and reacted positively to the introduction. He spoke freely, although at times he showed apprehension or nervousness.

The group leader conducted the first portion of the interview and did so incisively and with surprising success. Spark was taken through various reports step by step and a pattern emerged, not only for the group, but for Spark. The pattern showed a propensity for personal vendettas against citizens who had challenged Spark's supremacy on his beat. These vendettas invariably culminated in a relatively petty arrest in which Spark used the municipal code to assert himself vis-à-vis his opponents. The following are excerpts in which the summarizer (Jones) details the manifestations of the pattern:

> When we discussed his first report, I noticed that he kept track of a witness and he stated, "I didn't particularly like her." So he's been running a warrant check on her about every month and he finally came up with a $39 warrant which he is bent on serving. This brings up the personal involvement that he gets in these things, and I think this leads him to having difficulty. He also stated in that report that he can't stop doing the job because a suspect has a gun, which leads to an element of danger, and he has the attitude that he's going to get the guy no matter what.
>
> In the second report...he was challenged on how much officers will take in the eyes of the public.... And then he reacts with arresting somebody for something.... They weren't using profanity so he couldn't use that for a crutch. So he used littering when somebody picked up some papers and threw them on the ground again. He also wrote the driver eight violations on this second stop, after he'd already cited him for speeding.
>
> Going on to the next report, it was a high-speed chase. The driver gave him a funny look; he explained that he thought that the driver was hoping that he wouldn't notice and wouldn't turn around and chase him. He almost begged for a high-speed chase—he turned the red light on two blocks behind him. And he stated that he hadn't been in a chase for a while and he was kind of hoping that the guy would run. This sort of indicates to me that he appears to go looking for trouble.

Jones characterizes the pattern as he sees it. In doing so he includes concepts adopted by our first-generation officers (e.g., "playing in the opponent's ballpark"), which have spread to our new trainees:

> At this point it was appearing to me that he was being drawn into the other guy's ballpark, and he was trying to win in his ballpark when actually he wasn't, and he was looking very bad. He stated that the cop is the ultimate authority, and this is the way he works. That's his Territory and he's the guy who's going to run the show, although going over these reports, he's running the show rather badly. And he's not playing in his own ballpark, although he thinks he is.

> Again, when he loses control in a situation, he reverts to an arrest. This seems to be the only out that he can use. . . . These were personal challenges: the first one on the 415. This gal that he's running the warrant on called him a "motherfucking pig," I believe it was. And he was challenged there. The funny look on the driver's face in the high-speed chase challenged him. He takes all these things personally. He's using these personal challenges, and the way he wins them is by arresting these people on anything he can think of.

The process of elucidating Spark's motivation through interview, after study of his reports, proved to be especially instructive. Hypotheses based on the written material were helpful in directing the questioning, but had to be reformulated as new data emerged. One officer summarized the positive contribution of this experience by saying:

> We had a lot of material to work with, we had a good background study last night, and I personally felt good with myself because I began to pick out these traits of people that are being interviewed. And [with] some of the other people in the group [that] had been interviewed I had had a little bit of trouble finding the things that they did leading to the problem that they had. And of course Spark had some pretty glaring problems that weren't too hard to follow, and I think this has helped me find these traits and be able to follow them to a problem.

The discrepancy between the written and interview versions of the incident led to relevant speculations about the function of the written report. Here the "official" version of the incident was seen as a rationalization of the private encounter — not only for the benefit of superiors, but also for the man's own use:

OFFICER: There's a lot of things you wouldn't put in a report, like the kids — he declared war on them. He told them that they were fair game several days, months, or weeks before. "I'll have you — I'll get you — I'll take care of you at a later date."

STAFF: I think part of the pattern is the real stuff never goes on his report. Because he uses the letter of the law to accomplish some other purpose, and that other purpose is only in his mind and it cannot go on the report. He cannot say, "I got this guy for turning around this corner because I wanted to curb prostitution." He can't say that. He has to say, "failure to signal." He has to say, "litter." He couldn't say, "I was in a war against these kids and that's the first excuse they gave me." The report is the excuse he uses. What we got today was the reason why he's in this business, which is to get people. And it's to get people who have shamed him in public or who he disapproves of because they are making a mess of his turf there. Which he's in charge of. And there is no way you can put that in a report.

Another learning experience was related to the issue of insight and change. The first part of Spark's interview was insight-centered, with

Spark responding like a textbook case. At the conclusion of this interaction, when Spark warmly thanked the group for helping him to understand his past conduct, the leader moved to terminate the interview. The group, however, continued it, focusing on Spark's current practices and his future plans. The leader, who retreated somewhat into the background, later complained:

> I thought, "Goddamn. We won this battle—we really did. And now we're blowing it. Because we're giving him too much room for justification." Now that was my opinion. However, it was explained to me, and we talked about it quite a bit over lunch, that there had to be some way that we could go into future contacts that Spark would be having with people on the street and somehow relate them to past contacts which have resulted in a whole pile of 148s. I didn't see that—I didn't see that.

Group members noted that while Spark was freely conceptualizing his past conduct, he showed little indication of willingness to extrapolate from these concepts. As a staff member put it, Spark

> was filling in a picture which was neatly detailed, made absolute sense, was completely coherent, and every additional piece of information he gave us tied into it. And it's quite understandable that when one has it all together, one should say, "Well, thank you and goodbye." What happened, however, is that we kept on saying yesterday, as you'll remember, "If we can break this guy, we can break anybody." And we lost sight of a couple of little cues. Namely, he kept on saying, for instance, "Yeah, that's the way I used to be." And the clear implication was "that ain't the way I am now." Obviously if that's not the way I am now, then all of this is history and it doesn't have any relevance. Except you're giving me some pretty good insights into the way I was when I was young and inexperienced and green.

Indeed, as the interview progressed, Spark showed an exasperating propensity for justifying his escapades and for refusing to acknowledge the contribution of psychological factors to his current problems. As the interview concluded, the group felt that they understood Spark, but that they had made no impact on his conduct. They felt elated at their success in securing data for analysis and at their role as interviewers. The co-leader (generally predisposed to skepticism) asserted that

> The main thing that I could see tonight was that we did achieve the purpose that we set out to do. That is, that we had an interview with someone with regard to the 148's that he's been involved in. And after Bill's initial introduction, probing and discussion, everybody here did enter into it in some degree. And this is what the hell it's all about. It was real good. Then after it was over it was even better in that everybody had an awful lot to say about what went on—what they saw developing or happening. We had a real good discussion.

He stated the feeling of the group in noting that the information secured from Spark testified—among other things—to developing interviewing skills:

> And I think that if we had an interview with anybody now, that any three or four members in the group, regardless who they were, could conduct an interview and keep it moving.... He threw out some real big stuff that wasn't in those reports. And that was after we started chipping away. And I think maybe we tonight were working on our own particular M.O., our own interviewing M.O., in that you get a guy talking and there's a hell of a lot not written in that report that he will tell you. Like I say, there were large gaps in most of these reports, yet when we went back through them chipping away on some of the little stuff, picking through and going back through the hours and the location and were there other people around, what was the crowd situation....

As for failure to produce impact on the interviewee, questions were raised about how much of this could be expected. A staff member noted that

> The element which may have been a little hidden by what happened today is that somehow, despite all the guff yesterday about this is the last man we expect to change, everybody came in here today deep down inside expecting a tremendous conversion to take place in this room. Now actually we got a long ways toward something happening. That is, we got some insight here. And we got the guy on the defensive here and there. And we just have a large question mark here as to what's going on in his mind.

He pointed out that

> We needn't castigate ourselves for not getting him to walk out of here a convert and a changed man. I think we have given him some room for thought. I think he did say some things in this room that he has never said before. I think we have made a good start.

He added that

> We'll have an opportunity, since [Spark is] going to be with us in the next month or so, to do a little more observing and see the results, if any, of our session with him. I suspect there are bound to be some. I think we shook him up. We'll also have an opportunity, if we like, to bring him in for a follow-up interview anytime that he feels he's ready.

In addition to discussing the possibility for reinterviewing Spark, the group considered candidates for further "practice" interviews. One such candidate, a notoriously troublesome officer, had been recruited as volunteer in a neighborhood tavern the previous evening. The group decided to invite him next. Other prospective candidates were also named and discussed. The profusion of subjects—and the feeling that the group knew what it was about—produced much self-congratulation. Officer Graham, who announced his departure for two weeks of military training, said in parting that

> I can remember about a week ago Paul and I came in here with a stunned look on our face, like it's hopeless. Two officers just talked to us and condemned

the hell out of us—it's hopeless, we'll never get anybody up here. But my last thought as I'm preparing to go out the door is, there are more people right now during this test time than we have time to prepare for. Volunteers. We've got more people right now that may want to hold a mock interview to learn how we're going to do this in effect than you have time to prepare for them. We're already talking about, "No, you can't have him Monday. We don't have time to prepare for it." And you've got another one lined up who I'm totally surprised is coming up here no matter what game he thinks he's going to play. . . if you have him in here that's a hell of a start right there. So I'm totally encouraged once again with the idea of the VPU board.

The group's ratings of the session divided between "high" and "very high"; the leading adjectives were "promising" and "valuable." The group had developed a sense of purpose and an awareness of its potency.

THE MAN WHO CAME TO DINNER

The next session put the group's self-confidence to a solid test. They faced their first outside interviewee, and—as if this were insufficient—their subject was an officer whose record of activity (and to some extent, of physical involvements) had made him a legend in the department.

Officer Beam had volunteered for the interview, with some persuasion from Bill, the group leader. As one member put it (the preceding evening):

Last night at the Public House over his Ballantine scotch that Bill bought him after losing a game of dice to an unnamed officer, he very skillfully directed this officer into coming up here. I was a little surprised that he thinks that he volunteered to come up here.

The origin of the idea aside, Officer Beam expressed interest in serving as a subject and did so for his own ends. His ends included clearing his reputation by demonstrating the objective necessity of his physical encounters; pointing to changes in his conduct (but maintaining that these had not sprung from changed attitudes), rectifying false impressions about the nature of police work, and being of help to others who might have problems.

Whichever the dominant motive, Beam's appearance was self-defined as that of an expert witness, a man without problems who had wisdom and information to impart. In the face of this fact, the group set out to analyze Beam's pattern of conduct with a view to arriving at some understanding of it. The result was a Mexican standoff that left both parties satisfied. Whereas Beam departed with the conviction that he had enlightened the group, the officers (in their postinterview analysis) felt that they had arrived at meaningful diagnosis.

Descriptively, Beam's pattern involved a propensity for arresting narcotics users and a tendency to physical interactions with some of them at the point of arrest. In the words of the officer summarizer:

> People that he has arrested, and has had problems with, have been people that he has known or knows to be using narcotics. And this appears to be a very important thing with him. All through his interview he repeatedly referred to people who used narcotics and the way that they will act, and the way that he handles narcotics when he is going to arrest them. He stated that he makes the first move on a hype "If I think I'm going to have to fight them, because they're nervous, paranoid, and overall dangerous." He also stated anyone who doesn't cuff a hype either is a fool or the bravest person on earth. "They're all fighters" — and he emphasized this over and over — all hypes are fighters. They're the most dangerous people. He says, "I'm always prepared to fight, I'm careful, and I've never been nailed" — meaning that he's never been hit by one.

In an extended lecture, Beam defended the proposition that narcotics users were unpredictably violent persons, dangerous to deal with, and that it became necessary, at times, to act to prevent injury. He admitted to being "specialized" in his interest in narcotics users. Bill, the group leader, classified this as a "crusade" or "war," and this characterization resulted in a brisk exchange, with Beam defending his activity as rational and objective. According to the summarizer:

> He said, "Everybody's happy including me, because I put this person in jail and I've solved some burglaries and maybe some robberies and maybe some violence, plus I've also got this narcotic that no one else could catch but me."

The group inquired into the origin of Beam's interest, and he referred to two precipitating events:

> We got into why he developed this interest in narcotics. And he related an incident about when he first was on the street that he arrested a person that was high on narcotics and this person told him that if he would have arrested him 15 minutes earlier that the guy would have probably killed him. This made him think about people that are on narcotics, and he became concerned about the violence of these people, and also the narcotics problem. . . . Again, in his background, he evidently went home to Boston and he was talking to this sister and some friends about drugs, and he found that his sister had been using drugs a little bit, and some of his friends were now in prison for serious crimes because of their narcotics use. And he has a feeling that he must protect them from their own actions.

During the analysis session, the group speculated about the role that fear — and its suppression — might play in producing Beam's pattern of conduct. As one officer (the group co-leader) put it:

> Maybe I'm all wet in this little analysis that I have here, but I think that he's operating out of fear. I think that he's so goddamn afraid that he probably came into police work to prove that he could overcome this, which he does —

and I think that's one of the reasons I have so much respect for him. I think he's got the shit scared out of him, and that's the main reason he's chosen narcotics work and specialized in it. But he's not a dummy; he's armed himself with all the laws on narcotics and a hell of a lot of information, a lot more than normal patrol procedure calls for out on the street. He's always talking about snatching people first and never losing control of the situation, and then going through with some physical thing to restrain a guy—getting the handcuffs on him, getting him out of circulation real quick. And I think the reason he does this is also based on fear.

Another officer (Bill) pointed out that Beam

always is attacking individuals, or the problems of individuals who he has built up mentally to be sort of invulnerable creatures of strength, incomparable demons in narcotics. I really believe he believes that, although I don't buy his story about being scared to death by a hype in a men's room, and this is why he's on this personal vendetta. I think that's some sort of mental justification.

This analysis was elaborated, later in the session, by one of the staff members, who argued that

In a way he's built up the drug addict here as the real fiend. . .he's obviously sold himself. To the extent he's conning, he's conning himself on that. It would fit, if you're trying to prove to yourself that you're real tough. And remember, as Bill said, he wasn't a tough guy back in his neighborhood—he was a con. A real crucial question is when he stopped being just a con. He obviously hasn't given it up. And this image of being physically aggressive really took over. And Bill made some suggestion that it might have been with getting in the uniform. Anyhow, if you were trying to build a case of, "How do I handle this feeling in myself, that I can't rise to challenges, that I've got to make up a challenge where I can really overprove to myself that I really can make it, that I really can do it," it would seem to me that he's done a rather beautiful job. And we all agree he's bright, and he's made up a bright rationale here of the evil of these guys who use drugs. And then for a safeguard he puts in this, "I hit first."

You've certainly got a beautiful pattern here for actually getting a physical confrontation over and over again. We don't understand enough of it, but from what he's been telling us, giving himself reassurance that he can take on challenges and can meet them. And I would think of the drug addict as actually a relatively safe challenge. I don't know that I'd buy that he's really taking on anything that's rough.

Another staff member, in a fairly lengthy statement, produced a different version of Beam's hypothesized vulnerability. He reminded the group that

One thing we have already brought out—I think Bob brought it out—is the element of physical detection. That is, it's sort of like witch-hunting. When people hunted witches they prided themselves in being able to locate witches by marks that were left under their crotch or under the armpit or by various little indications that they gave. Beam considers himself an expert at locating these bad guys with a physical indication. He's able to separate them from the rest of the world, and goes about this business very assiduously. And it's extremely important to him to separate them from the rest of the world, which means that he has the world sort of divided and the people who are drug users—the ones that he can locate as bad guys—represent something very intimate to him that upsets him terribly. And he has to control them, which means, I think, that he has to control whatever it is in himself that he somehow senses in them. Now, I guess it's Bob who said before Beam came up here, "It must have something to do with his neighborhood, and the people he grew up with." And then that proved to be an extremely well-confirmed hypothesis because it's one of the few things that Beam was quite willing to answer...he started talking about what it is that really was the occasion for this need to control hypes, as he calls them, and it had to do with two friends he had whom he was apparently close to who ended up in serious difficulties after they started using, or he thought they started using, and his sister. I don't know what to make of his sister, and we might think about that a little bit, but one can venture two possible guesses as to what it was about his friends. The first one was that he felt acutely disappointed by them. Now, that doesn't seem very plausible. The second one was that he said to himself, "There but for the grace of God go I." That is, "These are people that grew up with me and this is how they ended up, and whatever it is in them, I got to fight it in myself." And he fights it in himself by fighting it out there in the world.

He recalled that Beam had presented as a reason for his campaign the fact that narcotics users do harm to themselves. The staff member suggested that

Part of what that means is that they are extremely vulnerable, which means, "I'm extremely vulnerable." Then the other part of the answer I think is related to that, in that they become very "irrational." Their mind gets tampered with. They lose control. They become aggressive. They become evil. They become stupid. They become irresponsible. Which means that I guess in part what he's saying is that "In order for me to keep control over my mind," and the fear element may enter in this, "I've got to fight like hell this tendency for people to have their minds tampered with, and to become irrational monsters, which I can become myself given half the chance."

The discussion later returned to this point, stimulated by an afterthought:

STAFF: I just want to throw in one additional word that he uses here that gives me a feeling that sort of supports my hunch about him, and that is one of the key words in his talking about these hypes is the word "control." That is, he says that he's in the business of controlling them. Now I would suspect, Phil's discussion of the rehabilitation rate of addicts would have very little bearing on what he means by "control." I think he means "subdue." I think he means "suppress."

KENT: He said their personality changes when they use it, they resent authority, and you can't tell them what to do.

LEADER: He did in fact talk about suppression.

STAFF: Which may kind of lend some support to the feeling that this is sort of a metaphor. That is, that he is really trying to control what he thinks of as the drug problem, which is the change in a person's mind from rational to irrational. And this is a very intimate, personal type thing.

OFFICER: That's where someone like Jim has an advantage. He has the answers.

LEADER: Yeah, but you see he doesn't have the alternatives to his answers. And furthermore he doesn't believe they exist—that's the problem. I think he might think about it.

The group concluded that Beam might be relatively difficult to change—and that the interview would have made relatively little impact on him:

> What he essentially wants to do is go out there and fight his private crusade, or as Bill put it, his private war. And he would like as much approval as he can for this. He would like to convince as many people of the rightness of his cause. But if he can't, he'll do it irrespective. There's no amount of pressure today that has had much effect, simply because the sources of the pressure are irrelevant, because people he feels justifiably don't have any feeling for this crusade that he's on. And he's right. They don't.

The group also agreed, however, that if any officer was worth preservation and utilization, it was Beam. As one officer put the case:

> I have a hell of a lot of respect for him, because in each line of work somewhere along the line there's something outstanding in whatever he does. Most people just go along and they do a job. There are people who play violins and then there's people who are damn good violin players. And then there are guys who are policemen. There are some 700 policemen, and then there's Beam.

One staff member, who had never encountered Officer Beam before, urged:

> I sure hope that you people that know this guy can stay with him, because of all people, you hate to see him go down the tube when you get to know him. This is a very powerful guy. . . . It seems to me besides talking, there ought to be some strategy developed to get him to be a real participant.

The group concluded that further interviews and other follow-up activities involving Beam were well worth the effort, even if Beam—like Spark—was admittedly a "tough nut to crack."

Ratings of the Beam interview testified to the feeling that the time had been constructively invested. The "productivity" line reached a peak unequaled except for the first session. Group morale was rated unprecedentedly high. And members felt they had participated fully. They also felt they had learned much, and classified the experience as "instructive" and "informative," as well as "constructive" and "valuable."

A Command Appearance

During the group's next meeting they found themselves faced—at the initiative of another group—with the opportunity of a "summit" meeting with the chief. They arrived at this encounter completely unprepared and were unable to present their ideas. As a result, the chief occupied himself with other matters. He responded to questions from members of a second group and (during a lapse in the questions) reported on his recent experiences with a police department in another city. As Bill summarized the situation later:

> With the chief, you can't give him 30 seconds of silence, because the man is extremely intelligent, he manipulates group conversation. He dominates it because he's extremely brilliant and he's a very eloquent man. He is; there's no doubt about it. And that's what happened. He shot the whole thing. He carried the ball the whole time. He's never in a corner. Joe drew a beautiful picture of a Southern Pacific Railroad Roundhouse, and let me tell you something. He was in the middle and we were all revolving around him like the earth and the sun.

As a constructive by-product of the debacle, there was strong incentive to structure the review panel idea in proposal form. In response to Kent's vague description, the chief replied that he'd like to know more. As Joe (the co-leader) pointed out:

> He stated several times "that's a great idea—you guys work up the finished package and show it to me." And I think that's what we're going to have to do. I think before you get anything across it can't be a generality or any vague idea. It's got to be the specific facts, a finished product all ready for him to sign and send on or it's not going to get anyplace.

Kent, who felt personally responsible for the failure to inform the chief, immediately set to work drafting his proposal. Amid much pleasantry and aimless conversation, he sat grimly formulating the document. As a staff member observed in the summary:

> Kent has made a great deal of headway there—he is well on his way to writing this proposal. We can give it to the chief as soon as it's done. So we may have in fact moved faster in this area than if Bill had been eloquent, although it's quite obvious that the chief would have listened, and from what several of us know about the way he thinks, he would have been extremely sympathetic and supportive and excited.

The group, however was still largely discouraged. Their session ratings reached an all-time low and hovered around "average." The two main rating terms were "fun" and "exasperating." Similar ambivalence was reflected in words such as "rambling," "irritating," "monotonous," and "enjoyable." The meeting had offered entertainment, but the group did not feel materially furthered in its mission, nor was it proud of its accomplishment.

A STUDY IN COMPLEXITY

During its next session the group was back on course, with another volunteer interview. The subject, Officer Kennedy, advertised himself as a changed-but-unreformed practitioner of violence. Kennedy had had contact with our original group in the context of research into a battle with Hell's Angels. At that time Officer Kennedy had impressed the group with his willingness and ability to conceptualize events. Thus, when he declared his interest in assisting in subsequent inquiries, the offer was welcomed.

Officer Kennedy is a brilliant young man, with a distinguished academic record (including a graduate degree). Despite his excellent mind, Kennedy had placed a premium on muscular prowess, with emphasis on boxing. He had also accumulated a reputation for explosiveness, which he was working (successfully) to overcome.

Kennedy is a self-styled Violent Man:

> He stated that violence is attractive to him. He liked the idea of street justice. He liked to draw people in to make them move so that he would have an excuse to hit them when he decided that they would have to go. He said that he must restrain himself in violent situations. He has an impulse to strike out when he is mad.

Kennedy's recipe for producing violence is to "come on soft" so as to give the impression that he is a "pushover." This encourages prospective opponents to assert themselves and provides occasion for attack. In confrontations like these, Kennedy asserts, he has never been beaten:

> He said, "I will always fight to the end. I will never be beat. If I am beat that time I will remember the person and I will get him later. I can't lose." [He recalled] some of his high school days when he was in a tough crowd and it was kind of a big thing and you got into a beef and won the fight. Also, when he was in the Marine Corps he evidently didn't lose too many fights.

In his early associations, Kennedy recalled, his physical confrontations had brought status with his peers:

> He said that he fought for status and he mentioned the codes. The code that he had in the Marine Corps and the code he had here dictated that he must fight for his status, that he had to demonstrate his fighting ability, to acquire his status here or in high school or in the service. And this status was what his peers expected, or this is what he feels is expected. He feels that in order to be worthy of their expectations, he'd have to be a competent fighter.

He asserted that the same circumstances obtain in the police:

> He thinks there is a code among police officers, probably gathered from the locker room, that you are cool because you got into a beef and you beat the crap out of somebody. This makes you feel good and you talk about it and everybody looks up to you.

Simultaneously, he felt that the police organization—particularly at the command level—kept the level of violence in line and suppressed it:

> And were it not for this pressure, the pressure of command and the pressure of Internal Affairs, he would conduct himself as he sees the police, and that is as commandoes. I guess that's kind of the bit where you swing from the ropes and kick down the doors and go in there with machine guns blazing, and you leave the bodies there for the Graves and Registrations Crew to come through and pick them up.

The same characterization of unnaturally suppressed violence ran through Kennedy's discussion of individual motivation and, particularly, of his own. He indicated that when a status issue arises—when he is challenged—this liberates "anger" or impulses and permits him to fight:

> His violent encounters start when someone is running away to avoid arrest or when someone is degrading the uniform and he becomes upset. He says that "I hit people when it is necessary and I lose my cool." When "I've lost my cool or when I'm angry, I'm letting that person know who is the boss."

The model Kennedy sketched of himself was that of a suppressed volcano, with a propensity for occasional eruptions. The result of eruptions, in addition to satisfying violent impulses, is the consolidation of status or dominance:

> Another quote here: "these violent urges." He seems to equate these violent urges also, I notice constantly, with the adrenaline flowing. With the flow of the adrenaline comes the violent desire. And he used words, for instance, "challenge," "dominate," "conquer," "beat into the ground," "John Wayne has got to win," "it's to win."

The problem becomes compounded when Kennedy claims that he reacts against the eruptions of others, but, as one of our group members notes, the paradox is resolved if one considers the suppression of others as indirect self-control (This explanation, as may be recalled, had come up in connection with the previous interview.):

> He said things like "control these impulses in me," "anger gives way to violence." He constantly mentions when you act in a violent way, this is giving way to some animalistic tendency. Real animals doing vicious things are violent themselves. All men are animals down inside. And he says when he sees somebody acting in this animalistic nature, it gets on his nerves, and he tries to stop it. And maybe it's because he has the fear of the same thing in himself. And by doing so, he comes to fight the fire with fire, fight the animal on his own terms of being an animal, and yet feeling bad maybe that he has to do it that way.

Lastly, Officer Kennedy made a strong point to the group of his assumption that the department had checked his violent propensities, and that he could expect no further physical involvements on the street. "I go out of my way to avoid fights," he maintained. "I don't want brutal cops on the street." With respect to this stance, one of our officers (Kent) speculated:

> I think he came up here to tell us that he had changed. And to give us some sort of reasoning for his sort of joining the Establishment. I think he was looking for approval from us. I think maybe one reason for this is that because he had changed, he had already decided that he had to change in order to advance, that maybe he wasn't finding the peer group approval from the locker room. So he had to find it somewhere. And even more so, I don't know—like I said, the guy is no dummy—maybe in the back of his mind he felt that this information would get passed on somewhere else, the fact that he's changed his approach. I think the reason that we saw so many of the contradictory statements was that he's still got to maintain a partial identity of the tough guy with the peer group that he finds down in the locker room. And this is where we find our contradictions.

Given this explanation, there were other complexities and inconsistencies in Kennedy's self-portrait. Bill, the group leader, categorized some of the themes in Kennedy's interview, three of which he labeled "the idealistic tough guy," "the introspective marshmallow," and "the justifier." There was some speculation that at least some of these roles were being played for the benefit of our group:

> Here's a guy saying, "I enjoy violence," and some of us get upset. And we say to him, "Don't you see all these alternatives? And how can you enjoy violence, and isn't this terribly shocking?" And I think at that juncture what was happening to us is we had a game of honesty played on us, where the fellow says, "I'm going to be completely honest with you" and then proceeds to say all kinds of really deep dark things about himself and at times you almost want to stop him and say, "Look, I've got to protect you because you're really exposing all kinds of terrible things." And he says, "Well, you know, I'm making sort of a monster out of myself," with a little snicker. And sure enough, you take a look and the guy is making a monster out of himself— there he is, "I'm enjoying violence, I've got all these deep dark urges. When I repress them I sit there clenching my teeth and have my hands in my pockets and I've got to go to a sex orgy to let all this energy out, because that's the kind of guy I am." You start having the feeling that you're being tested, that you're being goaded just like these people out in the street. You're being goaded this way because you're the Violence Prevention Unit and this is the way that you can be goaded, by my saying, "I am the Violent Man—I'm what you're fighting." But then you also have this business where he is trying to suck us in. He says "I enjoy violence, we all enjoy violence." Meaning, "you guys enjoy violence." And, "What nerve do you have having me up here for being a guy who joins the police force to get a little action when it's quite obvious we all do. Let's all cop out to how we are all really violent and the only thing that's keeping us from being violent is Internal Affairs."

Role-playing aside, the picture presented to the group was clearly paradoxical and considerably more complex than the patterns emerging from previous interviews. The group considered various ways of reconciling disparate elements. One of these was summarized by a staff member:

> Now this commando or Green Beret model of policing that he has is a little odd, because he gets something here that says each of us is sort of an uncontrollable force and it's the job of the police department to squelch us. And it sounds like if that happens you can be proud both of being potentially violent and also of being squelched, so that you can't really lose. Because essentially Kennedy can say, "Look, I am still capable of winning fights, and the only reason why I don't win them is because the police department is not permitting me to fight. And I don't mind in one sense the police department not permitting me to fight because I am also in this police game. That is, I don't like people out there stirring up trouble. But at the same time I myself am still capable of doing the things that I have been doing. And it's only the system that keeps me from doing them." Which I think is sort of in miniature the feeling he has about himself. That is, that he is sort of controlling himself, although he's capable of exploding at any minute. There's all that adrenaline there that is flowing. But still, there is the mind over matter bit, and he emphasized this very early in the game. He says, "I don't lose my cool—I choose to lose my cool. And now I don't choose to lose my cool as much as I chose to lose my cool before." So he has to feel that he's in control, but he also has to feel that he can get out of control and can have these highs and can have this fun and can be this monster, whenever he can get away with it. That is, he does not like the self-image of being a guy who had the controlling forces in command. It's got to be sort of a precarious balance at all times. A constant battle, where the only time you can be nonviolent is when you can give yourself some pretty solid reasons for being nonviolent. Then you can stand there saying, "There but for the grace of God goes another corpse. And it's only the system, or these things that I choose to give way to, that keeps this guy from being a corpse." And that way, save face. I must say he has me convinced when he comes in and says, "I am a violent man, I am a monster." I think he is. I think, however, that's just one part of the picture. I also think he's a guy who's very capable to coping with this, but in a situation in which he doesn't get any excuses for coping with it, he isn't going to. I think that's part of what he was trying to tell us.

The group decided that some of Kennedy's self-description was more revealing than he suspected. Thus one of the officers observed:

> Whenever Kennedy gets into any kind of a confrontation like he was here tonight, you'll notice that right around his collar line it starts a brilliant red color, and it creeps right up. I was watching it as he started taking us on here tonight. It finally covered his whole face. Evidently there's some physiological change that goes here and maybe this is this apprehension that we're talking about.

Except for "group participation" ratings, the session brought the quantitative indices back into the "high" category, with the group feeling that it was developing its procedure and learning much. The most frequently checked adjective was "valuable," followed by "thought pro-voking" and "constructive"; other recurrent rating terms were "challenging," "promising," and "informative."

BACK TO THE DRAWING BOARD

The next meeting was a two-part working session. During the first half, the group met with a captain who had requested that one of his men be interviewed. The purpose of this session was to brief the group on the interviewee's problem, as assessed by the captain.

The group was pleased by this session on two counts. First, there was pride in having been perceived as a resource, particularly by a member of management:

> I think we can be flattered somewhat that a command officer sat down and told us that he has exhausted just about every means that he has available to him in an attempt to help this officer, and now finds himself [working with] patrolmen who have come up with a proposal that might do the job better than he himself can do it. And, I think that is something to be damn proud of. I really think that it is something that we can kind of wallow in for a while.

The second source of satisfaction was the fact that a commanding officer might become sufficiently concerned with helping a patrolman to take the trouble to explore available resources. Simultaneously, the group felt that the department might face a general problem in not having supervisors equipped with information or skills relevant to the diagnosis of problems. The group discussed the possibility that the supervisor's role might make it difficult to exercise constructive influence:

> Like he was aware of several danger signs, he went through the standard procedure of calling a man in and talking to him, not really having any plan or pattern or any idea what was bugging the guy, what the man's individual problems were. And it's an indication to me that something's lacking around here in all ranks. That possibly a training program could remedy.

In the second half of the session the group broke up into subgroups to work on the details of projects. One of these subgroups, chaired by Kent, worked on the review panel idea. The other group dealt with a questionnaire exploring possibilities for using lineup time for short-term remedial training. The lineup survey group reported progress, but added that "everybody subverted each other all night long." The action review group characterized their session as "an agonizing exercise" from which they "emerged a bit torn up mentally."

Session ratings ranged widely, with some men classifying the evening as productive and pleasant and others declaring themselves exhausted. The most frequently used adjectives were "thought provoking," "challenging," and "inconclusive."

RUNNING OUT OF STEAM

At the next meeting the group was faced with the prospect of more planning and collective thought. No activity was scheduled, nor was there a consuming pending task. One concrete assignment was the planning session relating to an interview the following night. The remainder of the time was occupied with drafting and discussion. This portion of the meeting was somewhat slow. Its most negative assessment came from one group member, who said that

> After lunch I felt that we all fell apart. As I looked around the room, I found everyone...doing something other than the work that was going on or should have been. We spent an unproductive second period of joking, doodling, and making obscene gestures at one another.

The group leader viewed the session somewhat more favorably. He observed:

> There comes a time when you kind of think you run out of things to do and rather than think about something and rather than really push yourself on it, you have a tendency to want to not do anything. And I think we were damn near at that point tonight, because that's how I felt. I seem to relate everything to how I feel. And I wrote down that the group seemed to move tonight simply because it wanted to. I really didn't think I'd be able to get on board tonight, but I found it really easy when things started moving. And it was merely because you guys started participating and producing something.

A staff member's assessment fell somewhere in between:

> I think Bill put it very accurately—it was a tough session, we had a lot of thinking to do today; we didn't have anything entertaining to do, like interviewing somebody. And we sat around for eight hours, and we did some solid talking and thinking and looking at information and reading, and we got through it and we survived it and we got some ideas to take with us that we didn't have when we arrived.

The interview planning session did capture the interest of the group. It produced some observations, but no conclusion:

> We sensed that there was a person here who has a tendency to put himself in a situation where some people have given him some warnings that they're going to be unfriendly if he orders them to do things that they're not going to do. And then he jumps on them when they predictably respond, or fail to respond. There is still a certain amount of mystery about this which is healthy, because it kind of shows the point to which one can proceed with

these preliminary reviews and the gaps that are left, which is a lesson that we have to learn. And we will learn it filling in tomorrow.

The group also decided to adopt a new member, Officer Spark. Spark belonged to another group, where he had become the focus of tensions. Adopting Spark was a calculated risk, and the group took it freely and lightly. Several members observed that as things stood they need not fear potentially destructive influences. The group felt that it could proudly regard itself as a regenerating environment.

Except for morale ratings (which were high) the officers were disinclined to boast about their accomplishments. Nor did they despair. Almost all rated the meeting as "constructive," and some thought it was "creative" and "valuable." However, there were complaints about occasional "rambling."

ACCOMPLISHMENT

In a sense, the interview of Officer Fels represented movement from the sandbox into the battlefield. Whereas previous subjects had presented themselves as volunteers and as participants in the design of the project, Fels was neither. Here was a man who had been ordered up for an interview, with reason to be wary and resentful. The order had emanated from a superior who had previously voiced strong reservations about Fels' conduct—who had remonstrated with him, ordered, cajoled, sermonized, and threatened. Officer Fels suspected that his conduct was the issue, and assumed that the proceeding was adversary. He knew nothing about the group, nor had he more than superficial past contact with any of its members.

Not surprisingly, Fels entered into the situation coldly, sullenly, and determined to remain silent. He started by refusing to read his reports, and responded "I don't recall" to every one of Bill's questions. According to an outline chronology by Kent, the first hour and a quarter of the interview transpired as follows:

> My first entry on this little conglomeration of notes that I keep says, "he's extremely defensive, stern." At 8:05, this is 5 minutes after he sat down, I wrote, "his responses will be like testimony." At 8:12 I made a notation, "things are going bad." At 8:20 I made a notation, "Bill sounds like a cross-examination." Also, I put down the first report in this case that we thought was a good report was bad actually, I think. Because it put him way on the defensive. We picked up a few things. At 8:45 I made a notation that we were belaboring that first report. Then we go to the second report; then we jumped right to the third one. This is 9:15.

Fels's initial reluctance to respond had an adverse impact on the questioning. The issue began to revolve around a concerted effort to wring a concession or acknowledgment from Fels. In one report, for instance, the group worried about Fels's reluctance to permit an intoxicated woman to be taken to her nearby home. As one officer (Graham) summarized this incident:

> In an attempt to get him to open up, everyone kind of got on a bad bag. Whether they couldn't find another one or not, or what it was, but you wanted to try to make him open up and think about alternatives. So you're trying to come up with an alternative in this drunk case. And you couldn't get him to come up with one, so you suggested one, and then everybody took it on and you wanted him to admit something which he didn't believe. And everyone kept bringing up the aspect of possibly letting the suspect go, which may have been an alternative. But nothing else was mentioned, and then it went on with "haven't you ever done this before?" "let her go, let her go, let her go." I kept hearing this cry from the group. And he kept sitting over there saying, "Well, I don't see why I'd have to let her go—isn't there any other alternative? Is that all you've come up with?" And I felt that possibly at that time, that he might, since he's new and hasn't heard all this, be thinking along the lines of, "Is that their alternative, period?" No "s" on the end. "Do you have to make these arrests just because she's a little drunk?"

Eventually, after an indigestible Mexican lunch that produced innumerable complaints from the group, the atmosphere began gradually to relax and Fels talked. He started "remembering" details, including those not entered in the report. He began to speculate about motives and to discuss his premises. He became, ultimately, voluble. It became clear, as Bill later noted, that Fels "was ready to talk to somebody...really wanted to talk to somebody."

Fels speculated that at some juncture he had developed a pattern of reacting personally to suspects and bystanders. He indicated that he had permitted people to "get under his skin"; "respect" had been an emotion-laden issue. He confessed to feeling "challenged" by lack of respect and to creating confrontations: "He was out there thinking of himself as having to uphold the whole legal structure when anybody defied it by saying something to him or by not responding to him."

The group was not surprised by this analysis because it corresponded to hypotheses formulated the previous evening in the review of Fels's reports:

> We did a very good job confirming all the hunches that we built up during the agonizing four to eight hours that we looked over this stuff. That is, almost everything that he told us about himself we had thought through, and in a sense this was a kind of confirming session.... Which meant we did some solid thinking. It was right to the point.

Like Kennedy, Fels presented a picture of having been suppressed and controlled. He produced two versions of this sequence. His first model was that of a "pendulum" movement, which he thought was fairly general with policemen:

> He definitely thought when he was coming on and he first came on he was very susceptible and quite liberal and open-minded. And then some training officers in the peer group and some of the observations got to him, and also his personality, as he puts it, got molded to the point where he was taking these things personally.... And then he was able to get out of this into another period in which now he can view things more dispassionately.

In this model, Fels attributed his transition to education:

> He said he had been taking college courses and reading black literature. His view had broadened. He can see why blacks act the way they do and how they view the police. And this affects the way he acts.

He described the result as a set of insights, and indicated that he had found them to be valid assumptions, confirmed through experience:

> He used to utilize the law to enforce respect for the law. "Now I know it won't change them, it doesn't change me and it doesn't work. You can't force respect on people...." Fels has realized recently that he approaches people different. He talks and listens, he smiles more, he can get their view as to their actions and get their side of the story. And he can relate to them better. His first words made a difference. He tries to give the person an out.... He has gotten over some of these premises...like for instance this business of "It used to be my attitude if I am saying it, you better do it. Now I feel I ought to explain." He said, "How can somebody call you an MF if you walk up smiling?"

Fels's second version of change represents a strict compliance model, in which the new pattern results completely from administrative pressure:

> He's changed not really because of any changing in his mind, but he's changed because of administrative pressure here, which he thinks is unfair. He realizes that this is the environment that he's living in. If he wants to stay here he's going to have to do certain things.

In elaborating this model, Fels characterized himself as apathetic, and asserted that he was working less hard and enjoying it less:

> He says, "I enjoy the job less. I don't go after crime like I used to. I don't know how to be aggressive and keep out of 148s." ...He said he hadn't thought about any alternatives to being aggressive and being effective and staying out of 148s. He says now he doesn't have any initiative.... "The department is telling me I'm bad because I have a lot of 148s. Yet I don't think the department has the facts."

According to Fels, the reason for his low productivity consisted of the blanket nature of the censure to which he was subjected. By subjecting his street conduct to criticism, the department had failed to distinguish between his constructive activity and his corollary problem behavior:

> He definitely feels like he's in a straitjacket when he's going out there.... The point he made several times [is] that just telling him that he has a lot of 148s without any explanation made him very angry, especially because when somebody tells you that you have a great many 148s they also say you're a bad police officer. They don't distinguish that 148s and the quality of police work are definitely tied together.

In the course of the interview, the group discussed the difference between low-quality (violence-related) productivity and general activity. They pointed out to Fels that his supervisor was concerned with his problem, as witnessed by his high opinion of Fels and his desire to "save" him. Fels acknowledged that these arguments were reasonable, and indicated that the discussion had been helpful. In general, he reacted to the group very positively and appreciatively. As he left the session, he said that he was prepared to support the review panel project, which he viewed as necessary and constructive.

The group, in turn, was elated. Bill, the leader, introduced his summary by indicating that he had been "trying to think of how I can talk into the tape...without sounding like a kid who just woke up on Christmas morning." Jones, on his reaction form, waxed lyrical ("it's been shown that a rough road can end at a beautiful meadow"). Officer Spark, the new group member, characterized the review unit as "great," and expressed the hope that he could be used on future panels.

Productivity ratings averaged "very high," as in the first session of the summer. Almost everyone rated the session as both "tense" and "constructive." Other adjectives (in order) were "enjoyable" and "purposeful"; "valuable," "relevant," and "promising"; "instructive," "inspiring," and "beautiful." The summer had reached its climax.

AN INTERLUDE OF ALIENATION

Joe, the co-leader, introduced his contribution to the next session's summary by saying:

> We really didn't have anything going that anybody wanted to bring out right off the bat. There are a lot of things that are on policemen's minds today and we brought some of them out...

As another officer put it (on his reaction form):

> The before-lunch session *screamed* many frustrating things felt by policemen today.

The "frustrating things" had to do with recent snipings at police officers in various major cities. Once this subject came up, it branched into increasingly remote areas. At first, there was concern about the sufficiency of protection—was there enough "backing"? Then there were issues of priorities, strictures, arbitrariness of rules, lack of appreciation. At one acrimonious juncture, Joe advanced the proposition that

> It's going to be a hell of a thing to sell a violence-reduction program in police work when you're getting policemen snuffed out left and right all over the country.

Bill, who had tried (unsuccessfully) to curb the discussion, "dropped out" of it, and became a low participant. Eventually, the group returned to business and turned to reviewing the records of its next prospective interviewee.

In the summary the evening was penitently reviewed, with the only positive note injected by a staff member, who indicated that the evening's discussion might have some bearing on the concerns of several interviewees:

> The idea is, "Well, they...are trying to make me stop doing work." Which then gets to the issues of is this police department or is the chief really serious about doing police work? Or is he in the community relations business? And although the discussion itself may not have been terribly relevant, the more I think about it, the more it's obvious that there are some indications in this kind of discussion that are relevant. They have to do with the issue of good people like Fels for one, and maybe even possibly at some juncture Spark, saying "I feel like I'm being forced into a position of not being able to do my job. And I'm going to be unhappy and I'm going to be inactive and I'm going to view this department as in a sense not designed to get the job done." And on another level it relates to the feeling of maybe they aren't serious about protecting me from snipers. Or maybe the Chief isn't really on our side, maybe he's just a politician as opposed to a guy who's out there trying to facilitate our work. So in a sense the theme is related.

But the group remained depressed. The session was rated relatively low, and the adjectives reflected considerable ambivalence of feeling. The top four rating terms, for instance, were "enjoyable," "constructive," "inconclusive," and "rambling"; these were followed by "valuable," "frustrating," and "subversive." The group had permitted itself a cathartic experience and was now determined to return to business.

THE INTERVIEWER AS THEORIST

The next session was that of September 1, the last group session of the summer and the penultimate meeting of the project.

The evening started off somewhat disappointingly, with the scheduled interviewee, for whom preparations had been made, not appearing. Fortunately, Officer Chico Bond, a member of group 2, had stayed in the building and volunteered for an interview. The group spent an hour getting ready for Bond and then subjected him to a review session. In the final portion of the meeting the conclusions reached about Bond were compared with those obtained with other subjects, and some general assumptions of a theoretical nature were advanced and discussed.

Chico Bond is a relatively young, slight officer, whose physical encounters had taken place almost exclusively with suspects of Mexican-American extraction, most of them youths. Officer Bond admitted that he sometimes felt personally challenged by these persons, and that he felt compelled to respond:

> He said... "The suspects failed to comply." "The suspect appeared hostile — looked like he was mad at being stopped."
> He felt that he was being challenged at the time. This young man was a threat to him. He says, "I played his game and I met his challenge. I put myself in a position to lose face if this suspect didn't leave." And also the suspect would lose face if he did leave, so they had kind of a standoff here.

At the simplest level, the hypothesis about Bond was that he sensed a similarity between himself and his Mexican-American suspects, which he then set out to disprove:

> With all the problems he has with Mexican-Americans it was perfectly plausible to me that there's a great deal of similarity between some of these Mexican-American teenagers and Chico Bond. He isn't in some respects an imposing, muscular physical specimen. And it's entirely possible to speculate that he's also out there occasionally trying to make a case for his being an imposing figure. And he runs into other people who have the same case to make. You get a collision there, on account of there's only one imposing physical figure at any given altercation of this kind. And there is not room for both unless there is some kind of compromise possible. And you don't get the feeling that there was much compromise.

A more sophisticated (and more general) formulation was advanced by Officer Kent, who summarized it as follows:

> What I've noticed here, and I don't know if it's going to come out with the rest of the people we're dealing with, but the word I've got here again... is fear. Here you have fear of Mexican-Americans just like earlier we saw fear of hypes, fear of Negroes, fear of the crowd inciter, and now we have fear of a Latin-American. It seems to follow a pattern. And I'm wondering if when he has this particular fear when he approaches a person on the street, a person tends to get tense, and when he's tense because he has this fear that he's trying to control, if this causes a breakdown in his ability to verbally communicate with somebody. And when you have the breakdown of this verbal communication — this willingness to get out and talk to the person on a police officer–citizen contact — it almost seems like it's going to be a corollary

that you will have physical contact, because you have this mutual misunderstanding. Because the citizen's going to be afraid of the policeman, too, at a particular point. And consequently, if you have just orders coming out and he doesn't want to comply, you have both people that are nervous, tense, tight, and sooner or later somebody's going to take some sort of action. Because obviously the verbal communication is broken down.

The application of this view was elaborated by one of the staff members:

> I do think there may be something to this fear bit.... That when Chico gets afraid he becomes a different person. That he isn't the mild, sweet gentle Chico we all love. And you kind of have the feeling that maybe the one game that is going on with these Mexican-Americans is that he is in effect challenging them. That is, he isn't so much being challenged as he is challenging them, and there is communication going on here, and they are getting the message. I'm impressed, by the way, by the fact that we are putting some life on this bone of people refusing to comply with orders, which is in fact how eight out of ten 148s start out according to the statistical analysis. The statistics just give you that fact. One thing you get from Chico is that very often the order that is given or the instruction that isn't being complied with is really impossible for the person to comply with, not physically but in terms of the way he has already pointed out in some way or other to the officer he's going to be able to act. And it seems to me that one thing that you get with Chico is he does present difficulties to the civilians that they can't resolve. And it isn't so much that he gets mad with people who don't follow his orders, like another guy we had up here, but he has a tendency to give people orders that are boxing them in and then he gets into trouble. It's interesting that in many of the instances, that is, at least those instances that we've looked at, you've got a 148 where there's no real grounds for arrest in the first place.

This formulation led to a long and spirited discussion among the group. Joe, the co-leader, demanded a dictionary definition of "fear"; Graham worried about the implication of manifest fear among police.

There followed a discussion in which officers who had been interviewed speculated about the role of fear in their incidents. Jones maintained that he could detect fear in his own encounters; Graham (in response to arguments from other officers) began to see a possible involvement of fear in some of his own incidents:

JONES: This reminds me of this incident that we've got on tape that I went over. Remember when I snatched the guy when he swung? This is probably the same type of thing that we're talking about here. I reacted so fast because of apprehension, fear of what might happen.

GRAHAM: Do I really need to prove myself when I go through the door, or is it because—well, I find that hard to believe about me...

OFFICER: You know, in your character, in your ideas about fear, you've rationalized in your own mind that you've corralled fear and you're able to rationalize any incident that comes about where fear should be a part of it...

GRAHAM: Well, there were two incidents like that...I mean I was already ready to pick myself up from the sidewalk and fly through the window...Why don't you expound on this fear thing? The group mentioned this as an observation about Beam. And then I just took it like an explanation. And now Kent is actually making a kind of theory out of it. And I don't know how you're bringing in fear, but I'm having a hard time imagining policemen out in the street afraid.

BILL: You've never been afraid?

GRAHAM: Not as a running emotion, as constant a factor as this theory suggests.

OFFICER: Every time I get in the car I've got it.

GRAHAM: Well, on a particular incident, yes, but I find the theory being presented as a constant.

BILL: Could the fact that an officer could or could not act out of fear be because he's in a position where he can't make an exit? I would say that if a person was in fear or afraid other than a policeman it's obviously possible for him to get the hell away. A cop can't do that; he's got to stay there, although he feels that fear. Which makes him act out of that fear. You can't leave the scene like a truck driver or a banker or an insurance salesman or anybody else. You've got to stay there; that's your job. It makes it pretty goddamn awesome at times.

GRAHAM: At times, but no one answered this question about the fear as a constant.

In response to Graham's request, a staff member elaborated on the possibility of behavioral patterns based on habitually suppressed fear:

All right, lets say it's a constant in some respect but not in others. For instance, forgetting for the moment about the fear but thinking about what would happen if it were there at some level, and at some level meaning you can't leave the scene, like Bill says.... One thing is you can run in there without cover just to show you're not afraid. Another is you can go out there and be a man of steel and exaggerate the danger of all these people, and the more danger the better. That's another thing you can do. Another thing you can do is pick the first little guy you come across and beat him up, which is as a matter of fact the most terrible way of all. That's the way bullies do it. That is, you make other people afraid, and the more afraid they are, the more you feel you're an inspirer of fear rather than a feeler of fear. Another thing you can do is brave it out, and this is where you get the Chico Bond type of thing. That is, you come on more harshly than you would if you weren't afraid. The point being that all of these maneuvers and some others are designed for two purposes. One is to fool yourself, in the sense of making it hard to view yourself as a guy who's capable of fear, and the other one is fooling the other people involved, or the spectators or the opposition.... It's possible that one of the main problems in the police business is how to make yourself accept fear as a perfectly decent, respectable emotion to have if it doesn't run away with you, obviously. Not panic—fear. Admitting it. You know, the locker room doesn't compensate you if you go in there and say, "You know, I was scared out of my pants today."

The staff member argued that the suppression of fear could be a reaction to a self-image that labels fear as a symptom of vulnerability or weakness:

> I think one thing we've got to understand is that when you say "fear" you're dealing with something that is sort of like the middle of a sandwich. That is, in these situations that the guy feels afraid...what he is feeling and what he is doing is fighting off fear. But on the other hand, that isn't the answer either, because then you can go on and say, "Why is that such a big issue?" And then you start getting some other answers. Like, for instance, if you can admit that you're afraid, you admit that you're *weak*. And you may have a big problem about feeling weak. So you can get the Man of Steel type thing, which really says, two steps removed..."I'm really not much of a guy, I'm really pretty vulnerable," and then you end up making yourself invulnerable. But in between is this feeling that you've got to fight off because it would make you admit what you don't want to admit.... But on top of everything else, this is a dangerous job. We've got fear running through this whole business and then we've got some guys who seem to have more of a thing here than others.

The group also returned to the fact that several interviewees (including Officer Bond) had reported that their conduct had changed. This led to a discussion of the review panel as a context in which constructive movement (whether real or fictitious) could be positively discussed and rehearsed:

> They wouldn't go around the locker room saying "I have changed." They say it here. And I think the exercise of saying "I have changed" and documenting it is healthy. That is, one of the purposes of this interview might in fact be to give an opportunity to a guy of emphasizing those things about him that are positive, which otherwise might be submerged again by talking about inactivity, which is quite popular. It's quite respectable. Even Joe would regard it as respectable for a guy to say, "Well, this department has gotten me down and so I'm not doing any work." No one in the locker room would look down on you for this. But if they are talking more, "And I used not to tell people much and now I talk to them," that doesn't strike me as something that would get you many pats on the back in the locker room.

The session had thus provided an opportunity to conceptualize further the role of the panel, to begin generalizing about the dynamics of problem officers, and to discuss concepts meaningful to the analysis of patterns.

Despite the fact that some of the discussion had involved personal conflict, and despite the abstract nature of the ideas, the group felt good about the session. The ratings were high. The only negative adjective was "puzzling." Other terms used to describe the session were "academic" (a positive attribute), "enjoyable," "sensible," "constructive," "relevant," "promising," and "thought provoking."

AN ACTIVITY PROFILE

Figure 2 presents a profile of quantitative ratings for activities of the group. The high point of the productivity graph are identified, and all relate to the review panel. Interviews and interview analyses produced favorable ratings, and interviews with "outsiders" ranked higher than the less worrisome "in-group" exercises.

The group morale rankings proved relatively stable, except for three "low-productivity" sessions, in which morale dropped, and the first group session, in which morale was uniquely high. Participation was often closely tied to productivity, but occasionally proved independent.

A GENERAL COMMENT

In Chapter 10 we shall attempt to evaluate the Action Review Unit as a contribution to the police and as an experiment in planned change. It now remains to discuss the brief life of our group as a functioning group.

The first impression that strikes an observer is this group's high degree of task orientation. It may be noted that almost every session has some relation to the main project. On the first day the stage is set and a preliminary rehearsal takes place; the discussion of the second meeting is germane; the idea is formalized in the third meeting. In almost every subsequent session a task is performed or concepts explored that feed directly into the review panel.

Several other projects were stillborn during this period. Their life consisted of explorations of rationale, discussion of practical problems, and, in one instance, the design of an instrument. In no case did a side project occupy more than a fragment of meeting time and a few members.

The success of the group (if we use summaries and rating forms as criteria) can be attributed to three factors. (1) Time was taken up with consuming practical tasks that were related to an objective that the group identified with. These tasks (the interviews) were intellectually stimulating, controversial and challenging, and productive of generalizable information. As the officers developed as interviewers, they attained insight into the conduct of their peers and into their own behavior, as well as becoming informed about their jobs. They increasingly saw the value of interviews; even the subjects saw the experience as useful for themselves and for others. (2) The group enjoyed sophisticated leadership. Not only were the sessions conducted with sensitivity to group and individual dynamics, but group leaders had acquired substantive background, which was deployed at critical junctures. Both

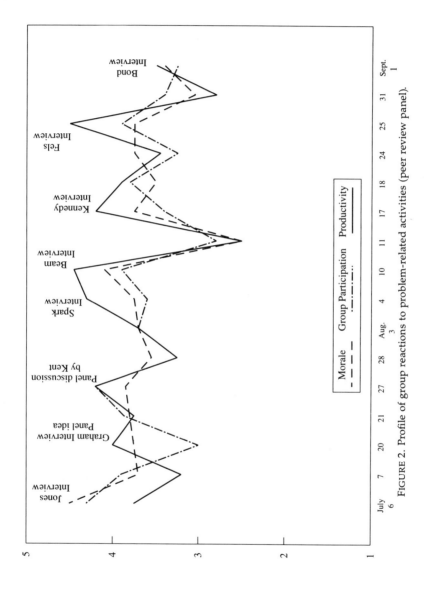

FIGURE 2. Profile of group reactions to problem-related activities (peer review panel).

leaders (especially the main leader) had perfected pattern-analytic and interview techniques before the project was born; both had become familiar with concepts that provided a framework for discussion; both had group experience that helped them deal with victories and defeats to which they were subjected. (3) The group contained key members who were stimulating and self-stimulating and who were able to originate ideas for the group and conceptualize them in detail. It is obvious that Kent would be a figure of power in any group. Somewhat less obviously, other permanent members (particularly Jones) and even some of the guests made critical theoretical contributions.

The role of staff members in the group was not that of nondirective observers. Typically, staff made two contributions: (1) they added to the analysis following interviews, by building on concepts advanced by group members; and (2) they produced observations about group process, especially in the summary. Staff members also participated in interviews, especially at first. In this connection, one important asset was the complete trust between staff and first-generation officers. This trust spread to the group, so that staff were considered full fellow members.

Group 1 enjoyed a happy, harmonious, and productive life. Its single-minded and effective dedication to its self-assigned task made this group a model problem-solving enterprise.

CONCLUDING NOTE

We started this chapter by noting that group 1 addressed the issue of Taylorism, which has to do with the assumption that police must be tightly managed to control misbehavior. The peer review concept, by contrast, implies that officers can monitor and control each other's behavior.

This assumption is crucial for problem-oriented policing, because it removes the most powerful objection to the exercise of discretion by rank-and-file officers, which has to occur in police problem-solving experiments. The review panel also makes misbehavior a problem like any other problem, which can be translated into a pattern, studied, understood, and remedied through interventions.

NOTES

1. Peer review means that workers quality control their own (or each other's) work. More broadly defined, the concept implies that workers can take over supervisory functions—such as monitoring and controlling performance—by having peer groups review the work of their members.

8

Addressing the Problem
Designing
Family Crisis Teams

The second problem-solving group whose work we review defined its mission differently from the first. Like the first group, it took an interest in police responses to street situations; but it evolved projects which were more variegated.

One of the projects originated by the group was not directly related to violence. We shall touch on this project briefly and trace its relationship to group process and productivity.

The second activity of the group, which we shall discuss in detail, is unique in several respects. For one, it represents an effort to adapt an experiment originating elsewhere. The adaptation is one that emphasizes systematic data gathering and analysis, and invokes peer influence as a training tool. The project also carried the group from the conference table to the field, where it conducted live tests of project feasibility. In addition, the group used help and information sources from outside the department, from agencies and groups in the Oakland community.

The quantitative profile of the group is displayed in Figure 3, where the high and low points are identified. The high-ranked experiences were those relating to field experiments, to encounters with outside professionals, and to project planning and project implementation. The low points include sessions in which data were tabulated and analyzed and reports were drafted. We shall return to this pattern at a later point in our discussion.

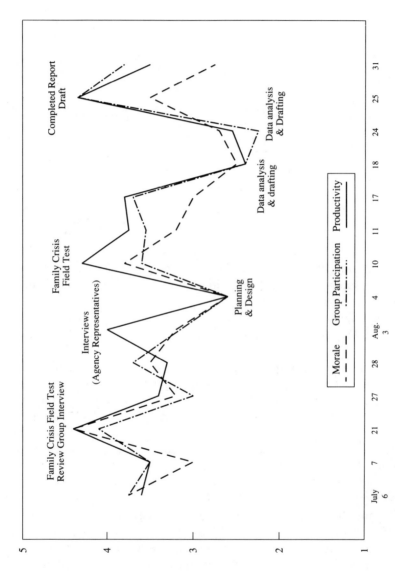

FIGURE 3. Profile of group reactions to problem-related activities (family crisis intervention).

PRELIMINARY EXPLORATIONS

The group did not embark on its career with a spurt of enthusiasm. Instead, the first session ranged casually over several areas. This included an exchange of ideas relating to violence, a general "gripe" session, and a firmly formulated project proposal.

The discussion relating to violence was initiated by a group member (Officer House) who questioned the rationale of the unit. His manner of posing the problem is reflected in the summary:

> The issue that we did get hot and heavy on right before lunch was the question of "Why keep talking with a suspect when you have wasted two minutes on him already and he has failed the attitude test?" And we had a wide range of issues here and I think we still are fairly sharply divided on these issues, and it's going to take us several weeks I'm sure before we can get House on our side... I might say, at last count House was holding forth in a kind of eulogy to the John Birch Society, so we have not really made what you would regard as a substantial dent in him.

A more positive outcome was achieved in another debate, in which the group addressed the problems of an officer faced with partners bent on "street justice." This discussion was stimulated by Spark, who recalled an incident in which some angry colleagues had apparently beaten a suspect. The group stipulated that "street justice" was undesirable and worried about its causes and consequences. They showed particular concern for the "witnessing" officer, who stood between the frying pan of his conscience (and departmental orders) and the fire of peer pressure:

> We went off on a second subject which engaged us quite actively, and it came from an experience which one of us had very recently, in which at the tail end of a very exciting high-speed chase, a number of officers who had arrived on the scene fairly late took it upon themselves to very forcibly restrain the suspect. And there was some question as to whether all this forcible restraining was really absolutely necessary. And this took us on a fairly intensive discussion on when does one and does one not have the right to lose one's cool; what about the officer who engages in street justice; some subdivisions of street justice (such as those that leave lumps and those that don't); what are the repercussions for the rest of the department of somebody having dispensed street justice at some stage.... And again we didn't resolve these questions completely, but we had the issues quite nicely posed and we were beginning to talk about, if we did take the position that at least some type of punishing on the street after a person has been restrained is not good police work, how do we go about making this clear to people who have been doing this or might be tempted to do this...
>
> We did also, I think, worry a little bit about the officer in whose presence that type of thing is committed. Who obviously, in terms of what's right, has some kind of obligation here to intercede or try to prevent this kind

of thing from happening again, but who on the other hand is under fairly strong pressure from the peer group—and speaking of pressure from the peer group, we talked some about the locker room and its emulation of officers who have good war stories to tell.

The ventilation of complaints occurred late in the session, and ranged from injustices in the world to immediate, "housekeeping" gripes:

We also talked some about the criminal justice system and the prevalence of negotiated pleas and light sentences and so on, and we had a number of standard gripes in this area. . . We ended up with the number of chairs in the report writing room, and then it suddenly occurred to us that maybe we were off the subject.

The proposal that came before the group originated with Caspar White, a trade-union-oriented officer. White harbored a long-standing concern with the problems presented by reserve officers—a category of parttime police volunteer who functions in restricted capacities, mainly on weekends. White's feelings about reserve officers, mainly negative ones, were couched in the form of questions about their training, qualifications, performance, and level of integration into the department. The other officers agreed to pursue these questions, since these involved research and could lead to constructive change. The group resolved to interview some reserves, as well as the sergeant in charge of the reserve unit.

The ratings for the first session represented average rankings for the summer ("high minus"); the adjective most often involved was "honest." This was followed by "enjoyable," "constructive," "creative," "inconclusive," and "rambling."

TOOLING UP

Except for a brief, abortive effort to continue the previous day's griping, the second meeting was task oriented.

Part of the time was invested in the reserve study and in the design of a questionnaire dealing with reserves. A portion was taken up with a projected four-hour field exercise in which the group intended to respond to family crisis calls in order to collect tapes. The rest of the session was occupied with a review and discussion of street incidents.

Officer White was the key figure in planning for the reserve study. He presented the substance of a report he had prepared about the program. This report contained background information supplemented with personal observations. Although these were tendentious, White advocated an objective inquiry with meticulous concern for methodological safeguards. The group invested considerable effort in drafting items for a questionnaire. Each member wrote several items, and the pool went to a staff member for editing and collation. The officers also designated a sample of respondents, stratified by assignment and time on the force. White proposed that the critical-incident questionnaire (put together by our original group) be administered to the reserve force:

WHITE: If we're concerned with reserves, why not a questionnaire for the reserves, to get their feelings on this thing? Did any of the reserves fill out this critical-incident report?

STAFF: No.

WHITE: That might be worthwhile, to have them do that.

LEADER: Boy, this guy does a hell of a job!

STAFF: It ought to be very interesting to see how they stack up against experienced officers, recruits. Joe's guess would be, I gather, that they'd talk very glibly about moving into all kinds of situations in which an experienced officer does not. Although we have the other hypothesis now that they do just the opposite.

The exercise in methodology contrasts with the group's casual approach to other projects. The officers decided to spend four hours on the street, in specialized cars that would respond to family crisis calls. This outing was partially motivated by a desire for variety and was not viewed as a prelude to further effort. The group's most salient concern was with mechanical matters and administrative detail.

SHAPING A GROUP MISSION

When the group reconvened two weeks later, it had two key experiences to digest. One was a retreat we had held, which included a discussion with Dr. Bard of the family crisis experiment in the New York police. The second was an evening spent answering family crisis calls. As part of its session, the group also interviewed three members of the reserve unit.

In reviewing the activities of the previous day, the group listened to two tapes of situations the officers had encountered. Both tapes evoked questions relating to outcome of the calls. The men decided to answer these questions empirically by contacting the complainants. In both cases, telephone interviews yielded testimonials about the handling of the incidents.

One call had begun alarmingly with a report of a man who had attacked two persons with a knife. The officers discovered that injuries were negligible and that the assailant had suffered a share of damage. The incident had featured a three-way altercation between husband, wife, and wife's son. The wife had been scraped on the forehead with an ice pick, the son had been menaced with a knife, and the husband had secured a black eye. The wife at first demanded that her husband be arrested and jailed:

WOMAN: My head is bleeding. See, ice picks bleed inside.

OFFICER: Yeah, well, if it penetrates at all, it will bleed inside. Well, this is a serious accusation you're making. Would you be willing to go through with a formal complaint?

WOMAN: I sure will!

OFFICER: Even if it has Conrad doing about 5 to 20 years in the penitentiary?

WOMAN: I don't care! I do not care. You see that ice pick—he threw that.

At length, the woman declared her willingness to entertain permanent separation from her husband, and indicated that she would subsequently file charges against him:

OFFICER: You wouldn't be satisfied just to have Conrad leave for the night, huh?

WOMAN: I'd be satisfied if you'd have Conrad leave for good.

OFFICER: Well, are you starting any legal proceedings against him?

WOMAN: Yes I am, because he threw a knife on my teenage son.

The husband, in turn, agreed to leave, but he insisted on an impromptu property settlement, including the right to remove household furnishings.

OFFICER: Your wife says if you take off out of here and don't come back for the night...

MAN: Well, I can't do it in five minutes. I've got to call people. I've got more furniture in here than she's got.

OFFICER: Well, you're not going to take your furniture tonight. You don't have any place to put it tonight.... If you're not out of here in two minutes, I'm going to let your wife press the charges.

MAN: Well, I can't go anywhere in two minutes!

OFFICER: That doesn't mean gathering your goods. That means gathering your clothes and get ready to go. Tomorrow or some other time you can arrange to pick these things up.

The wife watched her husband depart without regret and with the expressed determination never to renew their relationship:

OFFICER: If he should come back tonight after we leave, you give us a call and he'll go to jail.

WOMAN: He can go to jail now.

OFFICER: You'd be in love with him again tomorrow.

WOMAN: I bet you I won't. You wouldn't be in love with your wife if she did what he did to me.

OFFICER: Your son tells me this happens all the time, ever since you've been married.

OFFICER: Where's he going to stay tonight?

WOMAN: I could care less.

OFFICER: Does he have some friends around the area?

WOMAN: I could care less.

As a symbolic gesture of irreversibility and finality, the husband was enjoined to deliver the keys to the house and to the family car:

OFFICER: You're about all ready, huh?

MAN: Yeah, I'm ready.

OFFICER: Well, let's start downstairs right now, O.K.?

WOMAN: I'm pressing charges.

OFFICER: Well, you think it over tonight, and if you decide to go through with it, you go down to the second floor tomorrow.

WOMAN: I will.

In discussing this incident, the group divided on its probable aftermath. Some officers took the taped verbalizations at face value and predicted a separation. The men who had handled the call argued for a probable reconciliation. The group's leader (who had been a responding officer) telephoned the wife, who indicated that she had rejoined her husband, with whom she declared herself in love. The police end of the conversation reads as follows:

OFFICER: You remember I talked to you last night? I just wanted to call up and see how everything's going. Good! You didn't sign a complaint then? Yeah. You and Conrad got back together? You talked to the police this morning? Good! Did—how do you think the officers did last night when they were there? You think so? O.K. Do you think that they should have arrested Conrad when they were there? O.K. And you thought they handled themselves pretty well, then! Do you think that they should have done anything differently? O.K.

I wanted to ask you one more thing: Had the police ever been there before? He's called them on you before, but there's never been any problems? It never lasts too long, anyway? I just wanted to make sure the two of you were back together and that you weren't having any more problems. You shouldn't have any problems anymore, then, right? Real good, Mrs. Jones, thank you very much!

The second incident involved a minor disturbance between neighbors, with the complainant claiming trespass on her property.

The matter was handled by getting both sides of the story and by relaying information about the complaint to its subject. The callback revealed that false rumors had circulated about the actions by the officers and suggested that the complainant had endeavored to invoke police aid in a vendetta against "undesirables" in her neighborhood.

Both callback experiences left the group with the feelings (1) that they had successfully handled their calls, (2) that they had discovered a means for monitoring the solution of police problems, and (3) that much relevant information about the nature of crisis calls could be secured after the incident was resolved. The callback procedure was thus considered a constructive innovation, illustrating heretofore unexplored possibilities that the group could explore.

The group discussed the way incidents had been handled the previous day, including such matters as time spent, the desirability of separating the parties, and the merits of making an arrest. The idea arose of introducing systematic variations in street experiments, with the provisions that such variations would not include unnecessary arrests:

OFFICER 1: I would just like to make a suggestion on what we could do the next time we went out to make tapes. What I was thinking about was actually make an arrest where it was feasible and then call the complainant back and see what she thought about that. This was fine on kiss-offs, I mean on kiss-off assignments it seemed to work out pretty well, everyone was satisfied. I'm kind of interested to see what the complainant would think if we actually locked her hubby up, to see what she would think about the police department the very next day and to see if she followed up on it...

OFFICER 2: Well, I think there is a reason why we can't, and that is I think our main objective is to go out there and resolve these without an arrest. Now we're being kind of unfair if we go out there and say, "Well, tonight's the night we're going to arrest when we can."

OFFICER 1: What I'm saying is if the situation merits an arrest, why not make an arrest just to see what's going to happen, just to follow up on it?

OFFICER 3: By "merit an arrest" — I don't want us to get into the bag of if a guy commits an offense, an automatic arrest type thing.

OFFICER 1: It would appear to me that if you give these recruits nothing but kiss-off assignments, assignments where no arrests are made, the situations are adjusted without an arrest, they're going to form the opinion that you never make an arrest on a 415 situation.

Officer 4: I think there's an ethical question here. You get into the bag where you make an arrest just for the sake of making an arrest. I think if we just kind of cool this thing, eventually if we do enough of them we're going to come up with one where we're going to have to make an arrest anyway.

Officer 2: Even as you're making the decision, if you're in the call and you say, "O.K., I can make an arrest because she's got a lump on the side of her head. On the other hand, I could probably settle it by putting him out of the house, and she'd be just as happy with me," then I should put the guy out of the house and let her be happy, rather than to resolve it by arrest just to find out what the follow-up will bring.

Officer 4: If we do make an arrest on any of these 415s, why not follow up with a phone call like we did on the others?

One other thing on this Family Crisis Intervention Unit. I agree if we are going to have one, we might as well have as much to say about it as we can, rather than having somebody from the outside who doesn't really understand the problems of Oakland come in here and set up a prepatterned method of having a unit like this.

We can see that as the group discussed its experiences in handling family disturbances, it began to think in terms of a family crisis team experiment. No formal decision was made about adopting this project, nor was there a plan for pursuing it. The group simply started assuming that they were engaged in working on the problem of police response to family crises; previous to this juncture, they had viewed themselves as collecting tapes for training use.

The group discussed the fact that a university representative had approached their department about duplicating the Bard experiment. The officers expressed reservations about this approach.

They agreed that their use of tapes would insure a more sophisticated type of unit, and they anticipated the need for other innovations and modifications. They began to talk about the prospect of a formal proposal.

With regard to the reserve study, a group interview took place that explored the views and problems of reserve officers. The atmosphere was cordial, and questions (which had started as implied criticisms) became increasingly sympathetic.

Officer White, who had begun his inquiry as an antireserve campaign, initiated suggestions to improve the lot of reserves. He was especially impressed by the reserve sergeant (a black officer), and invited him to join him on patrol. (Previously, White had proclaimed that he would refuse to ride with reserves.) Officer White commented in the summary that

> These reserves are outstanding people, I think—especially Connelly. And I
> don't see why perhaps something couldn't be arranged to send Connelly to
> patrol to talk to the lineups, like was suggested. Just having him come up
> here and talk has opened my mind, somewhat.

There was discussion of the benefits of personal communications, especially when misunderstanding could arise based on incomplete data:

CO-LEADER: Last year when we had the Hell's Angels up here and we had CPU, the same thing happened. We had them up here purely for an interview. And it seems to me the greatest value this served was it opened up an avenue of communication, something we don't have in this department. And today, just like last year, I think it's regrettable that the only guys who get to experience it are us. And it's too bad that we couldn't figure out a way to afford a larger body of patrolmen to get involved in this.

STAFF: Why can't we?

CO-LEADER Well, we have. We've made a start. Now, if this reserve officer goes down to the lineup and he gives a little talk, this is a way around the chain of command, the letters, and all these interdepartmental things that confuse and hinder all these attempts for intradepartmental communication. And it would seem to me that this is one kind of thing that we're missing here—that is, a line of communication, direct communications. And if we could figure out a way to get it to the rest of the people, it would be invaluable.

In general the meeting had been lively, busy, and characterized by full participation. Even Officer House (who had shown a tendency to slumber or to leave the room for private excursions) entered into the discussion constructively. The group felt appropriately elated; ratings were the second highest of the summer, after the session in which proposals were presented. The most-used adjective was "valuable"; this was followed by "constructive" and "purposeful." Other adjectives invoked were "relevant," "though provoking," and "promising."

A DATA-PROCESSING SESSION

The officers entered the next meeting eager to begin work. They concluded within five minutes that they needed data to justify their family crisis proposal. Bard had suggested at the retreat that family fights, if unresolved, produced assaults and homicides. The group undertook to verify this trend.

Officer House, who confessed to experience in data processing, rushed off to obtain offense printouts and geographically distributed incident records. The men began to go over the information and to tabulate relationships. Part of this is described in the summary:

The information obtained from the IBM data sheets that House returned with is very complex. We passed around several IBM sheets—they contained dates, time, nature of complaints, arrest numbers, OPD numbers, addresses, and types of places at which the event had taken place. House understood, had a working understanding of the information given to him and attempted to explain to us exactly what the information was on each sheet.

We then sent an officer down to homicide to pick up a report on a recent 187 because we decided to research it. We then decided to check the assignment card to see how many times the police were dispatched in a family disturbance or other types of assignments. This is prior to the 187 itself. In choosing the report, we wanted to establish some kind of relationship between the deceased and the suspect.

At the conclusion of the operation, an officer reported that

We haven't had any particular correlations between police interventions and homicides, but we can see some trends in addresses, where in a one-month period there would be a number of calls for what would call for social services. And so we can get a very rough idea that in certain addresses, in certain places they are calling upon the police on a regular basis for handling family problems.

In addition to the work on a data base for the family crisis unit, the group also discussed arguments for the creation of specialized teams. The co-leader drafted a document in which he argued for advantages in terms of "better community relations, free the beat man for other work, lighten the work load with referrals to other agencies, and lessen the likelihood of injuries among the officers."

There was disagreement on other issues. Officer Young, the group leader, advocated a training function for family crisis units, including the cycling of recruits through the program. The group divided sharply on the merits of this procedure.

While the officers participated in this (and other) discussions, their interest lapsed during data inspection periods. A staff member observed that "there's been a lot of this running in and out of the room," and suggested:

If just two or three people are necessary for a given task, the others ought to be working on something else, not exchanging war stories or glancing at the ceiling over there on the other side of the table. That makes for a very boring session. I think in general we had a lesson today about how we've got to get more carefully organized.

The group seemed to concur. The session was rated "average," and adjectives such as "rambling," "slow," and "dry" crept into the descriptions.

FOUNDATION BUILDING

The next meeting was spent in additional data gathering and analysis; both projects gained shape and focus in relatively modest ways. The reserve project benefited from a discussion with the sergeant in charge of the unit, who discouraged the inquiry, but added facts of interest. In particular he added fuel to the group's concern with lines of communication by describing a feeling of isolation among the reserves.

In relation to family crisis management, the group discussed the distribution of calls and designed a radio room survey to provide exact information on concentrations of assignments. They then took up the matter of training needed by family crisis specialists. Unlike the New York model, the model that the officers evolved had no provision for civilian professionals; patrolmen would handle the training, and clinical tasks would be assumed by referral agencies.

Arrangements were then made to secure information about available referral agencies, and to establish links with key personnel:

> We set up for Monday morning an interview with a person from the Legal Aid Society who will enlighten us as to what the actual function of the Legal Aid Society is, and he's going to be raked over the coals for a couple of hours. On the afternoon of Monday, we're going to get a couple of people from welfare to tell us about the different agencies in welfare, what they do, what they will handle and won't handle.

The meeting was generally viewed as an improvement over the previous one, in terms of participation and morale. Since the bulk of time was invested in discussion, the "productivity" rating was low. The session was characterized "relevant," "informative," and "promising."

FORGING LINKS WITH OTHER AGENCIES

The following session was spent in interviews. The first part of the meeting dealt with the Legal Aid Society. The attorney who met with the group was obviously surprised at the client-centered nature of the group's concerns:

> We wanted to find out how we could open a channel of discussion, how we could open up a means of getting information back and forth. And we also wanted to find out what we could expect the Legal Aid Society to do for us and what their limits were, so we wouldn't make bad referrals. And also so that Legal Aid would know what we do.... We found out that they have confidentiality, which was already known about. Then we had a discussion on landlord versus tenants disputes, and we went into quite a bit of depth; we returned to this topic many times. We then talked about civil disputes,

and we wanted to find out where the policeman could go to get information on what he could do to change a particular abnormal situation, such as a house that was completely unfit in relation to landlord–tenants. Then we talked about the debts, the problems with people that are receiving aid of some type, getting themselves over their head in debts due to unjust business practices, and so on, and what could be handled from there.

After three hours of constructive information exchange, the group found itself sidetracked in a conversation about police image, black–white relations, and police brutality. This topic led to a short confrontation between the more militant members of the group and the attorney. With no hope of resolving the issue, the interview ended amicably.

After lunch the group's guest was an official of the welfare agency, who gave the officers a frank and detailed picture of problems and prospects in welfare management. The group asked many questions, and the interviewee, in turn, was fascinated by the prospect of collaboration in family crisis management. At one point during the interview, an offer was extended by the welfare representative of having volunteer service workers ride with the officers on their next field experiment:

> We were then advised that if we would like we could have, as a group, on some of our street problems that we will be going out on next week, a social worker in the car with us. This would be quite helpful to get immediate feedback, and also help us to find out where we can make some referrals that are proper referrals.

The officers accepted the proposal, and were excited by it. They were also delighted at the mass of information collected during the interviews. Session ratings were very high. Most frequently used adjectives were "constructive," "valuable," "practical," "informative," and "encouraging."

LOVELESS LABOR

No major business had been scheduled for the next session, and the group divided into task forces charged with detailed planning of projects. The task force involved in the reserve study worked on their questionnaire and readied it for administration. The family crisis subgroup wrote a section of their proposal and otherwise became enmeshed in minor details, such as the choice of card size for recording forms:

OFFICER: That's a 3×5 card; do you think maybe you could go to a 6×10 or something? I don't see how you could possibly get all the information you want to know on a 3×5.

OFFICER 2: Why don't we use a 3×5 card in the car for the officers responding to the call, and then we can have a more complete form in a separate file in the office for collecting data?

OFFICER 3: Oh, no, you want this information for when someone goes back the next time.

OFFICER: It seems what you're doing is just making an improved assignment card. You're going to put in writing what you already know now.

OFFICER 4: There's no reason for putting down all this other little stuff, like being an alcoholic. It's up to you, being the man on the unit, to put it down. You would know this. It's got to be discussed, but there's no reason for putting all that on the card.

OFFICER: Well, you'd have a summary, of course. I'm talking in terms of a check-off list, like marital status, sex, age—well, not the same questions, of course, but source of the case, employment, nature of the case. But it seems like there's a whole batch of things. You could have a bunch of things you could just check off rather than have to write it all in.

OFFICER 4: It would be an awful big piece of paper.

OFFICER: Well, you know a 6×10 isn't that much bigger—just need a wider box to keep it in.

The men not directly involved in these activities spent much of their time in idle conversation or in extended expeditions out of the room. As the co-leader characterized the situation:

> We lost it today. We didn't get a damn thing done except at the very end. In the beginning we didn't do very much. I don't know, but I was kind of pissed off about the whole thing today. And I think the best way to do it is the way we did it that last Tuesday. And if we're going to work on our project, four can have this room and four can have the other. Because all we did today was bullshit and screw around. We didn't get a damn thing done. All this stuff here written up about our proposal was written up in the last hour. So that's seven hours wasted and one hour of work. It's a waste if that's the best we can do.

The session ratings were low. The adjective list showed substantial variation. Highest-ranking terms were "slow," "wasteful," "frustrating," and "purposeful."

FERTILIZATION AND CROSS-FERTILIZATION

The following session consisted of another family crisis field test. This time, the group viewed their experience in terms of implications for a family crisis unit. They were concerned with possible follow-ups and referrals; they were intent on reviewing the quality of their performance. The observers who rode with the officers had been instructed to be critical and to provide critiques in a postride seminar.

Each of the social workers reported that he had learned a great deal, and several commented on the volume of calls during hours when conventional social services are unavailable:

> Everything does actually happen at night.... I couldn't believe it tonight. I said, "I've never seen so many children in all my life. The way they acted!"

The welfare workers declared themselves uniformly pleased by the way the officers handled assignments:

OBSERVER 1: I was just favorably impressed with the way the officers handled themselves tonight. Very clear about their roles with the people. They did their best, I think, to be very supportive to them, particularly on the first case with the drunken father and the family situation. The case where the man, I think, was unemployed and felt some loss of manhood at that point. Officers were very supportive, gave them every break, offered them a referral which he kind of refused. It was slow, but all in all, I had a very enjoyable time and I'd like to do it again.

OBSERVER 2: It sounds like we had quite a few 415s. It was one right after another. And after seeing what was going on, I definitely feel that it would help if you had a follow-up, of some sort. I was very impressed with the way it was handled.

The official who had met with the group the previous week, and who served as an observer, discussed liaison possibilities. He indicated that his department, as well as the officers, could benefit from future working relationships:

> I think if you can test this thing a little bit, you certainly can make the pitch to our department to work out some kind of liaison. After our meeting last Monday, I wrote a memo to our assistant director, and he passed it on to the director who called me today, and I just briefly indicated in the memo what had transpired in our meeting and what we were planning on doing this evening. And the director said this sounds great and he's interested in knowing what the follow-up was going to be, and he made the statement that he would like to incorporate something like this into our training program. What he means by this I don't know, whether it involved taking some of the more experienced social workers and utilizing them in a field placement kind of capacity so that the social worker would have a better awareness of what the police role is in the community, so that we would have better relations between social workers and policemen, or whether he's thinking in terms of bringing neophyte social workers and eligibility workers into the program just to see this particular aspect of what's going on in the community. One of the things I see as a possibility would be making a request of our department to use some of our professional social workers, some of our people with master's degrees who have some specialized education and quite a bit of experience, and perhaps utilizing them as resource people.

The officers were justifiably encouraged by these reactions and pleased by their own performance. They rated the session very highly and classified it as "enjoyable," "constructive," "instructive," and "valuable."

A SPONTANEOUS REVIEW PANEL

One of the officers who had participated in the street exercise was Officer Spark. Spark had been teamed up with Officer Young and with a staff member as observer. Young (as well as the observer) returned visibly shaken, complaining about Spark's violence-proneness. The next day, Young initiated a discussion of Spark's conduct, which developed into a group interview.

In the summary of the day's session, Young noted that

> Today we didn't get too far with projects or anything, because we spent all day interviewing Officer Spark. In any event, we discussed with Officer Spark some of the incidents that he's been involved with in the street.... I think we maybe made the point to him that if the opinion of many is that some of the things that he's doing are wrong, I think that maybe he should take that opinion, and maybe he will. I hope he will. I think he's going to get himself in trouble or get himself killed or somebody else killed if he doesn't analyze what he's doing out there and maybe find some different ways of doing it. That's basically what we talked about today.

Spark (who had defended himself vigorously all afternoon) ventured the view that "this was a pretty constructive session." He even expressed the feeling that "I got a lot more out of it than anybody would even think I did."

The fact remained that the Spark interview occupied the entire session. The officers met briefly with the chief, but at this meeting a hypothetical question referred critically to Spark's pattern of conduct. Some group members, who had been anxious to continue work on the family crisis project, complained about the preempted use of session time, and questioned the relevance of the exercise:

> I don't know if spending eight hours in a session like this—I shouldn't say it's not worth it. It just seems like it's a hell of a lot of time to try to get a point across, and I'm not sure we ever got it across, although Spark said we did. I think it would do if a few more of us would discuss some of our incidents. Instead of giving Spark all the pressure, I think we should spread it around as much as we can. But not at the eight-hour cost. That's too much time. We didn't do any project work today and we had some that we'd planned on doing. I think next Monday we're going to have to break up into groups almost immediately just to do some of the things that I know our group was planning on doing this morning.

The session rating was neither high nor low. The content of the meeting was described as "thought provoking" and "constructive," although there were individual ratings of "hopeless," "weird," "sad," "frustrating," and "exasperating."

PROCESS AND PRODUCT

At their next session the group became very output oriented. They divided into two task forces, which in turn subdivided. Each team had its assigned chores, all related to the production of reports. In one corner, two officers chewed on pencils as they bent over paper; elsewhere, a typewriter clattered and a dispute raged over the use of a second (borrowed) machine. Two men raided the computer for fresh data on the distribution of family fights.

The reserve officer subgroup (consisting of three men) had received some returns on their questionnaire to the troops and had tabulated them. They had also interviewed a deputy chief, who had commended them for their work. They spent their time writing up findings and drafting recommendations and concluded with this task at the end of the session. They then read their material into the tape recorder and expressed themselves satisfied.

The family crisis group, by contrast, had little to show for their labor. The computer data confirmed previous findings; the drafting subgroup was stalemated over the wording of several sentences in the preamble to their proposal. They had outlined their entire document, but reported that they then "started with the introduction and got bogged down considerably on the role of the police officer and how to (describe) it."

The combined group ratings for the session were relatively high, but this fact disguises differences between the task forces. The reserve officer ratings were "high" and "very high," with adjectives such as "constructive," "purposeful," "valuable," "enjoyable," "practical," "pleasant," and "relevant." The family crisis ratings tended toward "average"; the adjective list contained such terms as "frustrating," "irritating," "slow," "bland," and "monotonous." Whereas one group reviewed their work with pride (with the product in sight), the others were enmeshed in unfamiliar, strenuous work, and they could see little light at the end of their tunnel.

Paradoxically, the first group had reached precipitous closure, but the second group was beginning to lay groundwork for an innovative, high-quality product, although another week would pass before this product would strikingly emerge.

A TORTUOUS INTERLUDE: PART I

The next two sessions can be described as essentially a 16-hour marathon of clerical effort, with uneven participation.

The first of these sessions was again split. The reserve group had received more questionnaires, which they tabulated and summarized. They redrafted their introduction and improved its wording. But the group spent much time going over the same ground, or wondering what to do with itself.

The family crisis group made considerable progress on its report. The officers had pinpointed time and place of assignment and had collected all necessary baseline statistics for the evaluation of the unit's effectiveness. They had spelled out the organization of the unit and listed the categories of data to be monitored for effective evaluation:

> In the organization of this unit we've decided that first of all the cars should be two-man cars, with their responsibility being primarily the handling of 415fs. But they can be used in handling other 415s and as a cover unit, in order to keep the relationship with patrol division in a good frame of mind. The men should be picked for their expertise in handling 415s. The selection should be made by the peer group. Possibly the manner of selection would be a ballot election, and it should be a voluntary thing. They will be assigned to the Violence Prevention Unit, as we understand. Also in the organization would be the coordinator who, as we understand it, would also be assigned to the Violence Prevention Unit. Some of his responsibilities would be to appropriately coordinate the program as a whole. But in addition to that he'll have to coordinate the referral training on an ongoing basis to keep up a liaison with the referral agencies. He would have to maintain statistics on the number, location, etcetera of 415f assignments. He would have to set up and preside over period meetings with the units for purposes of discussing roles, changes in the program, and so on. He would have the responsibility for compiling and providing training materials and he would have the responsibility for making callbacks on 415f assignments and to check on the outcome of any referrals made to whatever agencies they were made to. Some of the research we think is necessary for an ongoing program would be (1) the number of 415fs over the year, including 415s, 242s, 245s, or the result of 415fs but dispatched otherwise. Some of the information we'll need will be the beat, the address, the name, the date, the time of day; (2) we would like to keep track of any injuries sustained by officers on 415fs to be broken down into three groups—those officers in the field crisis intervention unit, those officers arriving in normal patrol units, and those officers involved in crime prevention units, the wagon or otherwise; (3) would be our callbacks. We'd want to know what the complainants' impressions were of the services rendered. We'd want to know also what the outcome of the disturbance was after the officers had left; (4) would be the dispositions on 415fs. We'd want to know what arrests, if any, were made, misdemeanor citations issued, what happened as far as referrals go, and we want copies of all reports made.

These ideas were largely the work of Officer Johnson, the co-leader of the group. Johnson had also drafted the preamble to the proposal, the wording of which was now satisfactory to the group. This preamble read:

> Police departments have traditionally assumed the responsibility for handling family disturbances. The officer's role in such a disturbance has been one of preserving the peace while acting as an advisor, mediator, or counselor. The primary concern is to prevent violence and settle the obvious problem at that given time. Family disturbances are of such a complexity that they demand more time and consideration, yet the police officer's role remains the same—that of a law enforcer and as a buffer between the parties involved.
>
> It appears that the responsibility for handling the social need will remain that of the police department, and that in order to deal with it realistically the role of the police officers needs change. The emphasis should be less on law enforcement and more on solving the immediate as well as the underlying needs experienced by the parties involved. This can be made possible by having only those officers who exhibit a great degree of expertise in handling family disturbances handle all family disturbances and by developing means of bringing the parties involved into contact with whatever agencies could aid in the solving of their problems.

Despite the superlative performance of some of the officers, there were problems. Officer Johnson had worked with one teammate, and two other officers (Young and Spark) were left out in the cold; the ratings reflected this condition. Johnson and his partner (Officer Bond) rated the session highly and regarded it as "constructive," "purposeful," "relevant," "creative," and "encouraging" (Johnson also checked "weakening" and "annoying," though the latter word may have referred to the rest of the group). White—the leader of the reserve group—was also fairly satisfied. He declared the meeting "constructive," "practical," and "critical." (House's ratings were also high, but House had spent most of the meeting away on private business.)

The rest of the group characterized the session as a disaster. White's teammates produced ratings of "very low"; one of the two invoked a write-in-four-letter word. Spark and Young also expressed unhappiness. Spark used bottom ranks, and described the meeting as "monotonous" and "aimless"; Young wrote that

> I do not feel that four policemen, with very little interest in statistics and justification of projects, can produce what is expected. I feel staff personnel should do the research, make the proposals, and receive advice from the officer involved.

The session generally was ranked lower than any other in the series.

A TORTUOUS INTERLUDE: PART II

The next session witnessed a miscalculated intervention in the self-charted course of the group. But this move had no immediate impact on either the high productivity of high producers or on the unhappiness and alienation of the others.

The principal step consisted of Young (the nominal leader of the group) entering the session with the announcement that proposal drafting was boring and that more active projects were called for. Young describes his effort and its results in the following terms:

> I went in and told them that we're not that concerned about the deadline or having a finalized proposal, and this kind of really put a shot right in the ass of the project. "Here all this time we've been working on this thing we've been making an effort to get done, and now they say we don't care if we get it done." And I think that was the main thing. Maybe they felt that, "Well, these bastards are trying to have us work just to work and they don't care what we're doing, whether we're chopping wood or we're working on a violence-reducing proposal. They just want us in there doing something, keeping occupied. Here they stressed the importance of some of these proposals and now they're saying we don't give a shit about those proposals."

The second error was committed by a staff member, who took the opportunity (in midmeeting) of sharing with the group his ideas about an alternative organization for the family crisis activity. Young later described the group's reaction to this announcement:

> What happened there is that I think they had thought about something of that nature, or thought about what was best in their proposal, had written up what they thought should be done, and somebody came in the room and said, "We're not going to do it"—or maybe implied, or maybe they drew an inference, or maybe they felt as a result of what he said, you know, "We can't do it your way anyway" type of thing. And I think that, although it didn't have that much impact.

The group continued working on their proposals through the rest of the session, though they were increasingly alarmed at the possibility of having their ideas rejected. Again, productivity was not uniform. The reserve officer group was relatively inactive except as spectators. One member of the group participated in the analysis of one of his tapes and the others worked briefly on their proposal. The family crisis group was more active, including Young, who drafted a new section of the proposal. Officer Spark alone was unoccupied, and House (as usual) unavailable.

The session, again, was rated low. Spark pronounced the meeting a failure. White was absent at rating time, and his two cohorts ranked the session low. Johnson and Bond declared themselves satisfied with their own productivity, but not with the session. The staff member made a plea for efficiency. The group's rating terms included "frustrating," "weakening," "strange," "sad," "annoying," "tense," "irritating," "monotonous," "slow," "aimless," and "confusing."

THE END OF THE TUNNEL

The next day the group had undergone a transformation. The day was spent in an atmosphere suffused with constructive activity, and everyone (with the possible exception of House) appeared happy and productive. Johnson, in the summary, described the session as follows:

> Today we began right away working on the different projects that we were working on.... After a couple of hours of finishing up on some minor tasks that we had to do, we formulated or put together our proposals as best we could by putting them in the proper order and so forth. And I think we've got a fairly good package together. I don't know what an administrator or somebody who knows what they're doing would think about it. But it looks pretty good.... It's now at the point where you can look at it and tell what we're trying to say in the proposal. Next week we're having a meeting with the coordinator of social services in the area, and at that time we'll be able to gather data in regards to the agencies and services available to us and to families in need. And at that time we'll make a final insert for our proposal, and then it'll be just about at the final stages.

The reserve subgroup reported that, "All we do now is type the proposal up, make a few corrections in punctuation and so on and so forth, and we should be ready to roll with it next week."

Young, who in previous sessions had abdicated his leadership role, took a guiding position and helped organize the sequence of topics. He indicates that "I became more enthused, because I played a big part in helping to finally write (the proposal) up." Young explained the general change in atmosphere by observing that

> We're at a point now where everything we do is going to be an improvement rather than a wheel-spinner. We take that last draft that we've drawn up, we're going to improve on it, I'm sure. And we're going to be able to recognize the improvements. But if you take just one little area of that thing and improve on it, it doesn't look like the whole thing's improving. You're just kind of doing something that's worthless that's going to go in a whole package. But when you've got a package and you say, "We add this to it and it makes it better," fine. But when you've only got part of the package and you say, "We add this to it," it doesn't seem meaningful at all.... Monday we can sit down and take a long look at that draft. I know of a hundred different ways we can improve that—retyping, thinking about it. But now we've got it in a final stage. We can improve on a page and retype it. We can improve on the next page and retype it.

In retrospect, Young reconstructed the sequence of previous several sessions as a pattern, intrinsic to the development of any task:

> I think in a task like that, when you're trying to gather information and come up with something, you will run into low-morale and high-morale days. In the very beginning I would imagine the trend would be to be high. "Here we are, we're going to create a proposal, we're going to start gathering all sorts of information to do something good." Then all of a sudden you have all of this information and you don't know what to do with it. So bang, you're down and you're flat on your back. "What can I do with this? Do I have enough? Is the chief going to buy this?" We don't have any idea what the chief is going to like or dislike. So you're down there, and then all of a sudden you say, "Fuck it, I'm going to commit it anyway." So you finalize it, and we're up again, because even though the chief may not like it, we've done our share.

In fact, the group did feel a sense of accomplishment and pride. Ratings were the highest of the summer. Most frequently used adjectives were "constructive," "purposeful," "practical," "informative," and "creative." Other comments followed suit. The group generally concurred with Bond, who exclaimed at the end of the summary, "We made it, finally!"

A LOOSE END

During its last session the group met with a representative of the local social planning council, who gave it an overview of referral agencies. The woman, a sophisticated social worker, was also helpful with hints on referral management:

SOCIAL WORKER: If one person doesn't step out and take the initiative and really con the other departments into working with him, you can't get action. And this really amounts to getting on first-name terms with people in other departments, like sorting out who's the fellow that you can get to know as a real buddy over in welfare. And you call this fellow and say, "John, old boy, I've got a real problem going here now. I know you're the only fellow who can give me the right kind of help on this. How about it, old buddy, tell me, what should I do about this?" You get it down to those terms, with a couple of pals in health and a couple of pals in housing inspectors, and a couple in welfare, you can sort out these family things in a much better way. You really can.

YOUNG: Are there any specific individuals you can think of that we might want to talk to?

SOCIAL WORKER: No, I'd start out by calling and trying to make a buddy with the first person I meet. And if that doesn't work I'd say, "Well, you must know somebody in your department who'd be interested in this. Now, who would you recommend that I talk to?" And then on the next one, I'd try to get him to have lunch with me. Then I'd get a real chance to brainwash him.

I think that this is the most effective way. If you're going to work with ____, for example, phone him and ask him to come down and talk to you about family problems. Tell him you want to work with him. Tell him these things bug you and you don't have the tools to cope, and how's the best way to make referrals to him. And what are his suggestions? And keep him long enough so that you get to know him.

The interviewee predicted that the family crisis officers would find a limited number of agencies (which she specified) helpful, each in a major problem area:

SOCIAL WORKER: I'm suggesting to you that you really don't need a complete list of services. You need four or five hot numbers.

YOUNG: And get a real good coordination between the unit and these four or five.

SOCIAL WORKER: Yeah, make a real good relationship between you and the three or four places that you're going to make the main bulk of your referrals. And for the rest of the referrals, use ____ and get her to tell you what to do, and who to talk to. And that sort of simplifies it to the place where any officer who's personally good at separating warring couples can remember it in his head. He doesn't have to have a whole list to go looking up and down. Because that's not practical if you're trying to stop a beef. You can't say, "Wait till I look on page 31 and see which of these things I ought to send you to." I mean, that's for the birds. They're going to think you're nuts.

The group was receptive to these suggestions and incorporated them in their draft proposal. They rated the interview and the session high. Leading adjectives were "enjoyable," "constructive," "relevant," and "practical." Except for the anticlimactic nature of the experience, it marked a positive end to a partially frustrating summer.

FINAL COMMENT

The group was manifestly less successful than its mate, for several reasons. Probably its chief handicap was its division of functions. The early introduction of the reserve proposal split energy and personnel, weakened the group purpose, and introduced organizational problems. Subgroup development made the introduction of key experiences difficult and loosened the hold of leadership.

The sequence of tasks was also less than felicitous. There were sporadic sessions in which the group actively invoked concrete data sources which it found enjoyable and profitable. At other times, self-generated statistical exercises provided hours of taxing effort with little obvious payoff. Premature drafting tasks similarly involved painful, unfamiliar detail work with no obvious results. Moreover, the division of clerical tasks necessarily excluded some members, with no incentive for their reintegration into the group.

Group leadership was less than optimal. The principal leader became dispirited when he lost control, and refused to plan for activities that would have restored structure. The second leader refused to take up the slack, in part because he had found a consuming (more or less solitary) task in which he performed supremely well.

Group membership was another handicap. Three members were permitted to remain disinterested in the problem area. A fourth member was opposed to the goals of the group, but after the issue had been joined he was permitted to "drop out." A fifth member was subjected to strong group pressure, and then excluded by default.

If, despite these factors, the group produced a superlative proposal (and another, partially based on solid empirical data), this gives testimony to the resources available—and partially exploited—in the group. Most of the officers remained dedicated to project goals, insisted on a meaningful end product, and carried out the difficult steps to their self-assigned goals.

9

Implementing a Solution
Family Crisis Management

In our last chapter we traced the origins of Oakland's FCIU (Family Crisis Intervention Unit) proposal, which was then implemented, as an experiment. In this chapter we track the first stages of this experiment.

The group (see Chapter 8) had adopted the idea from a New York police department program, but the Oakland version was unique: There was to be no professional involvement; the team members were to be selected for their past expertise, and were to be trained "on the job." The program was also to be research oriented from the start. Baseline data for experimental and control beats were available; periodic review of key indices would document impact. The indices included need for callback, need for arrest, assault and homicide rates, and incidence of officer injury. There was also to be a cost analysis, covering amount of time and effort consumed and time and effort saved.

The third difference pertained to participation of outside agencies in the solution of family crisis problems. Whereas New York City had supplied referral rosters to its officers, it had done little else. As a result, agencies showed little inclination to cooperate even when clients appeared. In Oakland, the officers were scheduled to make their own referrals, to schedule appointments, to recontact agencies (and clients), and to keep a record of outcomes. The Oakland concept was one that stressed (1) exploring avenues of active collaboration toward joint problem solving, and (2) systematically evaluating the impact of new linking arrangements.

As a first step, an organizational meeting was called in the police building. This meeting was initiated by two officers, the sergeant of the Violence Prevention Unit and the coordinator of "experimental projects"

(Officer Bond). The participants were representatives sent by six key agencies.

A review of this organizational meeting may help to illustrate problems and prospects of the "outreach" phase of police problem solving.

CAVEATS AND REJOINDERS

Early in the meeting with agency personnel, resistances surfaced in the discussion. A supervisor representing one social agency announced:

> I'd like to raise a few questions that I have, and one of the reasons I'm here is I'd like to hear more from the officers about this. I wonder how treatable many of the people that you are going to be sending to us—how amenable they are going to be to the casework approach. I think you're probably coming in contact with really quite chronic kinds of situations, that people have acted out in this kind of a way over a period of years. I mean, this is the way they handle their problems, and when you make a referral to a family agency or to any other agency and some determination is made by the agency regarding the fact that these people are not amenable to treatment and are not seeking any kind of alleviation of the problem, what will the police do about this?

The sergeant (Bill, the ex-leader of group 1) responded by tracing the implications of a pessimistic stance. He said an option would be to give up the ship and arrest people wholesale. As an alternative, one could tailor-make change approaches to clients, excluding those agencies who failed and selecting "winning combinations" among the remaining resources:

> The other alternative is to arrest him, and nobody is "amenable" to arrest. So what we're saying is that I'm sure we're going to get people that don't like the case approach, that are not amenable to change and they may enjoy it—some people do—they don't want to get as personal as would be necessary with you, at least discussing their personal problems. But I don't really think that's the end of it. I think when you find a family, for instance, who can be referred to your agency and you don't seem to be filling the bill, we're talking about utilization of all of us. You know, us. Not the police department and the Catholic Service and the Jewish Family Service, and wage earner and welfare and health. We are us.

A representative of the welfare department (who had participated in one of our field experiments) rose in defense of casework as a solution:

> Now, I had the experience of going out with the Violence Prevention Unit one night—myself and two other social workers went out with them. And I have to disagree with you. The people that I met were in need of some kind of counseling.... And what myself and the other social workers pushed after we were out on the calls was exactly what we're getting right now. It's a

liaison thing, because these people are in great need and the police officers
are in great need of what we have to offer them.

The original dissenter, however, once more raised doubts about the
amenability of police clients to her agency's services:

> But I do think we get the kind of situation—that's what I don't know—this is
> my assumption—I've had no contact with the police in the past. I'm assum-
> ing that you get a lot of the kinds of cases that are going to come into our
> family agency, that are going to be the real sadomasochistic relationships
> that no one is going to intervene and break up. The community is going to be
> up in arms, but nobody is going to be able to put a stop to it.

The sergeant argued against precategorization, while conceding
that some clients might ultimately prove difficult:

> One thing we're trying to get across to policemen departmentally is that you
> kind of have to get rid of predetermined ideas that have emanated from your
> past experiences. For instance, there may be some "sadomasochistic" people
> and "sadists" that are referred to you for counseling. That's not to say that
> they can't be counseled.... There are some which the police must confront
> that are not amenable to anything and have to be taken into custody and
> locked up behind bars, which unfortunately sometimes is the only alterna-
> tive the officer has.

The dissenter demurred:

> But I just want to raise that I think we're going to deal with some people that
> in the past social agencies have tried working with and have not worked with
> very successfully, and this can make for complications.

At this juncture, two agency representatives warmly defended the
program. They pointed to "crisis management" objectives and to the
need to depart from a traditional view of available services:

REPRESENTATIVE 1: I will at the risk of being a little naive, however, look at this in
terms of the title of this program, which is family crisis intervention. To me,
I see possibilities not so much in terms of curing people of long-term mental
problems but rather in reducing the number of assaults within families and
upon policemen. And perhaps the greatest benefit, as I see it, might come in
lengthening the period that occurs in the repetitive offender and perhaps
reducing the overall number of offenses through the use of these policemen
who are specially appointed to this kind of work, and whatever help then
the referral agencies can give. I see this as more the ultimate goal, rather
than an attempt to give long-term therapy or something like that to people.

REPRESENTATIVE 2: I do see it as a way of perhaps doing just this to alleviate a
crisis, an immediate crisis. This is what I think it might be all about.

REPRESENTATIVE 1: First of all I'd like to say that I'm really impressed with the
fact that the police department is taking a step in this direction, and I think
in all of us being here that it does throw a responsibility on us of questioning

what we are doing. You know we are going to, if we accept referrals from this type of situation, see people that we don't typically see. Particularly certain types of agencies. In Psych Emergency at Highland you probably see a good percent of this type of person to begin with, but we'll probably be seeing more and different types. And I think rather than moving to "they may be untreatable," we need to look back at ourselves and say, "Yeah, we're going to be getting a new type of person that traditionally we haven't seen," and question how can we, what are new ways of interviewing. Now we all kind of point the finger at police, that they should be more service oriented, and here they're doing that and calling us in as a team to come and work together. And I think that's great, and I think we should look at our own agencies and when we say yes or no, we're willing to take that referral, say it with the fact in mind that, yeah, you may have to be doing something different than you did before. And maybe certain types of methods don't work, but to decide beforehand that it's going to be untreatable, I think we fall into a bad bag when we do that. And we throw certain people by the wayside when we do it.

A strong endorsement also came from the head of the Legal Aid Society who had participated in our group discussions:

> Let me say that I've talked to the officers here, I think this is the third time or fourth time, and I'm 1000% behind the program and I'd like to assist them in any way possible. I do dislike the attitude of pessimism that I've picked up, because I know that if you look at the police report for the city of Oakland last year, you'll find that 15,000 arrests were on alcoholism. That's almost a third of their arrests. I know that if you count assault and batteries, and so on as many times as I've had fights with my wife and I know about my neighbors and I know about a lot of people who have had disagreements, etcetera, that there is a problem. And I also know that there is probably a need for this type of service. So I'm 1000% behind the program.

The pessimism voiced by one person had mobilized others in the group to voice and to define support. It had furnished the occasion for a more detailed presentation of project objectives. Finally, it had demonstrated that previous contact (including riding in our field tests) had resulted in two-way conversations: whereas our officers had arrived at more sophisticated thinking about referral agencies, agency representatives had come to better see the need for the unit and the potential in working with it.

GROUP PROBLEM SOLVING

In the course of the meeting, the legal aid expert raised a hypothetical example. His incident involved an argument between husband and wife: "She wants me out of the house; and I say I'm broke, I don't have anywhere to go."

The first difficulty the example posed was that of transportation. The sergeant recalled that police cars could not carry civilians, except when arrested; he wondered about flexibility in this rule. He also raised a question about the availability of public transport tokens.

The central question in the example revolved around lodging:

LEGAL AID REPRESENTATIVE: See, I'm thinking about the situation where maybe he does want to leave, or she wants to leave. They have nowhere to go. No money.

OFFICER: Well, I think we could arrange somewhere to get him or her lodged.

SERGEANT: Well, is there an agent here that could do it?

L. A. REP.: That's the question I'm asking.

SERGEANT: Sure, yeah, we have something that's very nice, and would make anyone feel comfortable. It's called an accommodation booking and you sleep in jail. I don't want to do that. Now let's face it, those are our resources now. Of course there's homes for wayward men. And a guy walks in with a $95 sports coat and $50 shoes and they're going to say, "Wayward, hell. See you around." You're right. Now if anybody has any feedback to us, or any alternatives that we could use, I guess that's why we're here, to kind of talk about it. It sure as hell is a pointed question, and it's very relevant, because that's not an unusual circumstance.

The dilemma pointed to the need to involve other agencies, which were not represented. The officers noted the omission and resolved to remedy it:

REPRESENTATIVE: I see you didn't invite anybody from the Salvation Army.

SERGEANT: You're right, and that just hit me because I see the big sign here on 7th Street. Why didn't we invite the Salvation Army?

OFFICER: I overlooked it myself.

SERGEANT: Chico coordinates this project. We will contact the Salvation Army.

REP.: That might be the answer.

SERGEANT: It might very well be.

REP.: Especially if the family is willing to repay the Salvation Army afterward.

Another question concerned the availability of social services during peak problem periods. Again, the question originated among participants who had accompanied officers on their field tests:

REPRESENTATIVE 1: When I went on this excursion with the police officers it just dawned on me that nothing happens during the day. Everything happens at night. And if you have a client that tells you, "My husband beat me and broke my leg and my rib," which recently did happen to me, and you say, "When did this happen," they'll say, "Two weeks ago." I've never had a case—I've only been in social work for four years—where somebody told me, "Last night he beat me." So wait a couple of weeks or a couple of months and they tell you in passing, "My husband beat me." I think a lot of help can be had if at the time of the beating there's somebody they can talk to, about "why did you beat your wife?"

REPRESENTATIVE 2: If you looked into it, I think you'll find that the social service requirements actually require somewhere along the line that we do have 24-hour service.

The outcome of the discussion was once more to raise a problem-solving possibility that had not been previously explored:

REPRESENTATIVE: Yeah, I saw a very interesting program on television—last week I think it was. And it was showing a scene on the other side of the Bay, one of the counties, I've forgotten where, where a Protestant church had actually opened its doors to house people. Now I bring this out because I think that as a group we'd have to put all our inputs into this thing and if we do not have resources to help us, we've got to see what we can do to make new resources available to us. Maybe an approach to this is our individual contact with the people we know in the field; maybe another approach with the police department is their contacts with the Council of Churches, to see whether or not they would be available to intervene.

In addition to the suggestion about exploring churches, this second dilemma inspired a plea for the bringing of services to the client, conjointly with police:

REPRESENTATIVE 1: We've got quite a few representatives from the agencies and some of the agencies aren't here. But I say it to the agencies that are here: Are there any people in your agencies willing to volunteer at night with police officers and sign a release, because that's the first thing I was hit with, relieving the police department of anything that happens to you. Be with the police department and throw your professional jargon at these people. Because I'd be glad to do it. You know, we throw this professional jargon around like this. But this is two people trying to kill each other. And we just don't have the time to sit down and say, "You've got a sadomasochistic relationship."

This same suggestion also appeared in another context. Our group skeptic had argued that clients were apt not to appear for their appointments. How could this situation be remedied?

REPRESENTATIVE: Do you literally mean that you're going to make the appointment, or are you going to ask these people to call the agency you're referring them to?

OFFICER BOND: I would call and make the appointment for them, and call them. They would have the card.

REPRESENTATIVE: My experience is that when an appointment is made by the referring source, the likelihood is that the appointment is not kept. You have many more cancellations than when the client calls directly and makes his own appointment at the request of the referring source.

The sergeant mentioned reminders, but the questioner remained unsatisfied. This stimulated the hunch that police badges would deter absenteeism. It also brought a plea for agency participation "on the scene":

REPRESENTATIVE 2: Why do they have to go to the office? Why can't we go to them? This is what I'm saying. The last time I met with them I threw this idea out, I don't know whether they accepted it or not. But I suggested possibly...volunteers from the different agencies, from the graduate programs to be present at the welfare department with their own transportation. If something does happen that they do have radios in the cars and to make a call in and say, "Any of those professionals down there volunteering that can help us, then come up right now." I mean, they'd have to clear it, but you're talking about coming to our office. Why can't we go to them?

REPRESENTATIVE 3: The health department does. Our field staff makes home calls and our service is an outreach service rather than asking the client to see us. That's point number one. Point number two, I'm beginning to feel angry. I'm beginning to feel angry, I think, over this business of a client will not come to an agency, or how we're going to handle this thing. I would like to see the police department experiment. I see the police department as an authority, and I don't think the clients that the health department serves see the health department as an authority. And many times the health department has offered services and they have not come to us. They will lapse appointments. We have closed down our well-baby clinics because of this. They don't come in to us. But we are not an authority figure to them. And I think many of the clients that my nurses see in the health department feel as if the police department, at least, has some authority. And I think the response to you may be because the client sees you in this light. But I think you have to prove this to us, as a group. And I think it's worth a trial.

The prevailing mood, at the end of the meeting, was one of excitement and optimism. The group had dealt with doubts and resistances, had joined to consider options, and had evolved program extensions. It now showed itself ready to explore and eager to learn. As one member put it, "We're just going to have to try this project. We call it an experimental project. Well then, let us experiment!"

PEACEKEEPERS AS A HAPPY BREED

Having gained commitments from key community agencies, the Oakland Police Department started its experiment on a six-month trial basis. One of our Group 2 officers—who had acquired the title "Project Section Coordinator of the Violence Prevention Unit"—served as staff backup to two new field units. These units consisted of two-person interracial teams who operated in unmarked cars. The primary responsibility of these teams was family disturbance assignments, with a secondary responsibility to "respond to other disturbances of the peace, emergency dispatched assignments, and preventive patrol." The unit's hours of operation (7 PM to 3 AM, Wednesday through Sunday) and its patrol areas were based on statistics about past family crisis calls we had collected.[1] One of the districts of the city was maintained as a "control area," and records of family disputes the unit handled were kept for evaluation of the project.

The FCI team members were selected from among volunteers, and their attitudes are of interest because officers are prone to insist that "the police are not social workers." They like to boast about law enforcement escapades, and tend to downgrade human services as "not really police work." In our own groups (especially at first) several of the men had deplored calls that demanded peacekeeping functions; they had characterized these as a waste of their time.

Our family crisis team members had been cognizant of the fact that they would invest much effort in responses to peacekeeping calls. They were flattered by their selection and intrigued by the chance for innovating and contributing to professional development. They were curious and expectant, but they were not at first "sold" on the concept of their unit, nor on the definition of police work that it implied.

After six months, we discussed the teams with three of the men. They all recalled that previous to their membership in the FCI unit they had viewed family calls with a jaundiced eye. One officer pointed out:

> When you get certain family fights and arguments that you feel that's strictly in the realm of the civil, you get the feeling that you don't belong there anyway. You say, "Wow, something's going to happen down the street here," and you want to be there to try to prevent it or to arrest somebody; or you might have a team of burglars working on your beat, and the sergeant is coming down on you saying, "Where are you at when all this stuff is going down?"

A second officer expressed similar sentiments:

> In terms of the other things that I had out there, I hated 415s. I wanted to get out there and arrest people, make felony arrests and lock up burglars.

The men contended that the officers' anxiety about terminating contact is communicated to the client, who reacts adversely. The men attributed some of their client satisfaction to the department's implicit approval of a more leisurely approach:

> A police officer goes in and "let's kind of hurry up and settle the beef and get out." And it's kind of a rush atmosphere and they kind of get against it. And all of a sudden two officers completely snow them, they walk in and they sit down and "let's talk this thing out. . ."

In line with the philosophy of the group that designed the unit, the officers prized the long term solution of family problems. The currently unfashionable corollary of this emphasis was one that relegated arrest to the status of an undesirable, low-priority option:

OFFICER 1: I would say one of the differences is that now we can more or less say that we rely on arrest as a final-resort-type thing. But before it wasn't a final resort.

STAFF: What was it before?

OFFICER 1: Well, it was kind of high up on the priorities.

OFFICER 2: Number two.

STAFF: Right after kiss it off?

OFFICER 2: Yeah, if you can't kiss it off, lock somebody up.

In contrast to the premium on arrest, the officers saw themselves as rendering positive services. They saw themselves evaluated, and appreciated, in terms of this contrast:

> They say, "Wow, here's two policemen. I always thought these guys were mean, sadistic, and they were going to bang me over the head and take me to jail"—in the case of the man. Or in the case of the woman, that "The only thing this guy's really good for is to beat my husband and take him to jail. And here they're trying to offer us some kind of help, something that's going to help us get along better with one another, or to help save our marriage, or if they feel that there is some mental problem somewhere in the family, to see that the family member gets the proper help." And I think this gives them a warm feeling itself.

In a strange twist on the usual police theme of the "solid blue line" the team members have come to value their role as professional specialists, in the sense of emphasizing the difference between their own actions and those of nonspecialized officers:

OFFICER: Sometimes when we walk out they say, "You guys are different from the normal policeman."

STAFF: Oh, they do say that?

OFFICER: For example, we had one last night who said, "You guys really know what you're doing. We've had four different sets of policemen here within the last two weeks. And you guys are really different."

STAFF: Now, do they elaborate this in any way, do they say in some detail just what about. . .

OFFICER: Well, some said it seems like we understand the problem more and take more time. They are impressed with the time that we can spend with them. And we aren't taking any sides, or anything like this—we just seem like we understand the general problem, from a third-person standpoint.

The men have also developed a strong "we-feeling" and commitment, partly based on their recognized differentiation from the larger group:

> I think there's a certain amount of pride in the unit. Especially, you know, when we're called "those damned social workers," or something like that. It kind of brings you together by force if for no other reason.

In this connection the men are helped by the fact that although they may be sometimes condemned by other officers, they are also valued for their service:

OFFICER: I can see that quite a few guys out there really appreciate what we're doing.

STAFF: And do they sometimes say things to that effect or. . .

OFFICER: Not only do they say things, but a lot of times they'll call us in to handle a particular situation, where they couldn't.

STAFF: And just stand by until you get there.

OFFICER: Yeah, right.

The men are also aided by the fact that they have faith in their own effectiveness as specialists:

OFFICER: You said "confident," and that's exactly how I feel. I feel more confident. I know many times before when I went in, I felt that I really didn't belong there, especially if nobody wanted to make a formal complaint.

STAFF: You felt that you were sort of interfering in something that was none of your business.

OFFICER: Yes. And then many times I felt that my feelings were sort of out-front as a police officer. Because many times if you're there, and you don't have the elements for an actual arrest yourself, and maybe the husband or the wife or somebody in the family is very resentful of you being there in the home, and they're constantly telling you to get the hell out of here. "What are you doing in my home? You don't belong here." And they're constantly giving you this all the time, and they're threatening you. And they're talking about your brother officers and everything, you know, about "you pigs are all alike." And you just feel like "why am I here?"

The officers trace their confidence to their accumulated experience of success. They feel that they can analyze and break down their experience and share it among themselves. "A guy relates how he handled a particular call," one of the men recalls, "and in the back of my mind I say, 'hey, that's one hell of an approach. Maybe I'll try that next time.'"

By contrast, the men seem disinclined to grant that their skill could be disseminated among the rest of the force. They have a strong feeling about the benefits of specialization:

> The reason I don't think it's going to work is because I don't think most of the men on the street, or at least some of the men on the street are inclined to put the personal effort into it that we do.

The men obviously feel that their jobs have been enriched by their role as specialists. They want to do anything possible to enhance their impact. They have discussed the liability of approaching clients in police cars and uniforms. They know that civilian clothing would estrange them from other officers, but their primary concerns lie elsewhere. They value the approval of clients and social agencies. They are grateful for cooperation, but would like even faster responses:

OFFICER: Someone that you could refer them to immediately, and they wouldn't have time to equivocate, think about it overnight, and then be able to say, "Well, to hell with it, we've got our problems solved without going to this agency."

STAFF: I see, so what we actually need is somebody for immediate follow-up.

OFFICER: Right. Maybe a family services bureau available on a 24-hour basis, or some sort of marriage counseling service available on a 24-hour basis.

The officers take their work very much to heart. Off the job, they worry about some of their clients' problems and are apt to make unsolicited callbacks:

OFFICER: We go back strictly as interested parties, just to see how successful we were in quelling the problem.

STAFF: Do you select particular types of situations to go back to?

OFFICER: Not types so much as people. We see a situation where the people were about to kill each other and we go back a couple of days later to see if there are any bodies lying around.

STAFF: Are those largely the people about whom you have a little doubt in your mind? You know, "Did we really handle it right?"

OFFICER: Yeah, right.

As far as participants of this experiment were concerned, they were performing a vital function, and performing it uniquely and well. They had become advocates of their own role and of its expansion.

CONSUMER REACTION

The officers felt that they were favorably received and positively reacted to. But they had pride at stake. Would independent inquiry confirm their assessment?

With the cooperation of a professional school in Berkeley, a survey was run of a random sample of unit clients. The poll was a modest one, designed to furnish team members with some feedback. One student—a young black ex-offender who had grown up in Oakland—called on the families in the sample. As many callbacks were made as were necessary to make contact. Out of 26 persons contacted, 25 participated in the survey. This fact was encouraging, and seemed related to the questions being posed.

The interviewer's approach was weighted in the direction of eliciting criticism and reservations. He undertook his task with an explicit antipolice bias, pessimistic expectations, and no familiarity with the unit. In a postsurvey interview, he confessed:

INTERVIEWER: I was awful shocked to get the answers I did, to be truthful. I wasn't familiar with the Family Crisis Unit, and I didn't think I would get as many positive responses as I did.

STAFF: You mean pleasantly shocked?

INTERVIEWER: Right. Especially when I would say something like, "You know, in order for an officer to perform his job we take this interview, and your answers can help correct the mistakes the officer made with you." And I still didn't get too many negative answers.

In the survey, 23 out of 25 replies were favorable. Two respondents expressed reservations. One stated that he hated police, and the other was a lady whose reaction was quoted as follows:

INTERVIEWER: She said that the officers showed her no respect whatsoever. She was drunk at the time I was interviewing her, too. She was drunk at the time of the report.

SERGEANT: She was drunk at the time of the initial contact with FCIU. I would say that she's a drunk, just off the top of my head.

INTERVIEWER: She said they came into the room and she didn't have any clothes on and stuff like that. And they weren't courteous—they took her husband's side and everything. And really, I couldn't make out what she was really talking about.

The interviewer describes his impression of responses as especially eye-opening because he knew some respondents as lifelong antagonists of the police:

INTERVIEWER: Because some of the people I interviewed I had known from the past.

STAFF: Oh, you knew them personally?

INTERVIEWER: Right. And their opinion of policemen was all negative. And to hear them say something like this...

STAFF: Did this surprise you?

INTERVIEWER: Yes, it did.

He reiterated that respondents frequently had prior reservations about the police that had been removed through contact with team members. He indicated that "They view the police department as a better organization because of this."

The respondents were able to recall officers' actions that proved especially welcome. They listed a number of services that they felt had not usually been available from police:

> One of my questions states, "What did the officer actually do for you?" This is where I would get a lot of feedback from the people, and they would express themselves, where the officer would sit them down and talk to them, they would give them the law aspect from their standpoint, and in most cases most of the participants were satisfied that this was something that hadn't been done.

Finally, the interviewer inquired into long-range solutions to personal problems:

STAFF: Is there anything in there about their personal difficulties having been resolved as opposed to the immediate situation having been settled?

INTERVIEWER: Yes, there is. The last question states that. And they have gotten along 100% better. As a matter of fact, one lady, I couldn't even get out of the room because she wanted to come down here and congratulate the officer that was out there. I think it was Officer ____. Where she says now her husband, he's just beautiful. He was like a marriage counselor himself, the officer was.

The results of this minisurvey may not be conclusive, but they are concordant with the officers' version. Do they agree with observations by referral agencies?

THE REFERRAL AGENCIES: A VIEW FROM THE BRIDGE

The Oakland concept of family crisis teams placed emphasis on liaison with referral agencies. At the start of this chapter we summarized the first contact with the agencies. Six months later we sought agency reactions to the program.

We discussed FCIU with a representative of family services, who team members rank as cooperative and relevant. Thirty-four referrals have been made to this small agency; 23 families have availed themselves of its counseling services.

How does the agency's staff feel about FCIU? The representative tells us that

> Six different workers have been involved, have been interviewing. And I think that all six feel, I've been checking around, that it's a very valuable program. We have been tremendously impressed from many directions. Now many of the people we see we would not consider "motivated" clients. Most of them have come in to us with really not a very clear idea of what they wanted. But it seems to us that they've gotten a lot of clarification of exactly what their problem is just from talking to us even for one hour. And we suspect we will see many of these people again, maybe a year or two years later. The other thing we've gotten from them is that they are getting a very different view of the police department. I don't believe that we have had a single negative statement about the team that's come out to visit. And we have had numerous positive statements. They've said things like "you know, they sat down and talked to us for a whole hour, and this is the first time a policeman has ever spent this long." Time seems to be the important factor here, that they have time to give them. And also the clients seem to feel that the police were there to help and not there to punish.

Family services had made a special effort to obtain clients' reactions to the team's service. In response to the inquiry, according to the agency representative, "we really haven't gotten any outstanding negatives." A review of answers to the agency's question yields an impressive number of laudatory comments:

> Mr. and Mrs. B. specifically mentioned the sincerity and interest manifested by the officers in their problems, and the willingness to refer them to an agency which they felt could better help them with their problems. Mr. B. said that were it not for these factors he never would have come.... Mrs. B. specifically spoke of the time spent with the family and of the officer's wish to be helpful..." "...They were beautiful." Mr. P. mentioned the handling of this matter only briefly, stating that for the first time of the many times he's called the police on his wife, he felt that "the police officers were concerned and really wanted to help..." ...Mrs. S. was particularly pleased about the police dropping by a second time, and she mentioned the time they were able to be there. The officers were "helpful and understanding."

Do agency personnel get feelings about the police from their other clients?

> We get quite a bit. Usually it's a very negative kind of thing. But I think these people have all had contact with the police, particularly all of them have had some contact with the police before, and they speak of the difference, the difference being that, "Gee, these people really wanted to help." This one lady—I'm looking at her name—was terribly impressed; she has a very sick

son, and the son didn't get in to see me, and I don't know whatever is going to become of him. But he had a probation officer, and I talked to the probation officer at great length and let him know some of my impressions, even though they were second hand. The boy's terribly disturbed. But anyway, what she said was, "You know, they even came back a few nights later to see how things were." And just the feeling that somebody was out there who cared about her and her sick son was very reassuring. So it's been a very good feeling we've gotten.

Many FCIU clients seem to have altered opinions of the police as a result of contact with the teams. Can a similar point be made about agency staff?

There are those, I think, who had preconceived notions. We all have our prejudices, and that's one that an awful lot of people seem to have these days. But I do feel that the staff itself was surprised in the beginning that the police department would tackle this kind of thing, and very pleased that they were. At first the staff in general was a little dubious about getting in on this kind of thing. I think they were—some of the younger staff members—a little afraid that we were going to get violent people. What they have said is that we're getting the same kind of people we'd have gotten anyway, it's just that now we're getting them referred from the police department. But I think the whole feeling about what the police are trying to do has changed.

Changes have taken place in the agency as a result of the FCIU's operation. For one, provisions have been made in the shape of a weekly hour reserved for FCIU referrals:

We know when somebody's been battling on Sunday night, they really should be seen very shortly. Well, we couldn't always see them the next day, but what I asked each worker to do was to hold one hour that week that would be just for this. Now we didn't always fill them. Say on Wednesday if there was a Thursday opening that hadn't been filled, we'd fill it with something else. So it does mean, though, that the agency's holding time. I know you've worked with a lot of different agencies and I don't know how the other agencies have worked this out, but it seemed that the only way we could do it was by holding a block of time.

The agency has also found that its referrals called for a reappraisal of concepts and techniques:

We talked at great lengths among ourselves here about what techniques we use with people who "aren't motivated." And are our caseworkers, who are essentially trained to work with motivated clients, able to use the skills they do have or do they need to develop some new and very different skills? And we really haven't arrived at any firm conclusion. What we did arrive at was that we need to talk together more and present to each other more of the cases that have come and question how each other worked, and see if out of that we can get some information that might be helpful to all of us. I think that's one thing I can say, and that is that we have found we're very active in this sort of case, which very often we are not. But if you get a husband and wife in who are screaming at each other in the interview, there's no point in sitting for an hour letting them scream. So that I think already the caseworkers have learned that in this kind of case we might be much more vocal. Maybe have to interrupt more often, maybe have to call a halt to the screaming, and say, "Look, let me get in here for a minute." So that, yes, I think is has brought to our attention that we need to sharpen some of our own techniques. That can be very helpful to us in some of our other cases, too.

The agency at times has received useful information from police-sponsored meetings with the other agencies. In the discussion we summarized, for example, family services learned about the availability of a resource that had been unfamiliar to them:

It was just that I frankly didn't know much about this one, which was the Wage Earner's Plan, and we do talk with a lot of people who are having financial problems, and we refer them to all kinds of places. And I was not aware that we had not made any referrals to Wage Earner's Plan, but I came back and circulated information.

Agency representatives have also found personal encounters with the FCIU profitable, and would like to see more of them:

My only complaint is that I don't think we communicate enough with the police department. We've had group meetings three times. On the other hand, we don't have time. You know, nobody has time, and I keep feeling that we should be getting together more and talking about all this more.

Specifically, counselors and social workers had expressed interest in meeting team members. The representative notes that "they wanted to know who were the persons who were actually out there on the beat, and what they were like." There has been a demand for contact at the working level.

This development testifies to the viability of a team concept in the handling of peacekeeping crises. Shared clients can link patrolmen with partners in the human services. As the police reach out for resources and allies, social agencies come to view them as welcome bedfellows. The liaison is one from which everyone stands to gain.

THE POLICE AS REFERRAL AGENCY

The second agency whose impressions we gathered was the Legal Aid Society, whose contact with our project had predated the birth of the unit. Again, the assessment was a positive one. The director of the agency recalls that he has handled numerous referrals and has found them appropriate. He expressed himself positively about the teams, and praised the FCIU concept:

It's a wonderful thing. It's better than good. It's really great, I think. So far, I'm impressed. I've got the phone number right here, immediately available. Because I call them that often. So I have nothing but praise for the outfit, so far. And I'm not saying that because I know them personally, because I don't.

Paradoxically, Legal Aid is not much concerned with FCIU as a source of business. The unit is perceived as a resource and as a referral agency. This function, according to Legal Aid, fills a gap not only for the agency, but for the criminal justice system:

It's great to be able to say, "Can you send a police over here? Can you send someone to talk to this guy, he's killing my client." If I concentrate on going in for a restraining order every time a client asks me for a restraining order, I could jam that department 15, just me. I could do it, because there's that many. So I just kind of pacify them, cool them off, see if things can wait until I can have my main hearing, eventually getting a restraining order. And then by that time the emotions are already solved, and people go their way, and I don't even need a restraining order. But for immediate relief, I think this police Family Crisis Unit is it.

Legal Aid regards FCIU as a crisis-resolution device, and as a means of preventing time-consuming abuse of the courts:

I know that they're going to go in there and not arrest the man, because maybe that's not what's needed. But they'll talk to him, pacify him, at least where the emotions are high. And then tomorrow or a day later the husband will be back to normal, and save an arrest.

The availability of FCIU is a function that Legal Aid feels must not only be maintained, but expanded:

LEGAL AID REP.: I don't like it that the officers are only there from 5 to 12—I need it around the day. Remember this one, Jim, this morning? I needed a police unit to go in today, right now, in this particular case where this lady was booted out by her husband, yesterday, spent a night in a motel. She has no money, no relatives. She's afraid to go back to the house. The husband is not that violent that I think that he'll kill her, but at least violent enough to beat her twice in a row now. When was it, Tuesday night, she says, he jumped on her; last night, he jumped on her. That's two in a row.... If the police officers trained in this field could talk to the guy, cool him off for a while. If nothing else, at least give me time to prepare the complaint so I can get it in order. That would be great.

STAFF: This is something new! Actually, you're starting to make referrals to the police?

LEGAL AID REP.: Yeah, because I need immediate relief. She needs it. Maybe they could settle it, maybe they could save me the trouble of going through a divorce proceeding. I see there's a great need for this type of activity, but more so. Not just token amount, like I feel they have now. There's not enough officers involved in this family business.

A search of FCIU records indicates that the referral use of FCIU teams has been intensive and effective:

OFFICER: He's realizing now that he's got another tool to work with, so why not use it? He's found a little trust in the police department.

STAFF: Do you find it at all getting to be a headache, that he's calling you and really there isn't much you can do...

OFFICER: No, because they're pretty smart over there. They realize in one instance where we can't do anything, he's not going to turn around with the same particular circumstances and call us again. They're all usually pretty new incidents, and they're the ones, pretty much, that we can handle.

Beside Legal Aid, there are other agencies that have reversed the usual sequence of roles in the referral field:

> They have people that they're counseling and one of them goofs up one way or the other so they call, and if it's getting into a police problem—he's beat her up again, or he's beat the kids again, something like that—and they can't really handle it by counseling at that particular moment, then they will call us up. I remember one where we had been up there once before on a family problem, and referred them to family services. And family services counseled them for a couple of months, and then I guess their counseling session was over with.... And the problem started again, so family services referred them back to us. We went up there. It was the same problem, but it saves them from going out, and we're aware of the problem too.

The team concept has been a changing one. As the police reach into the community, they begin to be perceived as partners. The change is dramatic with Legal Aid, who had tended to see police as an adversary. The changed image is that of police as problem solvers. Concern and expertise are stipulated, and it is assumed that the police seek justice and equity. The next step is an accommodation, a division of labor toward a common goal. Agencies approach each other, share data, and request actions. They dovetail and intersect. Each raises the level of the other's service. As a result, the client discovers new and more effective help.

NOTES

1. The data that had been collected to document the need for the FCI Unit showed that in a six-month period Oakland officers had responded to 16,000 family disturbance calls. Assuming half-hour responses, this represented 8,000 hours of investment. Twenty-five percent of the assignments were return calls. As we mentioned, the majority of incidents occurred in the late evening, Wednesdays through Sundays. The geographical areas that originated most of the calls were districts densely populated by low income minority residents.

10

Implementing a Solution
The Peer Review Panel

In Chapter 7 we traced the evolution of the peer review panel idea. We summarized rehearsals of the procedure that helped the panel take shape.

These shaping experiences provided both positive and negative lessons. On the positive side, we discovered that even suspicious subjects could become cooperative. We discovered that the panel could be seen by supervisors as an adjunct to effective management. We discovered that novice panelists could become skilled interviewers. We discovered that the paper record could yield hypotheses that could channel questioning, without impeding discovery. We discovered that after half a dozen interviews, common denominators emerged that could expedite interview analysis. We discovered that patrolmen could act as scientists in evaluating data and as clinicians in reviewing clues to personality dynamics.

On the negative side, we faced the fact that single interviews may be more productive of insight than of changed conduct. True, some of our subjects showed improvement after their experience with the panel. But in these cases, the panel was one of several concurrent experiences; we can, at best, hope that it played a contributing role. With other subjects the prognosis following their one interview was guarded, particularly when the interviewee continued to defend his *modus operandi* after making concessions about his past. Such experiences led to the suggestion that the original procedure must undergo modifications to strengthen its impact.

In its original form, the review panel consisted of the following stages:

1. The necessity for the panel is documented. Typically, the process would be initiated when an officer reaches a threshold number of incidents on an up-to-date inventory of violent involvements. The number used would not be the number of raw incidents, but a refined index in which the active role of the subject had been established. It would exclude situations in which unwilling participation had been secured. It would include instances in which another officer had filed a report despite the subject's active role in bringing violence about.

   Other ways of mobilizing the review panel would include requests by supervisors or by the subjects themselves. In such cases, however, the record would have to bear out the man's eligibility by showing a substantial number of recent involvements.

2. A preparatory investigation for the interview is conducted. Data relating to the subject's performance on the street are obtained from available secondary sources. This includes interviews with supervisors, reports by peers, and all information on record. The investigation culminates in a "study group" where panelists formulate hypotheses and draft questions that streamline the panel session.

3. Then comes the interview itself, which can be subdivided into three stages:
   a. Key incidents are chronologically explored, including not only actions taken by all persons involved in the incident, but also their perceptions, assumptions, feelings, and motives.
   b. The summation of these data in the form of common denominators and patterns is undertaken primarily by the subject, with participation by the panelists. An effort is made to test the plausibility and relevance of the hypothesized patterns by extrapolating them into other involvements.
   c. The discussion of the pattern occurs last, and includes tracing its contribution to violence. This stage features the exploration of alternative approaches that might be conducive to more constructive solutions.

THE WALLS OF JERICHO

In Chapter 7, we saw panels rehearsed with two officers whose conduct was strongly motivated and well-established—men who showed little inclination to change their approach to police work. One of these officers was John Spark, a member of our project. Here was a bright, dedicated officer who detests unnecessary violence, perceives undesirable personal involvement in his past conduct, but considers his current activities as a necessary, objectively motivated strategy. His reaction, both to the interview and to other pressures for change, was to acknowledge the validity of criticisms without compromising his stance.

Officer Beam's case was even more discouraging. Here was a "supercop": tall, stately, calm, cool, self-possessed, serious, dedicated to the point of fanaticism, and extremely bright. Beam had volunteered for the interview as an exercise designed to educate panelists and to document the case for his one-man police force. Beam's interview yielded hypotheses. Beam, however, showed no inclination to consider these nor to abandon his self-image of privileged insight and superior performance.

Our group had no intention of giving up efforts to redirect Spark and Beam so as to insure the unimpeded availability of the talents of these men. But repeat interviews seemed as doomed as the original effort. Other strategies had to be evolved. In the remainder of this chapter, we'll review the efforts of the group to achieve impact on Officers Beam and Spark. These explorations will illustrate variations on the original review panel idea that can tailor-make a change campaign to even the most difficult, challenging, and obdurate subject.

KILL AND OVERKILL

After the expiration of our project, the Violence Prevention Unit began to monitor high-incident officers in the department, including those of our "graduates" who had returned to the street. Among their subjects, one of the most prominent was Officer Spark. The number of his involvements reached preproject proportions, and exceeded them. Moreover, the quality of his interactions was horrifying, even on the face of their description in official reports.

In one incident, Officer Spark had encountered a group of black juveniles and had stopped them for identification. He became physically involved after arresting one of the young men for not carrying his draft card. In another episode, Spark slammed his car door on the leg of a man who showed reluctance about entering his vehicle. Faced with obvious errors in judgment such as these (and several slightly less blatant ones), the panel coordinator resolved to attack Spark's case.

The strategy was to expand the review panel through the addition of prestigious outsiders. One of these (as we shall see later) was Officer Beam. Another was an investigating officer familiar with follow-up

problems in Spark's arrests. A third addition was a supervising sergeant. The panel was instructed to ask sharp, cross-examining questions to create "stress" in Spark. And they resolved (after preliminary
discussion) to maintain emphasis on quality (as opposed to quantity)
production.

A second procedure employed with Spark was to use him as a panel
member shortly after his experience as subject. This procedure, in part,
served to ameliorate the negative aspects of the previous step.

The results of the strategy were immediate and striking. Spark returned to the street and began an incidentless career. After several
months his record was "clean"; reports arrived from fellow officers of a
change in Spark's reputation. Persons who had refused to work with the
man now indicated that he was an asset. Others voiced incredulity at the
constructive work they witnessed in responding to Spark's calls.

THE NEW MAN

Four months after the last intervention, we asked Spark about the
review panel and its impact on him. Whereas the "old" Spark had been
tense and impatient, these qualities were no longer detectable. The interviewer was sufficiently impressed with Spark's demeanor to raise the
subject of "how much change?" Spark, in turn, confirmed the fact that
he now felt different:

STAFF: You know, I sort of get the feeling that you're awfully relaxed now compared with what you used to be.

SPARK: Well, yeah, I used to have something more to be nervous about. I'd really
have to defend myself in going over some of those sloppy reports and some
of those bad arrests that were made, and stuff. And you'd see reasons to
have to defend yourself.

STAFF: You mean deep down inside you were uneasy about it?

SPARK: Not deep down inside. Just plain uneasy about it. You know, a feeling of
guilt. Whether it was right or wrong, just a feeling of guilt. And at least now
when I go out there everytime I make an arrest, it's an arrest. I don't have to
feel guilty about anything. I think about it later, you know, "Did I do it right,
should I have done anything different?" But still, at the time I know that I've
tried 100% and if I've got to take the guy to jail, the guy's only going because
of himself and not because of me. So I just feel more relaxed when I have to
talk about it, because I know they're on the up and up.

Was the impression of a change related to reduced peer pressure?
Did Spark feel different about himself? He commented:

As a matter of fact, it seems kind of crazy—you probably won't believe this, I go home and I don't feel as tired. The pressure seems like it's off. I'm out there and I'm doing my job and I'm coasting along. I'm not picking up the free check for nothing. I mean I'm still out there doing my job but I feel good about it. And when I go home it just seems like I'm half as tired as I used to be.

Spark added, "My wife would vouch for (the change). I mean, I do more things around the house." He felt himself changed, not only as a police officer, but as a functioning person.

THE CHANGE SEQUENCE: A RETROSPECTIVE VIEW

Spark's initiation into a change-relevant atmosphere had not been overly auspicious:

> I guess my first reaction during the summer was when you enter a group like Violence Prevention Unit, just by the name you think everybody's going to be down on you. And then when you get in on it, you find out everybody is. I think I had a hard time in the group because I didn't get along with a lot of the guys and stuff, but I think a lot of the guys had legitimate reasons why they didn't get along with me.

According to Spark, the experience was an unsettling one. Even while Spark's street conduct remained the same, he had new second thoughts and disturbing doubts. His activity, while similar to previous conduct, was carried out with a divided mind:

STAFF: Are you saying that even while you might have been getting into some difficulties, like for instance to take a hypothetical example, you arrest a guy for not carrying a draft card, after it's over you think about it—that is, you thought about it in ways you wouldn't have before?

SPARK: Yeah, I don't know whether you'd say that was hypothetical or not. I arrested some guys for not carrying draft cards. But in a particular case like that, it was something where you feel pleasure for about five minutes while you're telling this Black Panther he's under arrest for not having a draft card, while Roosevelt Hilliard and the rest of the gang watch with blood in their eyes, and you feel real great. But then you think afterward of the rest of the people that were around watching you, and you think all these guys have to do is say, "See the harassment we're getting," and maybe they have some meat they can stick their teeth into when they can point that you're taking this guy for no draft card, and yet half the guys in Oakland don't carry them.

STAFF: And you're saying that after the summer now you were at the juncture where you were thinking like this, after the five minutes of pleasure, whereas before the summer you would not have?

SPARK: Yeah, that's probably right.

STAFF: But you were doing it anyway.

Why had Spark's experiences with the panel been of limited impact? He comments:

> Well, probably overall on every panel I've sat with—except maybe after the last one—I was thinking that they're out here trying to restrict me from really doing my job, really doing what you're paid for and stuff. . . Another negative thing would be, of course, nobody likes to be criticized, especially on your reports, when you go over your reports. To you it seems like that's the thing to do at the time and stuff.

Elsewhere, Spark describes himself as moving from (1) feeling his productivity attacked, to (2) admitting to differences in kind between his productivity and that of others, to (3) entertaining hypotheses about the reasons for his involvements, to (4) controlling his motives through variations in conduct:

> Well, my first thought was, when I was interviewed on all the violent capers that I've been involved in, my first thought was that it was only probably because I've encountered more crimes and maybe a few more calls than the average officer, that I had a high incidence of 148s and other violent crimes committed upon myself. And this is what I thought even after the first couple of meetings, the first couple of times that we've discussed. And then the more I talked with some of the other officers on the committee there and found that even percentagewise, they had had a lot fewer than I had, I figured that maybe I wasn't all right, which was kind of hard to take. And finally I thought the main reason I've been involved in so many of them, and which apparently turned out to be the reason because I haven't had any recently, was a sort of a fear of the situation getting out of hand, whenever you're handling something, whenever you're talking to somebody. And it's sort of— I guess you could call it self-confidence, when you're trying to make an arrest on somebody or when you're handling a family disturbance or anything. It's a lack of self-confidence in yourself being able to handle the situation, and your main objective is to get the guy under control, whether placing him in the police car or police wagon. And once you get them in control you feel relieved. And so I've tried to sort of avoid getting into that fearful state where you have to have the guy under complete control, and now I try to keep them under control by just talking with them and seeing if that doesn't work. And I've had terrific success, and I seem to enjoy the job more.

According to Spark, the final, crucial panel drove home the point of his atypicality by broadening the range of questioners and critics:

> I would say it did, it had an effect, because here I had been in front of a panel at least three times or so and different members all the time usually—at least a couple of different members, and you keep getting that feeling that even when they're bringing in outsiders like the last panel, these fellows feel the same way as the rest of the panel members. So you know it's not just the panel

members you've got against you. You've got two new fresh faces that you've hardly ever talked with before, and they say the same thing. So it's sort of like majority rules.

The panel had also invoked arguments about the impact of Spark's arrests that he found hard to evade:

SPARK: I think Lt. ____ brought it out the best at the last meeting, where he said, "When you make an arrest, just don't think of the immediate arrest. To you, all you have to do is you grab that body, you make out the arrest tag, you make out the report, and maybe at the most there's an hour shot. But then that report's got to be reviewed by an inspector or a sergeant who's got to spend a couple of more hours on it, who's got to get a complaint, meaning that the DA's got to spend a couple hours on it. Then the judge has to rule on the case, which means you're going to have to spend a couple of hours on that."

STAFF: And some of this is high-powered help.

SPARK: Yeah. Well, I consider myself high-powered help, but why waste everybody's time? Why get everybody to the extent where—on one thing where you could have hesitated for just a second before you jumped in, why waste maybe 10 or maybe even 50 hours of a lot of time? Especially the way the courts are tied up nowadays and the way our investigators are overloaded.

Spark also claims to have benefitted from "field trips" with other members of the unit, in which he had observed "model" resolution of problems that he might have mishandled. And there was membership in someone else's panel, which sharpened Spark's perspective on his own motives:

Like you bring me up on a panel, like last week, and I look at this fellow's reports and you read them over and you say, "Oh, my God, what's this guy doing?" And then you just remember back to some of your own capers and you say, "I would have done the same thing." But you can see on this fellow's report how he really fouled up, whereas looking at your own you try to avoid self-criticism and you don't see it so much.

Lastly, Spark had rehearsed alternative modes of conduct on the street, and discovered their advantage:

I don't know if it's good or not, but I can remember one 415, one of the first ones I went on after getting out of this pan. Over the gal who threw the lamp at the husband and the husband who threw the ashtray at the gal and we just stood there and talked, and we went away and about an hour later they were hand in hand and my God, that impressed me no end. And there was a case where six months—not even six months, probably two months prior to that I would have jumped on the guy and grabbed him and wrestled him, probably hurt my arm or something, and had him out in the car. Probably would have had to take her too, or something. If you see things that can be avoided, why add to the hassle?

Spark deliberately initiated his experimentation in one area (that of family disturbances), and then generalized the experience to other—more sensitive—situations:

SPARK: The reason why I said the 415 family hassles, that seems to be the one that you can really take yourself out of being personally involved.

STAFF: I see.

SPARK: And when you take yourself out of being personally involved in one thing, then why get personally involved in anything else, to the extent where it's going to tire you out, and run you down, and that's all you look for is to arrest this prostitute because she's peddling her butt on your beat, and it's a personal thing because it's your beat? But you start sort of losing that, it starts going away from you, and it's good.

STAFF: It's easier to see in 415s because you're less initially involved, huh?

SPARK: Yeah, right.

The positive feedback, according to Spark, not only consisted of results, but of newly discovered satisfactions. Nagging concerns (such as Spark's fear of victimization) were replaced by a sense of pleasure derived from constructive interactions:

SPARK: I think the whole matter is just a liking of the people, and by feeling that you sort of express it to them.

STAFF: That's great. You mean you actually find yourself liking them—I mean, after the ashtrays and the lamps.

SPARK: Oh, yeah. I mean anybody that you talk to for an hour, you sort of get to know.

STAFF: So another factor of what's happening now is you get to know a lot more people.

SPARK: Yeah.

OFFICER: You're looking at them now more as people, rather than annoyances, as a call?

SPARK: Yeah, that's right. It would always probably be the annoying that would get me, because why waste your time in a petty thing like that when you can be out doing something big. You know? And what's bigger—you leave these people and he kills her or she kills him, and then that's big, and you've got to take on that messy paperwork. It's just more enjoyable to me. You get to relate to the people's problems and stuff. I can't even remember making a 415 arrest in the last six months or so. And there's been plenty of cases where I know other officers would have made the arrest. So now it's sort of a challenge to me when I go in on a call. I'm going to see how I can get out of making this arrest, unless the gal's so bruised up or battered that you've got to take him. I figure I'm 100% success if I go in on a call and the gal's screaming "He's been trying to hit me, and he's been doing this and that," they'll both be sitting there watching TV, or both of them will just be in there. And then I consider it a halfway success if one of them just leaves, and I consider it no success if the fellow or the gal keeps complaining and wanting the other one arrested, or "why are you calling the pigs," and stuff. But I find in most of mine now, that most people stay.

FROM CHANGEE TO CHANGER

Spark's perspective on his own role has changed. He had seen himself as a dedicated officer, engaged in a solitary pursuit of criminal elements. He now sees himself (1) as part of an organization, with responsibilities to it; (2) as a member of a team, with concern for the conduct of teammates; (3) as a person who can exercise constructive influence on his teammates; and (4) as a positive problem solver on the street.

Having discovered both interest and skill in human relations, Spark views this as his principal asset, whose exercise gives him satisfaction. And having experienced the positive impact and rewards of his attributes, Spark senses their absence in others. Spark finds himself on occasion sufficiently disturbed by the conduct of others to intervene and to spread the benefit of new insights:

> It would bother me when I would see them do something that maybe I would have done six months ago, you know, but I'd be looking at it from a different viewpoint and it would look bad. And I'd even straighten out my beat partner sometimes when he'd do something that I don't think is right...

Spark is willing and anxious to formalize this concern through panel membership and through participation in training and retraining efforts. Having experienced the transition from "before" to "after," Spark has become conscious of the process and cognizant of its benefit. As a corollary of insight-centered change, the change object is a change expert. Ultimately, this role converts him into a sophisticated change agent.

THE IMPORTANCE OF BEING PERFECT

Whereas Spark's battle against change had been a rearguard engagement, Beam's was a counteroffensive. Beam began by billing himself as an Enlightening Influence; three transmutations later, he advertised this same role. He started by asserting his unimprovability; after numerous changes, he proclaimed vehemently that he was (and had always been) an ideal officer.

In Beam's case, the panel took the following steps: (1) after the first interview, the coordinator showed Beam a copy of the analysis by the panel; (2) the panel offered Beam the opportunity of a second interview, with stress on alternatives to violence; (3) Beam was used as a panelist in two other interviews; (4) Beam was recommended to the chief as a participant in a seven-week institute on community relations; (5) Beam was appointed to the Violence Prevention Unit, where he took responsibility for a study of police problem solving; and (6) Beam was given an assignment heading a neighborhood police team. Between the second interview and Beam's departure for the institute, his record was "clean." Again, informal word corroborated statistics. The sergeant of the Violence Prevention Unit reports:

> A fellow officer, presently the above interviewee's partner, asks in casual conversation, "What the hell did you guys do with him? He's different!" When asked about arrests and activity "He still makes arrests, but he operates in a different way. He doesn't have much trouble."

At the institute Beam became conspicuous by advocating community action; after his return he worked feverishly on projects designed to cement contact with neighborhood groups. He was involved in landlord–tenant cases in which underprivileged tenants were harassed. The prosecutor's office, which had experienced Beam's enthusiasm for jailing addicts, now witnessed with surprise Beam's new role as Defender of the Poor.

In a retrospective discussion, Beam belabored the assertion that he had experienced no movement so far. "From the time of the first interview," he proclaimed, "I felt one way, which hasn't changed. I still feel the same way." He recollects his panels as follows:

BEAM: The first one was the lecture, I think. The second one was where you were trying to find out why I had had this substantial decrease in violent encounters. Why had I changed? Right? And the second one was amusing again, because I hadn't changed.

OFFICER: You said you were amused. I'm just curious as to how you were amused.

BEAM: I got a kick out of it, because to me it was an exercise in frustration on your part. And it was probably perceived as me giving you a hard time or playing the dozens or just giving you a game, and I really wasn't. I was answering you honestly. Both times I was honest. It came right from the shoulder. The second time I was probably not indifferent; I would say I was a little bit aggravated that I had to have changed, because I hadn't. And I walked out of that meeting hoping maybe that there would be some concessions made to the fact that if you make a lot of narcotics arrests, then there is the opportunity for more violent encounters. The percentages go up. I hoped that I had gotten that point across. I also hoped that I had gotten the point across that I really hadn't changed, that maybe the fact that I was working a different area might have had something to do with it.

Beam recalls that he was "pissed off" by the analysis of his first panel. He consented to the second interview, with the intent of again providing advice and counsel:

> You people are trying to help me and I'm trying to help you. And a guy will believe a so-called good patrolman before he will a sergeant or his general orders or a training manual, because when you get street savvy, that's a hell of a lot more important than book learning. And so for that reason I'd always take an interest in something like this. Even if it's to keep the people involved in it in the proper perspective.

On the second occasion the panel was more forceful than in the first interview. Beam recalls that "I was accused of giving them the runaround and was told that I was full of shit." He adds, as a concession, "If I do give you the runaround, then it's unconsciously. Because things just aren't as literate or as linear as I'd like them to be."

Beam's feelings about the panel were not unambiguously negative. He continued informal contacts, including discussions of interview content. And he responded readily when invited to become a panel member. He recalls that he viewed his participation as an imprimatur, which would validate the panel in everyone's eyes. Beam's first step, he remembers, was to make sure that the panel merited his support:

OFFICER: I remember you came up and reviewed the reports, and went over them to get patterning and classifying behavioral patterns. And your recommendation to us before the interview was, "Maybe we should recommend this guy be fired." You said that outright. And I remember telling you "We're kind of in the game of getting the guys down in this setting with patrolmen and talking about..."

BEAM: I had reasons for saying that.

OFFICER: Sure, it was your initial reaction, "this guy was dangerous." There's no goddamn doubt about it.

BEAM: No, that wasn't my reaction at all. You were dangerous. I just wanted to see where you were going.

OFFICER: Yeah, that's good, sure, talk about that. You said that to test me?

BEAM: Well, to test the panel, yeah. I won't be a part of firing a policeman.

OFFICER: OK, good. How did you feel when you said that? What were your motives? This is what we want.

BEAM: What were my motives? Well, because I would have sunk you if that's what you would have done. I would have just gone down to patrol and just told them what's happening, "When you go up there you're going to Internal

Affairs, pal, only they're going to grease you out of here a lot faster than Internal Affairs would." I would tell them that the first time I thought it was true. I would tell them that now.

OFFICER: So you said, "I think this guy ought to be fired."

BEAM: I said, "This son of a bitch is crazy, we ought to can him right now."

OFFICER: OK. And you were waiting for what response?

BEAM: I was waiting for a response. And I was very concerned with what response. The response was favorable. "No, that's not what we want to do. That's why you're up here, we want to save him. We don't want to see him get fired." I could identify with that...

Beam found his first experience as panelist enjoyable and constructive. He says, "I felt it was good. And I felt that interview went real well...and I was glad to be a part of it, and optimistic of its success." The "part" that Beam assigns himself is (characteristically) the leading one:

STAFF: What were you doing during that interview? You participated fairly actively, didn't you?

BEAM: Well, I think I sold him on it, because I was sold on it myself. He knew me and knew of me, I think, rather than knowing me personally. And I was able to tell him to relax, that he could trust everybody there, and that I wouldn't be a part of it if he couldn't trust it. And he ought to know that, and I think he bought it. So I felt strongly enough about it to sell it.

STAFF: Did you feel that he was getting any help out of this?

BEAM: Yeah.

STAFF: In what way did you feel that you in particular were helping him? You know, after you had gotten him to work with them?

BEAM: Well, I don't know if this is conceit or not, but I think probably he can go back to the patrol division, and a lot of people trust me, and they say, "Well, if Jim Beam said that, then maybe you ought to listen to him."

STAFF: But in terms of giving advice, or in terms of understanding a little better what he's been doing—what in particular do you think he got out of this session?

BEAM: Well, I think he got a lot out of it, for a number of different reasons. There were a lot of things said that we didn't agree with, and then to his surprise that I didn't either. Where I would say, "You just can't do that," and all that. And I think he trusted us. I think it was successful. I think he believed what we were telling him. He realized, as he went through the sequential breakdown, that he was having problems.

STAFF: He did?

BEAM: Yeah, I'm sure he was aware of this. At the end of the interview he admitted it. He said, "Yeah, I've changed a little bit and I realize I have to change a little more." And I think he felt good because, I don't know if it was me or somebody else told him, "Well, that's a beginning."

Beam's reaction to the review panel had become one of enthusiasm. He took it upon himself—again, with a sense of his own potency—to "sell" the idea to others:

BEAM: Oh, the review panel I'm behind 100%. In fact, I'm selling it to the command officers finally. "You know, gee, this is good, and it should have been started years ago." I'm 100% behind it. I've got every goddamn patrolman I ever talked to behind it.

OFFICER: How do you do that? How do you get them on?

BEAM: I can talk to them a little bit differently than you can. But I have the advantage, I guess, of being a supercop. A lot of guys will feel that they can trust me, that's all. I've fought a few raps for a couple of guys. I've got a couple going now that I've fought the rap for.

Beam not only assigns himself the key role as panel "salesman," but recalls having informally used a type of "panel" approach himself:

BEAM: I can recognize certain patterns developing, that I seem to get in the shit the same way everytime. It's a breakdown, bang! When I see this happening, if I'm over to the Public House or I'm talking to some guy or something like this, at that point then I can see it a hell of a lot sooner now because I am convinced that patterns do arise, for one reason or another. And then at that point I will talk to them usually. And maybe very casual, not quite as obvious as it would be up here. Because it's not a stress situation. Bullshit is the word, with them. And pretty soon we'll just get down to the nitty-gritty of why.

STAFF: When did you start doing that?

BEAM: Well, let me see, maybe March of 1969.

STAFF: So you did really have a headstart on us, didn't you?

BEAM: Yeah, kind of. Now I would say that two things then are possible now, at this point. I don't know if this is defensive or not. That I have an inability to apply this to myself, or else it doesn't apply to me.

In any event, Beam had become an advocate of the review concept, and a strong and positive participant. His street conduct had improved. And at this point Beam was advised of the chief's decision to send him to the institute. This development was one for which Officer Beam had no ready explanation:

BEAM: I was surprised. I was really surprised. I was skeptical. And just wondering. I walked in there wondering, walked out wondering what was going on.

STAFF: You must admit that getting you wondering was a little victory for us, wasn't it? I mean we had you asking questions.

BEAM: Oh, well, there was a real diversity in how I was thinking. I was wondering, "Well, something's up and they're going to get me out of town." Or like, "What are they doing, why do I have to be out of Oakland for two months?"

STAFF: So, "they're trying to get me out of town..."?

BEAM: I don't know, I was concerned, I guess, curious, concerned, amazed, shocked is better. I felt a lot of things. And standing I guess in the forefront would be "why?" Which I still don't know, why.

Pressed for a reason, Beam speculates that his reputation would make him a unique asset to the program. No one could possibly see him as a "sellout," he argues: "Everybody says, nope, we trust you, you're the first one that went up there that we could trust." Beam concedes, however (as an afterthought), that his own development might have been an issue, "that I wasn't useful right off the street, that I had to have a little bit more awareness so that I could kind of fit into the thing."

In discussing his institute experience, Beam placed the emphasis on his own interventions and on their impact on other participants. In response to probes, Beam admits to having carried away from the experience a number of new premises, which he describes with considerable eloquence:

OFFICER: Well, we all have good ideas. I might have some that you don't and I'm sure you all have some that I don't and that's why we talk, right? Now what ideas did you get down there that you thought were applicable here, that you didn't have before? If any?

BEAM: One thing I did buy down there that I can identify with is that police departments are going to have to become more personal. I got a different perception of professionalism down there, a new definition.

OFFICER: What?

BEAM: Well, that it isn't necessary to spit polish—of course a hell of a lot more than that. That we took an oath, that there's a good deal more to do than throwing people in jail. That that isn't all we can do. Which is all I thought we ever could do. You know, just throw them in jail. Like a hype, throw them in jail, and who knows, maybe they'll get 90 days in Martinez to dry up. OK, fine. But I got an idea down there that there are people in this community who are stagnated by the system, that if we could plug into the police department and use them as a resource, that maybe we don't always have to arrest people. And this gets back to narcotics again. Because I see the narcotics addict as a nonentity in society, because there's no room for him. And the only other recourse is jail. But we can go into the community. And if I ever get a chance I can contact these people in L.A. and they can come up and sell the chief on it—so all of a sudden we're walking into places that were forbidden before. Because we're not only there to arrest people, but let's find out why they're there. Because they need help. They want to help somebody. I realized and became optimistic about doing a little more than changing substances of image. I then became aware of the necessity of and also the need for changing the reality itself, rather than the substance of the image, because that's artificial, that's phony.

It is interesting that despite the argument against arresting "hypes" (Beam's previous principal occupation), he asserts that there is nothing new here. He admits, however, that he has now become a change advocate, despite a past (well-publicized) stand against the possibility of reform:

STAFF: Before we had anything to do with you, I would guess you would have been fairly pessimistic about the possibility of inducing this department or anything else to change. Wouldn't you have been? You went along your own way feeling that sooner or later they might dump you but weren't offering very much hope of affecting anything.

BEAM: That would be a more than accurate statement, yeah.

STAFF: Do you still feel that way?

BEAM: No, I think it can be changed. I think I'm optimistic now. I'm optimistic that I, as a patrolman, and as only a patrolman, which is all I ever said down there, I realize I'm only a patrolman but—well, let's just say that I have reinforced something that I was beginning to lose as a police officer, and that's the power of oneness.

Beam has come to see himself, primarily and saliently, as a change source. As he puts it, "I can see myself coming up from the bowels of the earth, so to speak, to be reckoned with."

His views with respect to the change role are an amalgamation of alienation and liberalism, of struggle by the Little People (including the police) against a common enemy. Partly, Beam sees his role—as he always has—as that of the "supercop" overcoming institutional efforts to stymie and suppress. But the target of the suppression has shifted. In the forefront now is not crime fighting (and the arrest of addicts) but social problem fighting with emphasis on community self-help:

BEAM: I think we're going to have to be the conscience of the community, the spokesmen for the community. Because the community's been left out of the system too, so to speak. We happen to be—since we're being killed as the representatives of the system, then maybe we're going to have to actually play that role. But be the people's representatives. Rather than being the victims. Because most police officers will say, "Hey, listen, you're right. We're all being manipulated by the system, by the politicians."

STAFF: You mean "we have a lot in common."

BEAM: Yeah, we have a hell of a lot in common. I say that the community perceives us as very, very significant change agents, because we do change their lives when we make arrests and stuff like that. The community has a very valid frustration with the police department because all they ever do is hurt you. They never help you. Unfortunately, they perceive it as an apathy, an indifference—you don't want to help them. This is also the frustration of a police officer, because you can't help them. But I can see it, number one as a significant community relations effort. I can see it as a very, very necessary image change. And I can also see it as a vehicle for eliminating the impotence.

Beam's own role is still that of a one-man vanguard for others. He sees himself functioning in the change agent role at considerable personal sacrifice, but with a sense of unavoidable mission:

> There's a job to be done up here, and it's a job that somebody's got to do. And I think that I would be dishonest with myself and a discredit to them, the patrol officers, if I didn't do something.

THE BELATED REHABILITATION OF OFFICER WHITE

Officer White had been a member of our second group. One of the projects of this group was the investigation initiated by White into the problems of reserve officers. White's dedication to this activity reduced the time available for violence-related concerns. He himself tells us that he was not interested in family crisis management, nor motivated in areas other than the reserve program.

Ultimately—for White—the group had to stand or fall with the reserve study. And on this basis, the group failed. As White put it:

> [The reserve study] was the big thing to me, and it didn't go through, so to me the summer was a total waste almost. That's what I was working on. I put the effort in and nothing was coming back.

In retrospect, White's view of the summer is neither unhappy nor bitter. White assesses the police department with misgivings and expects nothing positive to originate with it:

> I fully expected what happened to happen. Because I have my own feelings about the way things go around here, and these type of things just reinforce it. I knew nothing was going to happen, in this particular regard anyways. Nothing was going to change.

It is surprising, given these facts, that a year after the end of our study, White requested that he be subjected to a review panel. The request came opportunely, because the record showed many violent encounters featuring White and his partner, and some intervention seemed necessary.

White tells us that he requested a panel because the summer had made him see some remote chance of salvation. He tells us:

> I remembered vaguely one of the other groups during the summer was work-
> ing on this panel and it sounded like a fairly good idea at the time to me. I
> was a little suspicious of it, but I had reached the point, up to about a month
> ago, I think, where I was just on the verge of blowing my cool, get myself
> fired or kill somebody or something. And I figured, "What the hell, I might
> as well come up and give it a try."

White anticipated the panel experience with a mixture of despair
(based on a feeling that he had reached a dead-end point) and of ten-
tative trust. He was determined to share his concerns, and to cooperate fully:

> When I asked for this thing, I figured, "What the hell, I'm going to just throw
> caution to the wind and tell it like it is and trust that everything will be all
> right." I figured there wasn't much that could happen because of it, from
> anything I might say up there, because what I was in fact doing was looking
> for help. I went up there with a basic understanding of what the whole thing
> was about, but I was just going to pour my guts out, so to speak, and let
> these guys do whatever was needed, whether it was to wring me out, or
> sympathize, or whatever.

In response to White's request a panel was immediately constituted. This group reviewed White's reports and concluded that these clus-
tered in clear-cut ways. The group summarized its findings and listed
its hypotheses:

1. It appeared that the officer would take immediate action (often
   physical in nature) when a subject would fail to comply immediately with his verbal directions.
2. The panel felt that the above was of extreme concern because the
   officer probably felt that his authority as an officer was being
   challenged by citizens when they failed to "immediately" comply with his verbal instructions.
3. The officer had numerous incidents degenerate into violent confrontations when crowd situations developed. Action was taken
   by the officer "to prevent a person from agitating or inciting the
   crowd." This occurred in areas where the appearance of a
   "crowd" should not have been a startling event.
4. In a large number of incidents, violent encounters erupted after
   the officer had made a car stop. In all of these incidents there was
   more than one person in the vehicle.
5. A disproportionate number of women were involved as suspects.
6. Contrary to the trend of most active officers, this interviewee
   had all types of arrest situations degenerate into violent confrontations. (The normal pattern being that there are more violent
   incidents related to misdemeanor arrests than in felony arrests.)

There is no transcript of panel discussions, but a summary of key points is available. The following is an excerpt from the White panel summary. It suggests that the main dimensions of White's problem (as hypothesized by the panel) were covered during the discussion:

> ...the interviewee stated that he was "sick and tired of taking things from the 'animals and social misfits' " he found on the street. He further stated that he now just does not have any tolerance when dealing with "these people." He further stated that he actually looks forward to when a person makes that error that is serious enough for him to effect an arrest.
>
> With further discussion along these lines, the officer stated that he was just tired of people not doing as he said or appreciating him. "After all, the policeman is supposed to be the 'good guy.' "
>
> It was then pointed out to the interviewee that on numerous reports that it appeared he took action that was probably not appropriate or necessary for that particular incident.
>
> There were several reports that appeared to have no crime committed until the citizen decided to disregard a simple direction of the interviewee.
>
> Several of the incidents involved pat searches, and the officer appears to have little patience with citizens who do not either immediately comply with his orders in these situations or understand the reason for a search and who question his authority to do so.
>
> It would appear that the officer's dealings with the citizenry is often blunt, overly direct, humorless, too quick, and unsympathetic.
>
> The interviewee became aware of some of the negative patterns that he had developed (specifically his overreaction to citizens when they failed to immediately comply with instructions or wishes).

Only time can tell whether Officer White, in response to this new, intensive, personalized contact with him, has overcome his diagnosed patterns. White feels he has insight into his difficulties and conceives of himself as regenerated. He specifically says that he has curbed the propensity to react emotionally when suspects don't heed commands or when they don't show respect:

> I know what my emotions are but I tend to control them. I don't know whether it's a don't-give-a-shit attitude, "do your eight hours and get out," or things are going to change or what. I don't know what it is, but at any rate I don't get that excited anymore. I detach myself a little more, I think. The name-calling, what have you, doesn't get to me anymore like it did. I think what happened was everything just blew up to a point, and maybe it was the panel that blew the top off. But at least I got it all out. I think I've got it pretty well out of my system now. I don't get too excited about it anymore.

White has become a panel advocate and has offered help in approaching subjects of future panels. White has interest in the reserve officer study and this raised the possibility of resuscitating the project.

In general, we can conceive of the sequence as cumulative. Each step increases trust, involvement in change, and commitment to a need for change. White has seen himself as the carrier of a problem, has stipulated the effectiveness of peer review, considers himself a partner with a stake in the enterprise. With each step the pace of White's personal development is increased. Also with each step, White becomes more of a problem solver who addresses the problems of his fellows.

MORE CONVINCING DOCUMENTATION[1]

So far, we have presented some case studies. These may sound convincing, but fall short of proving that the panel can modify behavior or that it would work for the average officer. What we needed were data about conflicts attendant upon arrests pre- and postpanel participation and comparable data for the department as a whole. Fortunately, Oakland had such data collected and had a group of social scientists who were able to analyze them.

The social scientists were all officers, and belonged to an entity our program had left in its wake. This entity was set up in 1970 and described in an information bulletin as follows:

The Violence Prevention Unit

Mission
The Violence Prevention Unit has as its major goal the reduction of violence during police–citizen contacts. Specifically, the unit will identify violence–producing situations and aid personnel found in these situations, undertake detailed analyses of circumstances and individuals, design and implement preventive and remedial approaches for violence reduction, and evaluate the success or failure of such approaches.

Organization
The Violence Prevention Unit is directly responsible to the chief of police. The unit is organizationally assigned to the office of the chief of police.

The unit consists of three sections. These are the action review section, the training research section, and the experimental projects section.

The action review section will analyze in a nonpunitive manner the activities of individuals who seem to be having difficulties during interpersonal contacts. Its activities will include the identification of such individuals, the review of their handling of interpersonal contacts, the convening of action review panels, the discussion of cases, and the recommendation of remedial actions.

The training research section will engage in a variety of developmental activities. It will plan, execute, and evaluate training programs dealing with violence reduction for clientele both inside and outside the department. Of particular importance will be the section's involvement in exploring new training approaches and applying them in the program of violence reduction.

The experimental projects section will design, execute, and evaluate new organizational approaches to the problem of violence. Operational activities in areas where there is a high potential for violence will receive considerable attention.

The analysis we present below is a joint effort, in which we provided technical support for the officers who had collected data they needed to subserve the above-defined mission.

THE INCIDENCE OF CONFLICTS

California has three charges referring to citizen–officer conflict: resisting arrest, a misdemeanor offense; battery or assault on a peace officer, a felony offense; and assault with a deadly weapon on a peace officer, also a felony offense. In the discussion below, these are referred to as "charged incidents."

Formal charges do not, of course, cover all instances of physical confrontations between citizens and officers. Many of these, in fact the majority, do not lead to a formal charge against the citizen; they become "invisible." In a special study undertaken by the Violence Prevention Unit, all arrest reports were reviewed and coded for the presence or absence of physical confrontations.[2] In the discussion below, these are referred to as "not-charged incidents."

Table 1 shows the incidence of each of the three charges for the years 1970 through 1973 and of the not-charged incidents for 1971 through 1973. The total charged incidents show a decline from year to year over the four-year period; this holds for the not-charged incidents (over a three-year period) as well. It will be seen that the drop in charged incidents is due to the decrease in misdemeanor charges (resisting arrest) rather than in the two more serious felony assault charges. The latter, it might be argued, result from situations that offer less room for officer discretion in whether or not to make a formal charge. However, since the not-charged incidents decreased as well, it cannot be argued that the drop in resisting-arrest charges represents a shift from the charged to the not-charged category. Nor can it be argued that the recording of actual incidents became more lax. The chief, very concerned with reducing the number of citizen complaints, had made it clear that any behavior of which a citizen might reasonably complain must be documented, whether with a formal charge or not, in the arrest report. The climate he set makes it reasonable to suppose that most, if not all, confrontations appeared in the department's records.

TABLE 1. Citizen–Officer Conflicts

Type of incident	1970	1971	1972	1973
Resisting arrest				
Total	630	489	469	326
Average/month	52.5	40.8	39.1	27.2
Battery				
Total	145	118	154	148
Average/month	12.1	9.8	12.8	12.3
Assault with deadly weapon				
Total	38	51	33	35
Average/month	3.2	4.2	2.8	2.9
All charged				
Total	813	658	656	509
Average/month	67.8	54.8	54.7	42.4
All not charged				
Total	NA	1,242[a]	1,007	724
Average/month	NA	103.5	83.9	60.3
All charged and not charged				
Total	NA	1,900	1,663	1,233
Average/month	NA	158.3	138.6	102.8

[a]The 1971 figures are extrapolations based on the data available for the last four months of that year.

INJURIES TO OFFICERS AND CITIZENS

Physical confrontations between citizens and officers may be more show than substance, but they sometimes result in real injuries—to officers, to suspects, or to both. Table 2 gives data on injuries to each group over each of the four kinds of incidents reported in Table 1.

As would be expected, injuries resulted from the misdemeanor offenses far less often than from the two felony offenses, and injuries resulted from the not-charged incidents less often than from the charged offenses. Unlike the year-to-year decrease in number of incidents, the proportion of these in which injuries occurred to one or both participants showed no such clear-cut trend. The number of injuries to officers rose somewhat from 1970 to 1972; the number of injuries to suspects, at least in the misdemeanor and not-charged incidents, showed a slight decrease. Both dropped sharply in 1973; we have no explanation for this sudden change.

In reviewing resisting-arrest injuries, we find that, although it is the citizen who is being charged and arrested, the *alleged aggressors' injuries exceeded (consistently) those of the officer-complainants.* The same point holds—though not as surprisingly—for uncharged violence.

TABLE 2. Injuries to Citizens and Officers in Citizen–Officer Conflicts

Type of incident	1970 Citizen	1970 Officer	1971 Citizen	1971 Officer	1972 Citizen	1972 Officer	1973[a] Citizen	1973[a] Officer
Resisting arrest								
Total	23	48	24	32	26	33	8	12
Percent	3.7	7.6	4.9	6.5	5.5	7.0	3.2	4.7
Battery								
Total	38	37	44	28	50	39	13	11
Percent	26.2	25.5	37.3	23.7	32.5	25.3	11.2	9.5
Assault with deadly weapon								
Total	9	8	10	11	9	6	1	4
Percent	23.7	21.1	19.6	21.6	27.3	18.2	3.7	14.8
All charged								
Total	70	93	78	71	85	78	22	27
Percent	8.6	11.4	11.9	10.8	13.0	11.9	5.5	6.8
All not charged								
Total	NA	NA	12[b]	54[b]	21	44	0	9
Percent	NA	NA	1.0	4.3	2.1	4.4	0.0	2.0
All charged and not charged								
Total	NA	NA	90	125	106	122	22	36
Percent	NA	NA	4.7	6.6	6.4	7.3	2.6	4.2

[a]Injury data were not collected after the first three quarters of 1973. The number and percent of injuries are for the first nine months.
[b]The 1971 figures are extrapolations based on the data available for the last four months of that year.

COMPLAINTS AGAINST THE POLICE

Under Chief Gain's administration, the department encouraged the receipt of complaints by citizens. Complaints were accepted in any form, including those made anonymously, by a central complaint office. Case records were kept on all complaints; feedback was given routinely to the officers who were the subject of complaints and, on request, to the citizens who made them.

Table 3 shows the complaint data for each year from 1970 to 1973. The total number of complaints made by citizens can be taken as a gross measure of citizen dissatisfaction with police. The number of complaints sustained (i.e., the number in which the department formally found a valid basis for the complaint) can be taken as a measure of inappropriate officer behavior. The percent sustained may be considered a minimum measure of the legitimacy of the complaints made.

It will be seen that total complaints dropped dramatically from 1970 to 1971 and continued a downward trend after that time; the total in 1973 is one third that of 1970. Despite encouragement to make complaints, this form of citizen dissatisfaction sharply decreased. The number of complaints that were found to have validity also decreased from year to year (differences are significant at the .01 level); the total sustained in 1973 is one quarter that of 1970. The percent sustained rose from 1970 to 1971, a result of the fact that total complaints made dropped far more sharply than did number sustained. The first may indicate the chief's success in working with the community; the second, his success in working with his officers. The latter came more slowly. After 1971, however, the percent of complaints sustained decreased.

THE INITIATION OF INTERACTION

A police officer may become involved with a citizen when dispatched on a call through the radio room or the officer may initiate the interaction. In the former situation the officer's interaction is not a matter

TABLE 3. Formal Citizen Complaints against Officers

Complaints	1970	1971	1972	1973
Number sustained	96	77	44	23
Percent sustained	14.9	21.6	17.5	11.2
Total number of complaints	645	357	251	206

Note: χ^2 test (number sustained v. number not sustained over four years); $p < 0.01$.

of choice. On-view incidents, on the other hand, are always "precipitated" by the officer in the sense of making a physical overture or contact. Table 4 shows the number of officer involvements in incidents in each type of citizen–officer conflict by the way in which the conflict was initiated.

The picture presented by Table 4 is striking and dramatic. In all categories, we see a strong, consistent decrease in the proportion of violence resulting from on-view incidents. In fact, we conclude that the time trends we have noted are disproportionately a function of on-view trends.

We also see that resisting-arrest incidents occurred more often with officer-initiated (on-view) activity than did felony-assault incidents; and of the latter two, assault on the officer occurred more often in officer-initiated actions than did assault on an officer with a deadly weapon. But for each of the three types of charge the ratio of officer-initiated to dispatched activities decreased from year to year over the four-year period. The same is true for the not-charged incidents.[3] Thus, it seems plausible to argue that the decrease in citizen–officer incidents reflected a decrease in field contacts or an improvement in field-interrogation conduct. In the resisting-arrest category the number as well as the percent resulting from officer-initiated activity decreased; the number resulting from dispatched actions actually showed a slight increase.[4]

THE TYPE OF ARREST

To what extent is the amount of citizen–officer conflict simply an expression of how active officers are? In the extreme case, if officers snooze or drive aimlessly about, they will clearly have no difficulties with citizens. The more work they do, the more risk they take of physical involvement with citizens. Thus, the decrease in conflicts over this four-year period may simply reflect a decrease in the number of arrests made.

Table 5 both confirms and disconfirms this argument. This table presents the percent change in the number of arrests made for each year from 1970 to 1973. Offenses are divided for this purpose into the reporting categories used for the FBI Uniform Crime Reports. Part I offenses include the major felonies (criminal homicide, forcible rape, robbery, aggravated assault, burglary, larceny, and auto theft). Part II offenses include victimless crimes (e.g., drunkenness, vagrancy, disorderly conduct, and drug, gambling, and prostitution offenses), some white-collar crimes (forgery, fraud, and embezzlement), and a variety of others (e.g., arson, simple assault, family or child neglect or abuse, vandalism, car-

TABLE 4. Initiation of Citizen–Officer Conflicts

Type of incident	1970 No.	1970 %	1971 No.	1971 %	1972 No.	1972 %	1973[a] No.	1973[a] %
Resisting arrest								
On-view[b]	474	50.1	383	42.6	352	41.5	147	27.2
Dispatched	415	43.9	458	50.9	449	52.9	392	72.6
Other[c]	57	6.0	58	6.5	47	5.5	1	0.2
Total[d]	946		899		848		540	
Battery								
On-view	116	46.2	90	38.3	144	38.4	53	20.5
Dispatched	113	45.0	121	51.5	205	54.7	206	79.5
Other	22	8.8	24	10.2	26	6.9	0	0.0
Total	251		235		375		259	
Assault with a deadly weapon								
On-view	21	35.6	33	34.7	26	28.6	17	22.1
Dispatched	31	52.5	53	55.8	59	64.8	58	75.3
Other	7	11.9	9	9.5	6	6.6	2	2.6
Total	59		95		91		77	
All charged								
On-view	611	48.6	506	41.2	522	39.7	217	24.8
Dispatched	559	44.5	632	51.4	713	54.3	656	74.9
Other	86	6.8	91	7.4	79	6.0	3	0.3
Total	1,256		1,229		1,314		876	
All not charged								
On-view	NA		846[e]	46.4[e]	784	38.8	425	35.2
Dispatched			906	49.7	1,174	58.0	781	64.6
Other			72	3.9	65	3.2	3	0.2
Total			1,824		2,023		1,209	
All charged and not charged								
On-view	NA		1,352	44.3	1,306	39.1	642	30.8
Dispatched			1,538	50.4	1,887	56.5	1,437	68.9
Other			163	5.3	144	4.3	6	0.3
Total			3,053		3,337		2,085	

Note: χ^2 test (on-view vs. dispatch over four years):
Resisting arrest $p < 0.005$.
Battery: $p < 0.005$.
Assault with deadly weapon: NS.
All charged: $p < 0.005$.
All not charged: $p < 0.005$.
All charged and not charged: $p < 0.005$.
[a]Data on initiation of conflict were not collected after the first three quarters of 1973. Thus the number and percent of incidents are for the first nine months.
[b]"On-view" refers to an officer-initiated interaction.
[c]"Other" refers to occasional situations in which the interaction neither is initiated by the officer in question nor results from a specific dispatch from the radio room: e.g., two officers may be dispatched on a call from the radio room, and a third makes a decision to join them on the call.
[d]Comparison with Table 1 will show larger "total" figures here. Figures presented here are for total number of *officer involvements* in incidents. Figures for Table 1 are for total number of *incidents* (which may have involved more than one officer).
[e]The 1971 figures are extrapolations based on the data available for the last four months of that year.

TABLE 5. Arrests by Type of Offense: Percent Change from Preceding Year

Type of offense	1970	1971	1972	1973	1970–1973
Part I					
Number	8,718	9,401	8,974	8,469	
Percent change	+ 12.8	+ 7.8	− 4.5	− 5.6	− 2.9
Part II					
Number	31,500	25,233	21,588	21,699	
Percent change	+ 0.2	− 19.9	− 14.4	+ 0.5	− 31.1
Total Part I and II					
Number	40,218	34,634	30,562	30,168	
Percent change	+ 2.7	− 13.9	− 11.8	− 1.3	− 25.0

rying illegal weapons, receiving stolen property, curfew violations, and runaways).

The table shows that total arrests were down considerably — 25% — over the four-year period from 1970 to 1973, but this decrease was almost solely due to a decrease in the part II offenses. Productivity in the sense of major crime fighting showed relatively little change over the four years. There was a marked decrease in arrests for the less severe criminal offenses, with drunkenness constituting 30–40% of these over this time period. The concomitant decrease in citizen–officer conflict seems thus to be related to a change in police behavior toward troublesome but not seriously criminal citizen activity. Such change is, of course, *precisely* the thrust of antilegalistic police reform.

The arrest figures we have cited must be evaluated in two contexts. The first is change within the department: the advent of new activities — an increase in nonarrest productivity (including such service innovations as family crisis intervention and landlord–tenant intervention); the desire for nonenforcement reactions to street situations formerly resulting in arrests (e.g., drunks, disturbance calls); and, to a lesser extent, the deployment of manpower into staff activities such as violence reduction, training, and other work concerned with reorienting the department.

The second context is the crime picture. As we note in Table 6, Oakland experienced a slight, but consistent decrease in reported crime from 1970 on, due mostly to a drop in larceny-theft and auto-theft offenses. An exception is aggravated assault, which spiraled steadily upward, doubling in number from 1970 to 1974. Thus, the decrease we find in police–citizen confrontations occurs against a backdrop of increased citizen–citizen conflict. This suggests an improvement in police response to assaultive citizens rather than a change in citizen assaults.

TABLE 6. Crimes Known to Police in Oakland, California

Year	Total Crime Index (using 1973 FBI formula)	Type of crime								
		Nonnegligent manslaughter	Negligent manslaughter	Forcible rape	Robbery	Aggravated assault	Burglary, breaking and entering	Larceny theft	Auto theft
1970	42,872	69	37	212	2,497	1,088	13,787	20,166	4,993
1971	42,699	89	26	220	2,932	1,224	14,311	18,528	5,395
1972	41,836	78	25	261	2,907	1,646	13,080	18,445	5,419
1973	41,595	100	11	220	2,879	1,853	14,734	17,063	4,746
1974	40,507	78	3	246	2,883	2,175	14,144	16,702	4,279

Source: Federal Bureau of Investigation, *Uniform Crime Reports, 1971–1975* (1976).

INDIVIDUAL PRODUCTIVITY AND VIOLENCE

What of the individual officers? Is the amount of their arrest activity related to the frequency with which they have trouble with citizens? Does their involvement in incidents increase with their productivity or with *certain kinds* of productivity?

Some law-enforcement personnel feel that citizen–officer conflict is more likely to occur in situations of serious criminal activity, that is, in association with felony arrests. Some research (Reiss, 1971; Toch, 1969; Westley, 1970) suggests that assaults are more likely to occur during misdemeanor arrests, in field contacts, and in police activity that might be construed as harassment.

To clarify this issue, a special study was undertaken to allow accumulation of arrest and conflict data for individual officers. The year selected was 1971. A count was made of the number of felony and of misdemeanor arrests for each of 489 officers and of the number of citizen–officer conflicts associated with each type. Officers were then classified as high or low in productivity for each type of arrest and for total arrests.

Table 7 presents the average number of citizen–officer conflicts during the year for officers classified as high and low in terms of various

TABLE 7. Citizen–Officer Conflicts
by Officers with High and Low Productivity, 1971

Level of productivity (median split)	Different productivity indices			
	Felony arrests	Misdemeanor arrests	Total arrests: felony and misdemeanor	Felony–misdemeanor ratio
High				
Number of officers	275	244	270	235
Average number of conflicts	3.2	3.3	3.1	2.8
Low				
Number of officers	214	245	219	254
Average number of conflicts	1.3	1.4	1.4	1.8
Total number of officers	489	489	489	489

Note: t-test (high vs. low production)
Felony arrests: $p<0.001$.
Misdemeanor arrests: $p<0.001$.
Total arrests: $p<0.001$.
Felony–misdemeanor: $p<0.001$.

measures of productivity: number of felony arrests, number of misdemeanor arrests, number of total arrests, and ratio of number of felony arrests to number of misdemeanor arrests.[5]

It is clear from the table that officers with more citizen (arrest) contacts *do* have more conflict with citizens. This holds for felony, for misdemeanor, and for total arrests. The differences between the average number of conflicts for officers with high- and low-arrest productivity are significant beyond the .001 level for each type of arrest and for the two types combined. Thus, while the data in Table 5, which show a large drop in the number of arrests for less serious offenses over the period when citizen–officer conflicts were decreasing, tend to support the argument that conflict is more likely to occur in connection with misdemeanor than with felony arrests, the data in Table 7 support the reverse position. One explanation for the discrepancy may be exposure: those officers assigned to areas with a high amount of criminal activity and thus more arrestable behavior had more opportunity for conflict with citizens.

The felony–misdemeanor argument raises the question of the *quality* of arrest as distinct from arrest productivity. If the law-enforcement function of the police is seen as one of attending to greater as opposed to lesser crimes, then an officer whose arrests are primarily for felony as opposed to misdemeanor offenses might be considered more effective than one whose arrests are primarily for the latter.[6] Conflict may be more common among the less effective officers when effectiveness is defined in terms of the quality of arrests that they make.

As a crude measure of the quality of arrest, we calculated the ratio of felony to misdemeanor arrests for each of the 489 officers during 1971. The officers were then divided into those with a felony–misdemeanor ratio equal to or less than 1.0 (i.e., those who had no more felony than misdemeanor arrests during the year) and those with a ratio larger than 1.0 (i.e., those who had more felony than misdemeanor arrests). According to our argument, the latter would be said to show more effective arrest quality and we would expect them to have fewer citizen–officer conflicts. They did not. The last column of Table 7 shows that the high felony–misdemeanor ratio group had an average of 2.8 citizen–officer confrontations during the year compared to 1.8 for the less effective (low felony–misdemeanor ratio) group. This difference is significant beyond the .001 level. Thus, citizen–officer conflicts were not associated with poorer rather than better quality of arrests (defined crudely by the felony–misdemeanor ratio). The data support the opposite position.

Let us look at the data again, however, across columns. Officers who made relatively few felony arrests tended to have relatively few conflicts with citizens. But officers whose number of felony arrests was low in relation to the number of misdemeanor arrests they made had substantially more conflicts. Officers who were high in felony-arrest productivity had a high number of citizen–officer conflicts; those whose number of felony arrests was high in relation to the number of misdemeanor arrests had somewhat fewer conflicts. This suggests that not all the variance in frequency of conflict is accounted for by a simple measure of arrest frequency, and that quality of arrest behavior contributes something to the variance in number of conflict incidents.

THE PEER REVIEW PANEL

Data we cited above tend to support the position that administrative policy change can make a difference in officer behavior. We turn now to consider the impact of the peer review panel.

The panel, after it was institutionalized, reviewed departmental arrest reports and maintained full records on every officer on street assignment. When any officer's level of "incidents" became statistically unacceptable, the officer was scheduled for a review session. The review session involved a rotating group of officers, with most being former panel subjects. Sessions were repeated if high incident levels persisted.

We find that there is evidence that panel experience had a positive effect on an officer's street behavior. Table 8 compares panel participants with nonparticipants in the frequency of citizen–officer conflicts for the

TABLE 8. Total Citizen–Officer Conflicts
Before and After Panel Participation: Participants versus Nonparticipants

Review panel	Before (Jan.–May 1970)	After (June 1970–July 1972)		Difference (expected vs. observed)
		Expected[a]	Observed	
Participants ($n = 72$)				
Average incidents/ officer	2.39	12.48	7.90	4.58
Average/month/officer	0.48	0.48	0.30	0.18
Nonparticipants ($n = 434$)				
Average incidents/ officer	0.64	3.38	2.44	0.94
Average/month/officer	0.13	0.13	0.09	0.04

[a]Expected figures were obtained by multiplying the average number of incidents per month by the number of months in the June 1970–July 1972 period.

5 months prior to instituting the review panel and the 26 months following. Only officers who were on street duty for the entire 31 months were used in the comparison.

Using the 5 months prior to the panel as a base, the average number of incidents expected for the next 26 months was determined. The actual number that occurred was less than the number expected for both the participants and the nonparticipants. The decrease was much greater, however, for the participating officers, their expected–observed discrepancy being 4½ times that of the nonparticipating officers. A covariance analysis shows that a difference of this magnitude has less than a .001 probability of occurring by chance. The conflict-prone officers who had designed the panel had developed an intervention that significantly reduced the incidence of such conflict.

Though the review panel began in June 1970, participation in the panel was spread over the months following. The figures reported for the participants for the "after" period in Table 8 include varying numbers of months prior to participation. More precise measures were obtained by taking each participant's average number of incidents for the actual months prior to and following participation in the panel. This analysis is reported in Table 9. The average monthly incidents for the participants dropped from .37 to .16 following participation. Monthly averages for the nonparticipants (using randomly assigned comparable time periods) dropped from .10 to .08. A covariance analysis shows that the differences among these averages have less than a .01 probability of occurring by chance.

TABLE 9. Average Monthly Citizen–Officer Conflicts
Before and After Panel Participation: Participants vs. Nonparticipants

Review panel	Before	After
Participants ($n = 88$)		
Average	0.37	0.16
Variance	0.13	0.02
Nonparticipants ($n = 434$)		
Average	0.10	0.08
Variance	0.03	0.02

Note: In contrast to the figures in Table 8, time before and after participation varied for each participant. Actual months on the street before and after participation were used to determine monthly averages. This allowed the inclusion of 16 additional officer–participants who could not be included in the analysis reported in Table 8 because they were not on the street for the full before and after periods.

Time is controlled for the nonparticipants by proportional random assignments, to correspond to the monthly proportions of participants.

WHAT COULD WE CONCLUDE?

In Chapters 6 through 8 we described how we worked with groups of officers as co-students of a problem that had meaning both for them and for us and how we assisted their planning of interventions to cope with it. One concern for the department was the high number of physical confrontations between officers and citizens, leading to tensions with the community, and the concentration of those incidents among relatively few officers.

One of our assignments was to help the officers assess the result of their interventions. In assessing the panel intervention, we followed one kind of officer behavior, participation in physical conflict with citizens, over a period when the department was undergoing rapid policy and administrative change.[7] We have shown that police–citizen conflict can decrease sharply with a deemphasis of legalism and that citizen resentment (as expressed in complaints to the police) can also decrease. We have found that this decrease is associated with changes in kind of arresting behavior, with less emphasis placed on the less serious offenses and on-view stops. We found these changes occurring against a background of an increase in total assaultive crimes by citizens.

We found a link between productivity and police–citizen conflict. This link is neither surprising nor disheartening. It confirms that productivity, even if refined, entails paying a price in violence. It tells us that a police force of any orientation must precariously balance its values. It must decide how much to prize arrests and how much to "trade" for them. Not all trade-offs are inevitable, and moderation in arresting—as elsewhere—pays decent dividends.

We found some evidence that frequency of conflict may be associated with arrest quality. This last is an issue that needs to be explored more fully. We need arrest-productivity indices (such as conviction rates) and ratings of nonarrest productivity. We need to know more about different types of officers and about different patterns of productivity. We need to know how these patterns change when change is imposed from without and when it comes from within.

Finally, we found that officer behavior can be changed by an intervention designed and implemented by other officers. While incidents were decreasing in the department as a whole, officers who participated in the peer review panel showed a larger decrease in incidents than officers who did not. The panel could not have been implemented without the background of change in the department, but its relative success is a testament to the importance of involving the officers themselves in change efforts.

BUT WAS IT PROBLEM-ORIENTED POLICING?

Peer review panels do not sound like a problem-oriented intervention dealing with what Goldstein (1979) referred to as police problems. For Goldstein, police problems are troublesome events in the community that must be addressed in the community. The panels by contrast are an intervention inside the police department. Panels did not deal with citizens, nor could they involve citizens as panelists. But what defined a "problem" for the panels were arrests that occurred in the community. Such arrests do not make a different pattern from one of disruptive acts that became police business.

Of course, the panels are not the beginning of our story. We started with concern about a wave of incidents involving conflicts between police and suspects. These incidents created tensions in the community and adverse publicity and complaints. Some of the incidents inspired lawsuits and others cost officers their jobs. This was indisputably a problem for the community. It was also a problem for the police.

The problem could have—and sometimes has—been defined as an offender-related problem, as one of patterns in the behavior of violence-prone civilians (Toch, 1969). There are suspects who replay the same attacks against officers time after time. One could think of interventions that anticipate the level of risk posed by such suspects or that attempt to reform recidivistic assaulters. One could try to stage peer review panels—or something like them—for offenders.

Our officers had a mandate to study violent incidents and to ascertain their patterns and causes. The officers would have loved to blame most of the violence on suspects. But in the end they did not do so. Honesty prevented the officers from taking the route, because the data pointed elsewhere. In this respect the officers proceeded as we had hoped they would proceed. Our studies, and those of the police department, had highlighted individual officer contributions to the incident variance. The groups rediscovered this contribution in their turn.

There were other reasons why we were delighted with the outcome of the study. One reason was a strategic one: The logistics of intervening by working with officers were mercifully simple. Locating suspects in prisons and on the streets would be an inordinately difficult enterprise and not cost-effective. Other intervention options, such as safety training, have been found to have limited payoff.

Our second reason had to do with problem-oriented policing, which we see as a process that enables officers to develop and learn as they evolve solutions. We especially selected violence-involved officers for our project, hoping that they would combine their experience with science to evolve expertise. Such expertise, we felt, could then be transmitted to others, as through training. Problem-solving skills could similarly be applied to future problems.

Our third reason for being pleased was because review panels transfer a traditional managerial function (quality control) to officers. This matters more in policing than elsewhere because many people feel that officers cannot be given discretion because they tend to abuse it, and resist managerial monitoring and controls.

Finally, it was our view that an intervention like review panels makes a strong case for problem-oriented reforms. If police can accept the import of self-critical data, their capacity to intervene after dispassionately studying problems is established. There are few institutions in our society that can match the commitment shown by the police and by our officers to the problem-oriented process. The officer's uninhibited exploration of intervention options yielded a departure from familiar responses. In problem-oriented thinking, this is not a liability, but a plus.

NOTES

1. Most of the data in the following were collected under NIMH Grant MH 20757 ("Research on Violence Prevention by Police") from the Center for Studies of Crime and Delinquency. We are indebted for this support.
2. Elements of resistance, battery, or assault with a deadly weapon were present in the arrest report but not charged by the arresting officer.
3. Differences between the proportion of on-view and dispatched incidents over time are significant at the .005 level for all but "Assault with a deadly weapon."
4. As noted in Table 4, 1973 figures are based on 9 months only. Extrapolating to the full year would give 96 on-view and 523 dispatched incidents in the resisting-arrest category.
5. The data were compiled originally for a study of officers who participated, or were eligible for participation, in the peer review panel during its first year of operation. These constituted 171 of the total. The remaining 318 formed the criterion group for determining high and low productivity: high in each case being all numbers above the median for this group, low being all numbers at or below the median.
6. It is recognized that this does not take into account the nature of an officer's assignment—its location and time of day—which may have an influence on the primary type of arrest the officer makes.
7. Police departments do not commonly keep the kinds of records that allow systematic study of change efforts nor the tracking of individual officer behavior. The Conflict Management Unit (rebaptized Violence Prevention Unit) had to set up an information system that allowed study of the citizen–officer conflict problem over time. The data presented in this chapter derive from this system.

11

Community Problem-Oriented Policing

The Brave New World as it is envisaged by leaders in the police field may be a world of problem-oriented policing, a world of community-oriented policing, or a combination of the two. The distinction between fashionable concepts is not neat; there are many students who at times regard one concept as subservient to the other. Trojanowicz and Bucqueroux (1990a), for example, write that "in essence, solving problems is an important aspect of Community Policing, and a department that encourages its officers to use Problem-Oriented techniques can make greater use of their potential as part of a Community Policing approach" (p. 10). Goldstein (1987) has similarly written that "I would argue that a fully developed concept of what we now allude to by "community policing" could provide the umbrella under which a more integrated strategy for improving the quality of policing could be constructed" (p. 8).[1]

Another problem lies in the fact that "community policing" has a wide range of connotations. Wycoff (1988) points out that

> "Community-oriented" is one of those terms that simultaneously suggests so much that is general and so little that is specific that it risks being a barrier rather than a bridge to discourse about developments in policing. Unfortunately, the barrier can assume the illusory shape of a bridge... People...can converse at length before discovering they are talking about different entities bearing the same name.
>
> This seems currently to be the risk in trying to discuss different experiences of what various observers may refer to as community-oriented policing. (pp. 103–104)

Some partisans of community policing see the approach as a composite of social work, community organizing, and sainthood, with a

247

deemphasis of traditional enforcement. Trojanowicz and Bucqueroux (1990a) define the goal of community policing as "to solve the problems of crime, fear of crime, physical and social disorder, and neighborhood decay." They write that the community police officer (CPO) must be a person of tremendous ingenuity. He or she must be a leader because "solutions to contemporary community problems demand freeing both people and police to explore creative, new ways to address neighborhood concerns beyond a narrow focus on individual crime incidents." The CPO must be "a new breed of line officer... the direct link between the police and people in the community." The linkage "demands continuous, sustained contact with the law abiding people in the community so that together they can explore creative new solutions to local concerns involving crime, fear of crime, disorder, and decay, with private citizens serving as unpaid volunteers" (p. xiii).

look at wider society

Community police officers are often seen as mobilizers of citizens, as "creators of community" in neighborhoods in which disorganization and apathy are endemic. One assumption here is that crime problems can come to interest neighborhood people to such an extent that they can be energized into collective action. In an editorial supportive of community policing, for example, the *New York Times* proclaimed that

> The need grows ever more obvious. Like other cities, all of New York suffers profoundly from the collapse of institutions in poor neighborhoods. And many residents now find urgent, fundamental reasons to re-establish them around the issues of drugs and crime. Community policing programs are designed to develop that process. (February 7, 1990)

Elsewhere, the *New York Times* wrote of the introduction of CPOs that "at best they can help create a more orderly neighborhood, freer of intimidation, where urban decay is stalled or turned back" (Malcolm, 1990).

Another set of associations lies in the proliferation of nostalgic connotations when "community" is attached to "policing."[2] The juxtaposition of these words evokes images of beat cops (usually with brogues) giving homespun and salubrious advice. It also evokes a view of lighted windows of storefronts in deteriorated neighborhoods where friendly persons in blazers protect the poor from predation.

In looking for common themes among the sorts of definitions that are—at least, implicitly—used by persons who run mainline community-oriented programs, Wycoff (1988) concludes that

> Philosophically, the programs tend to have in common the belief that police and citizens should experience a larger number of nonthreatening, supportive interactions that should include efforts by police to
> 1. Listen to citizens, including those who are neither victims nor perpetrators of crimes;

    2. Take seriously citizens' definitions of their problems, even when the problems they define might differ from ones the police would identify for them;

    3. Solve the problems that have been identified.

       Some programs go even further to incorporate the idea that

    4. Police and citizens should work together to solve problems. (p. 105)

Wycoff's composite definition requires that the problems that police attend to respond to the concerns of citizens. It also connotes—but does not require—that police should work with citizens in trying to solve citizen-nominated problems. A key verb for the officers is the verb "listen." Skolnick and Bayley (1986) refer to this listening process as "police–citizen reciprocity." Reciprocity "means that police must genuinely feel, and genuinely communicate a feeling, that the public they are serving has something to contribute to the enterprise of policing" (p. 212). Mastrofski (1988) points out that the requisite is rarely met as it is supposed to be in many police departments. He writes that

> Anyone who has observed a variety of community crime prevention programs readily ascertains that the bulk of the communication is from the police to the citizen, explaining and selling prepackaged strategies devised without the particular neighborhood and its residents' preferences in mind. Several evaluations of these programs show that they emphasize organizing to do crime prevention, not to stimulate the neighborhood to voice its demands in matters of police business. (p. 52)

Reciprocity, of course, is a two-way street, and denizens of some neighborhoods may be disinterested in crime problems and indifferent to what the police may do. Elsewhere, citizens may distrust police or view them as antagonists. Hostility is arguably worse than apathy, but at least it can motivate citizens to take an interest in trying to influence policing. Berkeley (California) residents, for example, reputedly mistrust police, but involve themselves in the smallest details of police work, such as the recent creation of a one-dog K-9 unit. Bishop (1990) reports that

> ...when faced with hiring its first police dog in decades to help combat a growing problem with crack, the city did what comes naturally here: it insisted on a politically correct pooch...
>
> While many cities with neighborhoods that are being torn apart by crack might welcome a lean, mean drug-fighting machine, the last thing Berkeley wants is a German shepherd with an attitude.
>
> After a talent search that lasted for months, the Berkeley Police Department has obtained Pepper, a 19-month-old Labrador that can sniff out stashes of crack even when drug dealers hide them outdoors under debris. And Pepper may be the prototype for the 1990s—a kinder, gentler police dog.

Where citizens take an interest in policing, it matters, of course, who the citizens are and what they want police officers to do. Police have a right to resist demands motivated by special interests or unrepresentative sentiments, and they have an obligation to reject political pressures and invitations to engage in unprofessional conduct.[3] Conversely, police cannot claim community input where there is neither community nor input. Weisburd and McElroy (1988) concluded that "perhaps scholars have romanticized the concept of community in their effort to develop a more community-oriented policing strategy" (p. 100).

The same charge about romanticized community conceptions has been lodged by other observers of organizing efforts in the ghetto. And it is certainly true that (1) some neighborhoods are hard to mobilize because they are disillusioned and demoralized, and (2) officers must often deal with unrepresentative elites, who cannot deliver constituencies (Mastrofski, 1988).[4] But if police totally relinquished the option of community organizing, the term "community policing" would have very limited connotations. It would suggest that citizens are permitted to help the police define services they receive, provided the police solicit advice and accept it. Such connotations hardly seem sufficiently broad to encompass citizen involvement in joint problem-solving activities in the community.

BEING ONE'S OWN POLICE CHIEF

Skolnick and Bayley (1986) have written that "a reciprocal understanding of crime prevention will ordinarily be linked closely with a strategy of areal decentralization of command" (p. 214). What Skolnick and Bayley mean by this pairing is that officers who listen to citizens must first come to know them, which is accomplished by remaining around the same neighborhood and the same people over time. Officers who are assigned to work in neighborhoods must be detached from assignments elsewhere and must be locally headquartered. They must be allowed to make decisions about local problems based on indigenous information. They must be permitted to use their own judgment in prioritizing their goals, with or without input from citizens.

A sense of what this means can be gleaned from the arrangements that were made to ensure officers' autonomy in the neighborhood police teams in which the decentralization movement had its inception in the 1970s. The Policy and Procedures Manual for a Team in Holyoke, Massachusetts, for example, was drafted by team members, and it provides that "changes in or additions to this manual can be initiated by the members of the Team" (Holyoke Police Department, 1970). The manual says that "questions concerning decision-making authority should normally be decided in favor of the most decentralized level consistent with the achievement of the objective of effective policing for the Team's jurisdiction." In case the import of this is not quite clear, the following sentence reads, "in cases where provisions of this manual conflict with the general policies and procedures of the Holyoke Police Department, the provisions of this manual will be followed by Team members except in emergencies when the Team control is returned to the regular departmental chain of command."

The Holyoke Team consisted of 15 members, including the director, who held the rank of captain. All 15 members had a vote in the Committee of the Whole, which was responsible for "Team organization and management matters." Specific topics were dealt with by standing and ad hoc committes of officers.

A Police–Community Relations Council, chaired by the team director, was made up of six neighborhood residents and two officers. The team director was to be "the principal liaison officer between the team and the remainder of the Police Department." He was officer in charge, but the manual says that "generally, the team's activities will be carried out as a group effort extensively employing the techniques of participating (sic) management." As an example, "in any instance where two-thirds of the Team members recommend dismissal of a Team member the Project Director shall respect their judgment and the officer shall be dropped from the team." The officers allocated themselves the task of reviewing and investigating charges of misconduct directed at team members.

The officers were not to be dispatched outside their turf (they had their own dispatcher), and "except in response to serious situations, officers of the Police Department who are not members of the Team shall not be dispatched to handle activities or situations occurring within the Team's area of responsibility." The team's turf was off-limits to Department members, except by request. If the Team requested assistance, however, "no officer of the Holyoke Police Department shall refuse...regardless of the area of assignment."

Team members could prepare proposals for obtaining grants and could "assist citizens, community groups and government agencies in their efforts to obtain financial support for programs related to reducing police problems and improving police service in the Team area." The team headquarters was open "for community members' use and service," and the team was instructed to "concentrate on a philosophy of service and prevention rather than suppression of crime and disorder." "Negative law enforcement techniques and force" were to be used as "a last resort."

The team could evaluate its performance and that of its members. It could set its own goals. Team members could even "wear a variety of uniform and nonuniform clothing," to symbolize their autonomy.

AUTONOMY IN PROBLEM-ORIENTED POLICING

The community-oriented officer needed decentralization so he or she could get to know people in a neighborhood and get to be known by them. The community-oriented officer also wanted to become familiar with local problems, which is a goal he or she shared with the problem-oriented officer. Goldstein (1990) points out that

> while some problems can be viewed as citywide and relatively uniform wherever they occur, most have a local character to them or may even be unique to a specific beat. It requires officers close to a community to identify them and to deal with them. (p. 160)

This view did not impress itself on traditional police chiefs, who valued standardization of policies and uniform procedures. Goldstein (1990) notes that

> upon reflection, the move to centralize control and standardize procedures undervalued the importance in policing of knowledge about the specific community being policed. It also undervalued the importance of the type of relationship maintained with the community. (p. 159)

Of course, the issue of standardization versus adaptation to local conditions is not an either/or issue. For many situations, across-the-board rules are appropriate, and they ensure evenhandedness, equity, and fairness. Due process concerns, for one, must always be uniformly observed, and citizens must be treated with invariant probity and decency.

Enforcement problems may be reasonably comparable across neighborhoods, and where this is so the response that is used in one neighborhood may be applicable to other neighborhoods. But problems often also vary to some degree from place to place and the "fit" of solutions can also vary, to the point of inappropriateness. The study of variations in problems tells us whether standard solutions are appropriate or variations in responses should be tried.

Problem-oriented policing addresses situations in which sensitivity to local conditions is important. In such situations officers who are familiar with localities are in a better position to study problems than staff assigned to planning and research units. That is not to say that decentralized problem solving is essential, but that it makes sense where problems vary from place to place. With decentralization, one can create combinations of community policing with problem-oriented policing, and kill two birds (community relations and closeness to data) with the same stone.

Does decentralization also require autonomy? Probably not, but groups of persons who work at a distance from headquarters often develop their own loyalties and esprit de corps. Moreover, they may resist instructions by central office executives who they feel are ignorant of local conditions. The executives, in turn, may fear that decentralization has the potential to increase the incidents of police running amok (Kelling, 1988, p. 7).

AUTONOMY AND MORALE

We have noted that problem-oriented officers often show very high morale and motivation; the same holds true of community-oriented officers. Geographical decentralization is one reason community police program participants tend to feel liberated and demonstrate high levels of morale. The Flint (Michigan) foot patrol program, an exemplar community policing venture, boasts about the fact that officers have turned down promotions to remain on the job. A questionnaire administered to the officers showed that

> Many of the foot officers saw themselves as the "chief of police" of their beat areas. Their expertise ranged from helping residents install burglar alarms to conducting meetings in order to determine the priorities on which to focus crime fighting activities. Some foot officers emphasized activities and programs for the elderly, while other officers worked with juveniles or spent much of their time in public education forums. They viewed themselves as "professionals" writing articles for community newsletters, interacting with other community agency professionals, both in their uniforms and out, and making statements and presentations to the media...
>
> The program promoted the development of a clear role identity among foot patrol officers legitimized by both the police department and the community. It also permitted a degree of autonomy in exercising the role. (Trojanowicz and Banas, 1985, pp. 11–12)

Goldstein (1987) paints a similar picture, speaking of community–policing programs across the country. He writes that

> Most striking, for me, have been my observations of the impact that community policing has had on the police officers involved in these programs. The officers with whom I have walked and talked express immense satisfaction in getting to know citizens more intimately, in following up on their initial contact, and in seeing the results of their efforts. They like being helpful. They enjoy the freedom and independence they are given to be creative and imaginative, and to take the initiative in dealing with problems. And perhaps most important, they appreciate the trust that the programs place in them. (p. 28)

Autonomy, of course, has a possible downside if it brings loss of organizational support. Some officers have tried to retain the admiration of peers by playing the supercop (enforcement-oriented) role. But where service goals are salient, peer support may be lost and a different equation must apply. In this equation the "community connection" must make up for attenuation of the "police connection." Citizen esteem must partly substitute for departmental and peer support relinquished by involvement in service-oriented community-centered policing. Trojanowicz and Banas (1985), for example, tell us that

> The foot officers began to view the community as the reference point for job enrichment and satisfaction rather then depending on the police subculture. Their sometimes cynical motor colleagues became less and less important as a necessary support group. The foot officers could be innovative and did not need to worry about bearing the brunt of criticism or ridicule from either their supervisors or community residents. (p. 12)

Any review of work motivation concepts (Chapter 3) suggests that persons who define their own jobs can have their self-esteem and actualization needs satisfied. They can also make or enhance their reputations. Some (Dirty Harry and his ilk) can get prestige from being headbusters; others (service-oriented officers) can gain the gratitude of service recipients. For some, the source of adulation is the peer group; for others, it is clients; in both cases, what the officer does is valued by others and earns admiration. It also becomes meaningful to the officer and is a source of satisfaction and pride.

Wycoff, who studied community-oriented programs, writes that officers can progress through a process that includes

- Officer recognition (to their surprise) that most citizens welcome the opportunity to interact with police;
- A feeling that patrol work could be more interesting than they had realized;
- A sense of pride in their work;
- A growth in their sense of efficacy and personal competence (example of this being the officer who, over the course of the project, ceased referring to himself as a "plain ole, dumb ole cop" and began instead to think of himself as a leader in the neighborhood he served);
- A recognition that there are many ways to approach policing; and
- An identification with the profession of policing, which extended beyond the officers' own organization, as they become aware of officers in other departments attempting to conduct similar programs. (p. 111)

The list of rewards can vary, but the principle is the same: autonomy permits officers to shape the work to maximize goals they feel matter because of the results that are achieved.

BUT WHAT OF QUALITY CONTROL?

Some police administrators find this picture enticing, but others regard it with reserve and remind us that freedom to do good is freedom to do harm. "A cop's morale tells you nothing," they note. "Dirty Harry loved the work. So, no doubt, did Jack the Ripper." As for community input, they might say, "Have you ever heard of Corruption? Who is it who does the bribing? And what of local prejudice? Should cops arrest neighborhood misfits to gain citizen approval? Use shortcuts and clobber people? Protect lawbreakers who are held in esteem? Community input is great, but is no substitute for principled supervision."

The point is that police are presumably a unique profession. Officers have the right to use force and can invoke or not invoke the law at their pleasure. Police actions can have tragic consequences. "If that team screws up," the chief asks, "who do you think takes the heat?" A further point is that autonomy can be regressive: "The nostalgia bit is apt," the chief might say, "it took 60 years to get professional police. Why turn the clock back?"

The view is not as Tayloristic as it sounds. Taylor's concern was with getting lazy people to work. Police management has a different worry, which has to do with honesty, integrity, law-abidingness, evenhandedness, self-control, and legality.[5] Chiefs will relinquish their concern with *quantity* of police product (incident accounting) but stand less ready to abrogate supervision of *quality* (monitoring of misbehavior), which has been a sore point for police managers.

The Oakland project we have reviewed is relevant and instructive, because it showed us that peer pressure can reduce misconduct, and a peer-run quality-control entity can modify behavior. This is doubly important because the subculture often opposes managerial monitoring and protects deviants to spite management (Westley, 1970). The subculture may not succeed in this effort (it often does not) and may disapprove of the behavior the manager has sanctioned (it mostly does), but morale suffers with interventions that come unilaterally from above.

Experience in industry has increasingly suggested (Ouichi, 1981) that the control of work quality can be exercised on assembly lines if responsibility is relegated to workers. Such transfer of responsibility does not involve an abrogation of power, since managers can monitor rank-and-file controls and can intervene where needed. But workers who are trusted to share concerns with quality of product (which is not an inborn monopoly of managers) do not react like workers who feel mistrusted and who are stereotyped as sloppy and corruptable.

Experiments in community policing require trust and arrangements in which quality control is left to officers with input from citizens. Officers must be assumed to care about quality policing, and this trust may be furthered by selecting the first officers carefully, and by preintervention training in which quality goals and methods are defined by groups of managers and officers. Subsequent redefining (possibly in joint groups) can cement trust over time.

Citizens must also be presumed to value the quality of police service. Where they do not show such concern, the hope must be that they are educable. However, where citizens continue to make demands that would lower quality of service, they must be politely rebuffed.

COMPOSITE STRATEGIES

Wycoff suggests (see p. 249) that community-oriented policing implies that "police and citizens should work together to solve problems." This sort of definition raises the question: Can problem-oriented policing be community-oriented policing, and vice versa? There are obviously instances where the answer is "yes." One program—the Community Patrol Officer (CPO) program in New York City—has even self-consciously and consistently seen itself as in the community-policing and problem-solving business. The program is envisaged as a hybrid by those who provide its technical support (the Vera Foundation), and it has been researched to see whether it lives up to the model. It is, moreover, a large-scale program, involving nine (sometimes, ten) officers in each of 75 police precincts in the city of New York.

An official manual of the CPO program proclaims that "of all functions of Community Patrol Officers, the most important, and the one that makes CPOP different from other Department deployment strategies, is problem solving. Without problem solving as its foundation, CPOP makes little sense" (Vera Institute of Justice, 1988, p. 4). Community police officers are instructed to follow a sequential process in which they (1) discover and identify a problem, (2) analyze the problem, (3) design a tailor-made response, (4) get support for the response, (5) implement the solution, (6) evaluate its effectiveness, and (7) repeat the sequence if necessary.

Community police officers are provided with a definition of "problem" to help them know a problem when they see one. The definition reads:

> Sometimes problems come right up and bite you. Other times you have to sneak up on them before you can realize that it is a real problem that you're dealing with. In the simplest terms, a problem is anything that can have a negative effect on the community you are working in—something that causes harm to members of the community or is a potential source of disorder. Problems are generally a source of great concern to residents of the community, and they are not likely to go away unless something is done to correct them. (Vera Institute of Justice, 1988, p. 5)

Community police officer team members are instructed to use citizens on their beats as a source of problem definition. They are also trained to use their powers of observation and to rely on other sources, such as fellow-officers, departmental records, agency representatives, and the press. They are told to do serious, formal pattern analyses and to "look for similarities in crime patterns, time distributions of crimes, locations, etc." (Vera Institute of Justice, 1988, p. 5). In tackling a pattern thus analyzed, the officers are told that "the strategy chosen must go beyond the incident and address the underlying problem" and that "the solution should provide a substantial improvement for the residents of the community, reducing both harm to them, and fear of future harm" (p. 13). As for the range of solutions, they are told that the sky is the limit, but that combinatory solutions are better than simple solutions. Moreover, the officers are told, "Don't be limited by traditional police responses. There is nothing wrong with enforcement as a tactic, but it has its limitations, and on some problems it just doesn't work" (p. 21).

The officers are assured that they need not work alone. They are told that "the solutions to some problems are within the capacity of the community to carry out themselves. Community police officers can play a critical role in helping citizens join together to work on a problem and in guiding them through the necessary steps" (p. 17). Officers are also enjoined to "reach out and network" (p. 20), to collaborate with other police and public and private agencies in solving problems. They are given instructions, such as with respect to

> Other City or Private Agencies: Here is where networking comes in—reaching out to find out who does what, and how, and if they don't, who you can call next. Don't be afraid of calling another agency. Begin at the level of execution (the workers) or their supervisors, and work your way up. Find out if they can do what it is you need done. Whose approval do they need? What's the process? Who has to be asked? Does it have to be in writing? Who has to sign the request? After you find all of this out, run it past the CPOP supervisor for his or her approval. (p. 24)

HOW DOES IT WORK?

The CPO program began on a limited scale and was assessed by outside observers. Two of the observers (Weisburd and McElroy, 1988) praised CPO problem-solving efforts, but noted a difference in the problems the officers faced over time. When the officers first arrived, residents made suggestions that the officers found helpful, and during this phase "most of the problems the CPOs focused upon were quality of life concerns that were seldom addressed by regular patrol officers" (p. 91). The quality-of-life emphasis may have seemed surprising, but "residents often told CPOs that they were more disturbed by these problems than by crimes, because the former represented constant annoyances" (p. 92).

Over time, the officers found the residents less discriminating in their suggestions and less helpful in setting priorities. As one officer put it,

> When you've solved a problem or addressed a problem and the community sees that it's addressed, they give you something else. I went from drug selling to beer drinking and loud radios down to the stupidest thing. Yesterday, a lady told me a Sanitation guy didn't pick up her trash. (cit. pp. 92–93)

The proliferation of parochial requests led officers to use other data sources (such as crime statistics) or to selectively address specialized concerns, such as those of senior citizens or teenagers. By this time, some officers made many observations of the neighborhood underworld, and they decided to become crime fighters. Drug-dealing emporia came to particularly engage their attention. Weisburd and McElroy (1988) observed that "officers devoted significant portions of patrol time to individual locations, during which they would use a series of aggressive patrol tactics against those they believed were involved in the drug trade" (p. 94). Though community police officers had been strongly enjoined to use a broad array of problem-solving strategies, they became extraordinarily enforcement oriented and made many arrests. One reason for this special focus was that, "in the view of the CPOs, these enforcement actions gained them respect and status from patrol officers and precinct supervisors" (p. 94).

The officers showed enthusiasm, ingenuity, and initiative in rousting small-time hoodlums. They "might surprise those involved by, for example, jumping out of the van after coming down a one-way street in the wrong direction" (p. 95). Such routines were satisfying to the officers and created discomfort to the miscreants, who were forced to change their work schedules and locations. But it would probably be hard to argue that neighborhood drug problems were being solved, except in the short run.

On the positive side, officers did manage to enlist help and often received support from citizens. In one case, for example,

> CPOs utilized beer drinkers in a local park to alleviate an ongoing drug problem there. They told a group of young men that they could continue to drink beer in the park only if they were neat and threw away the bottles after they were done. The CPOs added another condition to their bargain; that the beer drinkers get rid of the drug sellers in the park. The latter group was, in fact, convinced by the former to cease sales in that public area. (p. 97)

More prevalently, officers in the project complained about citizen passivity and confessed that they could not inspire much citizen action. Community organizing is a difficult task for police, and the same holds true for problem analysis in problem-oriented policing.

STUDYING PROBLEMS

To be problem oriented, a CPO program must involve officers in research; to be community oriented, a problem-solving program must involve citizens and be neighborhood-based. Most programs do not meet all these requisites, though the Baltimore County (COPE) program approximates the model, as does New York's CPO program. Our skid row unit (Chapter 1) comes similarly close.

How has the model been partly compromised in other interventions? One point of slippage is in the way police problems are studied. We have seen (Chapters 6 through 8) that doing social science work is not always enticing nor exciting to officers. Men and women of action prefer to take action, which does not mean perusing tables. A modest survey (say, on fear) may be fun for a time (Brown and Wycoff, 1987), but we have seen that some officers have not enjoyed it (Taft, 1986). Moreover, a mandate to do academic-sounding research, such as "study demographic profiles," may strain officers' patience and lower their morale. Chief Burgreen of the San Diego police made this point about a community problem-oriented experience he attempted to promote:

> What it did was take beat officers and have them do their jobs a little differently—have them become students of their community rather than just climb in a car and go police every day. They were to study the ethnicity, the demographics of the community, the crime problems, the social service and referral agencies available, the community leaders, community organizations, and to literally know everything that was on that beat, and then to attempt to interact with the community and community leaders to impact neighborhood problems....
>
> A year later we attempted to implement it department-wide, calling it Community-Oriented Policing.... We had some problems, which primarily revolved around the inability or the lack of desire of a lot of officers to become

students. In a focused, grant-type environment, we were able to generally gain the compliance and support of officers to become that really tough student of the beat, and do the homework required. But department-wide, we found there were some officers who enjoyed it and some who thought that they quit doing homework when they left high school...Now we are literally doing the work for them in providing them with the material so that they don't have to go out and develop it. We're also using videotapes to introduce the officers to their areas. (Burgreen, 1989, p. 12)

The San Diego police opted for a compromise solution in which some officers continued to do community policing and others (whom the chief called the "homework squad") gathered and analyzed data:

We have a staff of officers and analysts who work in our Operations Support Unit. Instead of everybody doing a little, we decided that we're going to take some people who are real good at this, and who understand what we're trying to do, and that's going to be their job. They're going to do it for everyone. Then we're going to have a training program where people are taught how to use this material. (p. 12)

The model is a defensible one but deprives its participants of certain benefits.[6] The operations support staff may lack feedback and closure, since they feed information to others and cannot tell whether it is used. The officers who receive information have no strong incentive to take it seriously, since it does not respond to questions they have asked. The applicability of demographics may not be obvious, though the chief had argued eloquently for the relevance of statistics:

People say, "What's this got to do with police work?" Well, it's got a lot to do with it. People who are poor, people who live in densely crowded housing, are much more likely to engage in certain kinds of conduct than other people are. People who live in upper-class neighborhoods are much more concerned about different issues. That gives you a basis from which to start understanding your community and work with them. (p. 14)

Another difficulty is that the word "problem" has become ambiguous and adaptable to predilections. Crack dealers in a building can be seen as a "problem" if fashionable language (as in the CPOP) makes them so. Unfortunately, the responses to a problem thus defined may be indistinguishable from those of incident-driven policing. A stakeout is a stakeout and a raid a raid, no matter who conducts them. A stakeout does not become "the exploration of a problem" because the responding officers are CPOs. Nor does it help for the officers to have invoked neighbors as problem definers if they learn nothing new from these neighbors. Citizens who are indifferent to drug transactions on their doorsteps are predictably difficult to come by and officers know this. For officers to poll citizens to obtain rubber-stamp confirmation is to belabor the obvious. Referring to citizen complaints is a ritual if it does not modify what officers do.

Citizen-informants do provide data, and CPOs are more likely to elicit them. They know their turfs intimately and can develop trust. They may also be skilled and ingenious at locating informants. For instance, "CPOs say that the answer often lies in finding the neighborhood *busybody,* often a retired person who keeps track of everything going on, including the neighborhood's drug problems" (Trojanowicz and Bucqueroux, 1989, p. 3). Such gambits improve the CPO's ability to do incident-driven policing, but one wonders what they do for problem-oriented policing.

A CPO can do all sorts of policing, of course, in all sorts of combinations. For instance, the officer may invoke problem-oriented policing in tandem with incident-driven policing. According to Trojanowicz and Bucqueroux (1989), drug crime fighting lends itself to a sequential approach, which moves from incident driven to problem centered:

> Most often, the first priority in many areas is to reduce open dealing, to stabilize the neighborhood, then focus on indiscreet dealing to maintain the pressure. As the area begins to improve, the CPO can brainstorm with people in the community about new ways to address the broader spectrum of drug problems. This might mean linking addicts to proper treatment. Or it could include working with area businesses to provide jobs for recovering addicts. (p. 5)

The activity in the example ends up problem oriented because it attacks underlying conditions by addressing employment issues and linking addicts to treatment. It is community oriented because it involves joint thinking by officers and citizens. It is also both in that what the officers and citizens "brainstorm" about are ways of dealing with underlying conditions ("the broad spectrum of drug problems"). The issue of what is problem oriented or not does not lie in the distinction between enforcement versus nonenforcement options, though there is somewhat of a correlation. Incident-driven goals are always short-term enforcement goals achievable through acts such as arresting dealers. Problem-oriented approaches have a wider range of goals (such as reducing addiction rates), which are easier to pursue when shorter-term goals have been met.

According to Goldstein (1990), all problem-oriented policing is an effort by police to address a problem. If citizens are involved, it is as co-students of the problem and partners in the effort to solve it. The citizens are in part enlisted because their help is needed: "If, in exploring the problem, the police conclude that it could be eliminated or significantly reduced by some form of community involvement, they then set out to bring about such involvement (p. 24)." Invoking citizens becomes especially profitable with longer-term goals. In incident-driven community policing, citizens are supportive (and sometimes bloodthirsty) cheerleaders, as is the chorus in a Greek play. This contribution cements relations and advances good will. It does not go beyond these benefits and no one is likely to learn to solve problems by being a cheerleader. Learning only occurs if citizens ask problem-oriented questions, such as, "How does one actually address the crack problem in this neighborhood, as opposed to inducing some of the dealers to take unscheduled vacations?"

Such questions are substantial and require the acquisition of knowledge, the drawing of inferences, the planning of action, and the monitoring of results. These activities promote enlarged perspectives and spark ingenuity. They foster learning in that the indigenous experience of citizens and the street experience of officers can be merged in thinking together. Learning can be further enhanced by doing research (such as interviewing drug users) or using social science data to the extent to which data are available. Citizen–officer study groups can work with police planning and research units. They can also benefit by inviting experts to whom they can pose grounded questions. The experts would be addressing persons who have practical experience, which means that they would have to be plausible (congruent with experience) in their analysis of problems. Should the experts pass such tests, they could learn a lot themselves and gain the benefit of having their knowledge used.

Solutions can be assessed in light of street knowledge (by citizens) and street sense (by officers). This means that the solutions cannot be faddish nostrums because they must make sense in terms of local conditions known to both officers and citizens, which are unfamiliar to bureaucrats and planners.

Officer–citizen problem-solving projects are experiments that could take many shapes, which include, (1) all sorts of variations in group composition, (2) separate (homogeneous) and combined (heterogeneous) sessions, (3) creation of task forces to explore special topics, (4) meetings with policy makers, officials, or service staff, (5) use of researchers to collect or process data, (6) joint presentations by officers and citizens to decision makers, and (7) networking among groups who explore comparable problems in different communities.

A strategy of this kind could be dramatically timely, given the endemic nature of some problems, such as drug-related crime (Chapter 12), which impinge painfully on many citizens, demand police action, and defy short-term solutions. Such problems cannot be solved without some concerted effort addressed at underlying conditions. And it makes sense for such efforts to be initiated (as they were decades ago in Oakland) by those who are closest to the problems, and have the greatest stake in ameliorating them.

LINKING BACKYARDS

Community policing is by definition local because that is what communities are. Though neighborhood boundaries may be evanescent boundaries, they exist psychologically. Citizens become most upset or angry about threats, such as crimes, that occur in their neighborhoods. Events on one's own side of one's border impinge on "us" or "the community;" events on the other side have less intimate significance.

Problems are often defined ethnocentrically or parochially, and so are solutions. In many communities, the winning of the drug war (see Chapter 12) means chasing drug dealers out of one's neighborhood into the next one. This delightful achievement becomes a cause for celebration, no matter what it does to folks who live outside the community.

Police who are assigned to a neighborhood can come to share this sort of perspective; in fact, police may be mandated to do so in community policing. But police agency responsibility straddles neighborhoods, and this leads to ambivalence where a community "solution" poses problems for other areas served by the police. The same dilemma faces service providers who serve broad categories of clients, including problem persons who can be chased across neighborhood frontiers.

The nature of the issue becomes clearest with "sundowning" (citizens who buy one-way bus tickets for undesirables) but it transcends the effect of shifting a problem from one location to another. Any time a group is concerned with only its own share of a problem, it implies indifference to those who have the problem elsewhere. NIMBY (not in my backyard) can come to mean IABYBM (in anyone's yard but mine); at minimum, it relegates the sweeping of backyards to those who occupy them.

Parochialism is inevitable in the short run, but it must be counteracted over time. As community policing has spread across neighborhoods and localities, its sponsors have built direct bridges from one experiment to another to enlarge the perspectives of officers and citizens. One means of doing this is to arrange for cluster conferences (Chapter 4) that link problem-oriented groups with each other. This linking is analogous to that of self-help therapy groups, where individuals discover that their problems are not unique and that it is possible for persons with the same problem to assist and support each other. If a solution that has been adopted in one neighborhood seems applicable to another, we can offer peer assistance to speed the second intervention and enhance its effectiveness. This process gains momentum over time: Two or three self-managed housing units or tutorial programs or indigenous construction efforts can be induced to form networks that help institutionalize an intervention.

This strategy works, but can create an in-group with a sectarian flavor rather than a cosmopolitan outlook. A network may not address the connection between problems and problem areas and smaller and larger solutions. This connection must be forged by members of the network who link it to the outside world. Police representatives can serve this role if they are trained as subject matter experts. An officer with expertise in homelessness or accident causation or family disturbances can assist a community that faces the problem by putting the local pattern in context, without shortchanging its unique character. In analogous fashion, service providers can tell community residents, "we are here to help solve your problem, but our mission is to ameliorate the problem wherever it occurs. In fact, we hope that your efforts, if they are successful, can make it easier for us to help others who share your problem."

Such messages carry two connotations. The first connotation (dramatized in *The Music Man*) has to do with defining the problem in such a way that local concerns become part of something larger than themselves. The invitation to a transcendent definition says, "River City's problem can best be appreciated if we take a look at the outside world. When we do, we can notice that billiard halls elsewhere have led to a proliferation of massage parlors and other manifestation of moral decay. Far from being alone, you people in River City fight shoulder to shoulder with other communities that are as concerned as you are about unsavory trends in the use of leisure time." The other connotation has to do with the importance of local achievements (such as the advent of the River City Marching Band), given the needs of other communities, who are desperate and hungry for ingenious ideas, such as the potential of musicianship as an antidote to licentiousness.

The war on drugs (Chapter 12) is an example of a successful problem definition. It makes an insular perspective difficult because the problem (drug/crime) has been publicized as of concern to everyone. The next challenge, which is harder, is to make communities who feel part of the problem also feel that they are contributors to solving the problem. This requires linking local drug-fighting efforts to the national war on drugs and not by working from above (by disseminating solutions devised by strategists). Instead, it means using local solutions and disseminating them, because for communities to feel that they are part of the war, they must see it as a guerrilla war. Such wars are won by deploying local strategies that have demonstrated success.

A community-oriented, problem-oriented approach lends itself to the type of drug war that this prescription implies, and we outline the approach in our next and last chapter.

NOTES

1. Skogan (1990) concurs with this view. In the first of several principles of community policing he advances he says that "Community Policing assumes a commitment to broadly-focused, problem-oriented policing" (p. 91). Such principles are statements of ideal, or desiderata. This becomes clear with Skogan's fourth principle, which reads, "Community Policing implies a commitment to helping neighborhoods help themselves, by serving as a catalyst for local organizing and education efforts" (p. 92). Skogan assumes this is the case, but has limited faith in the prospect of organizing deteriorated neighborhoods. (See Note 4.)

2. The nostalgia has a basis in fact. Historians have shown that "the urban police acquired welfare responsibilities as the (nineteenth) century progressed, and then lost them to specialist agencies around the beginning of the twentieth century (Emsley, 1983, p. 109). Monkkonen (1981) reports that

> Almost from their inception in the middle of the nineteenth century until the beginning of the twentieth, American police departments regularly provided a social service that from our perspective seems bizarrely out of character—they provided bed and, sometimes, board for homeless poor people, tramps. Year after year these "lodgers," as the police referred to them, swarmed to the police stations in most large cities, where they found accommodations ranging in quality from floors in hallways to clean bunkrooms. Often, especially in the winter or during depression years, there would be food, usually soup—nothing fancy, but something. During very bad depression years or harsh winters, the number of overnight lodgings provided by a police department exceeded all annual arrests. (pp. 86–87)

When social service agencies came into existence, the police helped them to perform former police functions. One service the police had been performing involved returning lost children to their parents. This task became the responsibility of child protective associations. According to Monkkonen (1981),

> A typical police–NYSPCC interaction involved the police discovering child abuse or neglect, or in some cases a child offender, after which the police asked the society to intervene and take the case. Often the society placed children in foster or orphan homes and actively aided in the criminal prosecution of parents. Concurrent with these forms of police–private cooperation, the police began more and more to use the society's assistance in dealing with lost children. In 1877, the society helped return only twenty-five lost children to their parents; twenty years later, the figure had leapt ten times to 2,810 lost children returned. Clearly, this private agency accounted for a substantial portion of the decline in the number of lost children returned by the police in New York. (p. 127)

3. Kelling (undated) pointed out that beat foot patrol officers in the nineteenth century were already seen as manifesting such problems. He writes that

> Integration of police into neighborhoods isolated officers from other police...Their sympathy with community norms and their ability to isolate themselves from the police organization led to other problems, including corruption and unequal enforcement. Both merchants and illegal liquor operators were in a position to pay police officers to "look the other way" when

unpopular antiliquor laws were broken. Many communities did not want "outsiders" (ethnically different people) to come into their neighborhoods. Often sympathetic to such feelings, police (and gangs) provided the means by which such outsiders were kept out. Local politicians interested in maintaining themselves in office often recruited police assistance to extend their tenure. (p. 2)

4. Skogan (1990) describes two sets of police interventions—one in Newark and the other in Houston—which showed impact favoring more receptive segments of the community. He concludes that "one of the greatest problems is that it is difficult to organize low-income, heterogeneous, deteriorating, high-turnover, disorderly neighborhoods" (p. 169).

5. Typical of mistrust from above that invites resentment below is a recent New York City Police decision to subject officers to random drug tests. Under the new rule, 10% of the force (2,600 officers) would be tested every year. The *New York Times* noted that "the proposal is expected to draw a strong reaction from the patrolmen's association" (McKinley, 1989). In the long run, actions such as this one, that are designed to control deviance, often boomerang. They tend to cement solidarity and promote norms (like silence) that protect deviants from scrutiny by management. This in turn limits information that management can get and inspires new surveillance efforts which escalate resistance.

6. The qualification applies to the officer-as-research-consumer model, not to the San Diego Police Department, which stands at the forefront of community policing and problem-oriented policing. The San Diego police have originated a plethora of ingenious solutions to problems encountered in their city and its vicinity.

12

A Problem-Oriented War on Drugs

The introduction to a recent report (Police Executive Research Forum, 1989b) includes the documented claim that "for tackling drug problems, the problem-oriented approach is an idea whose time has come" (p. 2). The report concludes by noting that "of greatest importance is the development of a thought process for police that fosters both creative and collaborative solutions to specific problems. This development stands in stark contrast to the application of global measures for all drug problems" (p. 18).

Actually, an effective antidrug program must combine several approaches if it is to make a difference. The first move is typically a traditional move and consists of a set of sweeps that clear the deck to make the problem manageable. Later moves must include community-policing components, because partnership with law-abiding citizens is a requisite for success in drug fighting. The problem definition in drug-related interventions must be long term, but the gains we accept must be incremental.

TOWARD A PROBLEM-ORIENTED PROCESS

One difference between the connotations of "problem oriented" and "problem solving" is that "to solve" has an optimistic, can-do flavor, implying a product (a solution) and a good chance of attaining it. The word "oriented" does not promise results, but suggests a directionality that can be sustained through stick-with-it perseverence.

The prospects of eliminating a problem are attractive, but there are limits to what police (or anyone else, for that matter) can do: social problems such as the drug problem are always connected to other social problems and often embedded in wider societal contexts over which localities—and the police that serve them—have little influence and control.

Such depressing thoughts do not bother us with standard enforcement activity, which has built-in payoffs. The payoff in drug sweeps lies in the capture of suspects who are swept off the street, and added payoff occurs if the sweepees are jailed, convicted, and imprisoned. The point is to "get" offenders and one can "get" them, which is a tangible result. It becomes irrelevant (though regrettable) if one discovers that neighborhood drug traffic is reinstated and that arrestees, who overcrowd prisons for a time, rejoin their trade with unabated vigor.

In "solving" problems, limited results can similarly be obtained by targeting short-term changes. Goals can be unambitiously defined and criteria of success (desired behavior change) can be modestly framed and circumscribed. For example:

> **The problem**   Shameless drug trafficking, corner Broadway and Seventh.
>
> **Analysis**   Drug bazaars have been set up at this location because it is dark and isolated. The corner offers privacy, which is a commodity prized by drug retailers.
>
> **Solution 1**   Patrol the area intensively for four weeks, as unpredictably as possible.
>
> **Results**   Bazaars shut down for seven weeks.
>
> **Solution 1A**   Repeat the process.
>
> **Results**   Bazaars shut down for ten weeks.
>
> **Solutions 1C, 1D**   Hit them again, Sam!
>
> **Results** (eventually):   Bazaars shut down and move to Broadway and Twelfth.

Or, alternatively, one can invoke another agency (the power company) and claim a commendable interagency solution:

> **Solution 2**   Arrange for installation of high-intensity-street lights.
>
> **Results**   Bazaars move to Broadway and Twelfth.

Or, even better,

> **Solution 2**   Arrange for high-intensity lights.
>
> **Results**   Bazaars move. Their present location is unknown.

Such "solutions" can be disseminated to other police departments so that streetlights can proliferate, while levels of drug trafficking are unaffected. The "solution" is a pseudo-solution, but it looks tangible and has circumvented the obduracy of the addiction problem as a target of change.

Interventions that are relevant to problems like addiction must consider the force fields in which the behavior is embedded and must "play into" motives that sustain or resist the behavior. Results one can attain are typically modest and depend on the validity of one's working assumptions. For example:

The problem As before, drug trafficking, corner Broadway and Seventh.

Analysis The bazaars happen to be located in an area of many Protestant churches noted for high religiosity. Young addicts would have had religious upbringing of recent vintage. Could religious beliefs predispose against addiction if they were mobilized?

Intervention 1 Arrange for church choirs to sing hymns on the corner during peak business hours.

Intervention 2 Install illuminated billboards with messages such as "The Cops May Not See You, But God Does." (Consult clergy and advertising council for content).

Hoped-for result Slight reduction in number of customers.

Levels of Causation and Intervention

Most of the social problems police have encountered in communities with problems are problems that must be tackled on various fronts before one can expect results. Our own Oakland experience (Chapters 5 through 10) was simple because a single variable—the contribution of maladaptive officers—responded to a salient intervention—regenerative peer influence—enough to make a difference. Even here, however, the achievement (conflict reduction) had unforeseen effects (diminished productivity) and the "solution" proved impermanent, as new variables (municipal budget constraints) entered the equation.

What makes the Oakland effort an amenable paradigm is the hypothesized level of causation (individual). This problem definition meant that the entry point to the problem could be the police locker room and that no change agents beyond police were required. If there is complexity to a problem, this implies more levels of causation and entry points. Causation levels and entry points in turn determine the types of change agents one needs to attack the problem. If the problem is one that is not structurally embedded, it might be a problem that still could be addressed with remedial services. If one wants to deal with drug addicts whose only problem is addiction, for example, our Family Crisis Intervention model may be applicable. A referral network of treatment programs can supplement concerned police as germane change agents. Where problems cannot be explained with individual-level types of explanations, community members are often needed as agents of change. Peer-centered interventions, for example, can tackle contracultural norms, such as those of drug-oriented gangs. Neighborhood groups can dispel apathy in a drug-ridden community, create new sources of people power, and channel activity into neighborhood revival and into demands for external resources that may be needed to get the job done.

The equation also holds in reverse. The more diversified the kinds of change agents one can press into service, the more complex the variables one can envisage as "handles" to one's problem. In this sense, problem analysis must accommodate prespecified complexity. Variables that one cannot affect (poverty, for instance, or drug overlords) are useless for analytic purposes. Such variables may illuminate causation, but do not help us when we try to define the problem-as-target. Interventionists need insights that help them deal with a problem they can address and cannot afford to see the "total," global problem, as an academic (or a person from Mars) may see it.

Interventionists must also preserve the integrity of problem-oriented science, which builds on experiments in which one reduces crime-related problems by attacking their hypothesized causes. Whenever we assault a variable we have nominated as causal, we hope the severity or incidence rate of symptoms will be reduced. And we must regard our analysis as validated where solutions that are based on our analysis work and invalidated where they do not work. When we cannot operationalize our variables, we cannot tell whether they are valid or invalid. Such variables, therefore, must be taken or discarded on faith, which is not a scientific enterprise.

Empirical knowledge does grow, but it grows incrementally. We can learn from community-oriented experiments individually, but we also learn from them cumulatively and in the aggregate. Police learn that given interventions work in some places but not in others.[1] Other interventions (such as Family Crisis Intervention Units) work across settings, despite differences of environment. Variations suggest specificity of cause; parallel experiences point to the existence of general principles, which can build a science of problem-oriented intervention.

Experiences in specific communities also instructively cumulate. To work on many problems in one setting builds setting-related expertise in interventionists, who learn from successes and failures what they must do to improve their community, using approaches that are applicable to new and different problems over time. Both types of experience are important because they allow for effort that is cumulative and ongoing. The point of such effort is not to "solve" problems but to engender "problem orientation" as a strategy for meaningful (as opposed to gimmicky) change.

BARRIERS TO CUMULATING KNOWLEDGE

At the current stage of the game, the war on drugs is a set of skirmishes that are separately fought. Each community that fights the war is on its own and must proceed on a trial-and-error basis to find a strategy that works. If such a strategy is found, the community that evolves it benefits, but the next one down the line may still have to start from scratch. This is so because the problems of each community are somewhat different. In other words,

> the responses of problem-solving officers are not generic: drug problems must be evaluated on an individual basis because what works in one situation will not necessarily work in another. (Police Executive Research Forum, 1989b, p. 5)

We have outlined how experiences can ultimately evolve into a science of drug fighting, given enough experiences and some way of coordinating them. In the words of one proposal, "an important goal...is to develop a flexible model that identifies what works and what doesn't" (Trojanowicz and Bucqueroux, 1990b, p. 1). The question in fact reads more like, "what works where and when, under what circumstances, and for whom?" To answer this question requires that we locate the key attributes of each intervention and the contextual factors that make them relevant. This makes it possible for interventionists to evolve a theory about why their intervention would work. A theory is something that says, "we propose to do A because the context is X and A will modify X. The reason we think A will modify X is.... "

One thing one must also know before one disseminates an intervention is "which contextual variable was relevant?" This enables the next community to ask, "is the important context in our case the same, or is it different?" Suppose that one community determines that drug dealing in their case is done by unemployed high-school students; the next community must ask whether the same holds true. The adopters must next remember that causation can vary for conditions that are superficially the same. In the first community, drug dealing may have stemmed from the unemployment of the youths. In the second case, it may result from the fact that the youths are addicted to drugs and unemployable. In the former case, providing that jobs were available (for instance, on the public payroll, or by providing incentives to employers), a training-cum-hiring intervention might have worked. Given the second scenario, this strategy could be painfully inadequate, though the situation at first glance looked identical. To take another example, one might fail to clean up an apartment complex with a program that envisaged drug-aversive tenants if the tenants turned out to be intimidated, complacent, alienated, or apathetic.

But even if we have transferable theories, this does not guarantee that strategies that are based on these theories will work when they are exported. One community may have skills or resources the second lacks or may offer a "secret ingredient" in its prescription that cannot be duplicated because it is unknown. A second reason for failure has to do with the process whereby ideas arise. An invented idea is powerful because the persons who implement it own it and have a stake in seeing it succeed. An adopted idea cannot inspire the same level of commitment and the same enthusiasm unless it is reinvented by its adopters.

A WAR ON WHAT?

Any war is fought on several fronts under the assumption that those who win on one front help those fighting on others and that this occurs at the expense of the same enemy. Reducing the demand for drugs hurts suppliers; cutting supply discomfits addicts. Both are "the enemy" in the war. It is also axiomatic that many frontline dealers are addicts and that no one cares which hat they wear when we snare them.

But not all goals are reciprocally helpful. Demand for drugs may attract supply, but the converse need not hold: We cannot create addicts by making drugs more available nor can we cure addicts by drying up supply. Closing down a dealer forces his clientele to patronize other dealers; if we close down the next dealers, the addicts look further afield. We can justify the strategy of pursuing dealers (and we shall), but not by arguing that we can thereby affect the consumption of drugs.

A good reason why we may want to discourage dealers from plying their trade is that it lets us stage a morality play for the benefit of their peer group. The war in this case is not against drugs, but against the demoralizing effect of drugs on the community—arguably a more sophisticated enemy than drugs (or drug crimes) themselves.

Harassing dealers becomes a way of encouraging self-regeneration in drug-infested communities. This goal can be an end in itself, but can also advance more traditional goals by inspiring community members to enlist in the war against drugs. The following hypothetical examples of composite interventions show how these goals can be accomplished:

> An eight-man team, the HAND (Harass Your Neighborhood Dealer) Unit, is established by the Midcity Police Department. This group is composed of officers who are lifetime weight lifters, have belts in Karate and ride motorcycles. Their assignment is to advertise their presence in a flamboyant manner wherever drugs are sold. The officers park in front of crack houses or sit on their stoop and issue citations, such as for littering or trespassing, when a customer appears. The officers also videotape dealers and customers, and chase reluctant tapees on their cycles. If officers enter a dealer's premises, they do so riding their motorcycles. If a subject resists, an officer wrestles him to the ground while the officer's partners distribute candy to neighborhood children who come to watch.

Groups of officers of this kind exist in various guises, and their purpose has been described as "to strike some fear into the hearts of drug dealers and users and maybe spark a flicker of hope in the minds of intimidated residents" (Malcolm, 1990). One such unit wears running shoes, and its members are chosen for their wit, resourcefulness, and size. Part of the group's mission is that of "psychological encouragement for law-abiding citizens" (Malcolm, 1990). Another unit uses mountain bicycles and sports bright yellow raincoats. Its goals is that of "chasing bad guys" and advancing community relations. Unit members, according to an observer, "can be seen in the basketball court of the community center, playing hoops with the children, as often as they are seen handcuffing a suspect" (Egan, 1990). Neighborhood fear is said to have diminished as a result of the fact that "these guys on bikes always seem to be around" (Egan, 1990).

Crime-fighting acts can be staged for the benefit of suspects and of the spectators one wants to energize. The point one wishes spectators to get is not only that police can protect them but that offenders can be ridiculed and intimidated, which means that they are not all-powerful and therefore need not set the neighborhood's climate. The point is not for citizens to gain confidence in police but to gain confidence in themselves. If the drug dealers are not as tough as they look, it follows that one need not acquiesce in their taking over one's neighborhood. Another message is that police have a double mission. While they pose threats to offenders, they are helpful to nonoffenders. They can therefore be talked to and worked with, if citizens wish to do something about drug trafficking themselves. Take another hypothetical example:

> Parishioners of the Midcity Mosque and the Midcity Baptist Church join to create the SOD (Stamp Out Drugs) Task Force, which approaches the police for advice and support. With police encouragement, the Task Force

organizes nightly SOD patrols. The nightly patrols are composed of three to five citizens who wear SOD hats and sweatshirts, are equipped with two-way radios, sport cameras and baseball bats, and come accompanied by large dogs that enjoy taking walks. The patrols watch for drug-related activities and alert the police when they have located suspects, so officers can be dispatched to join them at the scene. When officers arrive, SOD members take pictures of suspects, buildings, and vehicles. They are reinforced by other SOD members who arrive with homemade signs to picket the premises in which drug activity takes place. Picketing continues until drug trafficking is discouraged.

Citizen antidrug activity of this kind is increasingly occurring with help from the police. One observer of militant neighborhood groups notes that

The police have welcomed much of the new resident militancy, which is creating a new subculture of citizen involvement against drugs.... In many cases, the police have helped train anti-drug citizen groups and have informed them of what they can and cannot legally do in their fight against drug dealers. (Ayrs, 1989)

Civil libertarians are often upset at the unfettered enthusiasm displayed by citizens who become certified "good guys" in a war against the "bad guys," particularly when citizens have reason to feel vengeful and do not advertise strong concern for due process strictures. Police involvement with the groups does not reassure the civil libertarian critics because they do not trust the police. They see the public (and presumably, most of the courts) favoring an "anything goes" stance toward drug trafficking, which encourages the police to cut corners in this area (Mydans, 1989).[2]

But the enthusiasm that civil libertarians often deplore is essential for citizen groups, particularly in neighborhoods in which a sense of powerlessness or apathy has prevailed, and where activists may engage the displeasure of violent peers when they embark on their rounds. Citizen groups need to feel militant, they need appreciation and backing from the police, and all the help they can get. The last thing they need is to be equated with lynching mobs and lectured to and admonished. The same holds for the police, who are congenitally suspected of needing tight controls—including from their superiors—and who are for once liberated by the wider discretion accorded them in the units that operate in drug-infested neighborhoods.

The point that control-oriented critics miss is that the enthusiasm expressed in enterprises that engage in problem solving is a spur to the ingenuity such enterprises manifest. Though there are exceptions to the rule that enthusiasm is constructive (such as suspicious fires in one or two crack houses), the acts of the officers and citizens who are involved in drug fighting are mostly characterized by whimsy, humor, and surprising restraint. Suspects are mostly filmed with empty cameras, they are shamed rather than intimidated, and they are often arrested on minor charges instead of being prosecuted for felonies. Much thought is given by the officers in drug-fighting units to "psychological" strategies that can change the power balance in neighborhoods from dominance by drug offenders to the recapture of the streets of their law-abiding residents. The goal is to create a sense of community, and in this connection it is no coincidence that the police officers who spend time dogging the heels of nervous drug merchants spend the remainder of their time in public service-related pursuits. The quibbles of critics of police–citizen drug fighting miss the point of the war, which is self-empowerment and the promotion of grass roots democracy for citizens and the officers who assist them.

FORMAL PROBLEM-ORIENTED INTERVENTIONS

The police units we have discussed as examples are mostly not officially involved in problem-oriented policing. These units generate experience-based interventions, as did the skid row officers described in Chapter 1. Some of the units work more systematically than others, however, and some of these resemble police activities included in the landmark study in which problem-oriented police tackled the drug-crime problems of five large communities.

The study was a two-year program administered by the Police Executive Research Forum (1989b). The program included projects in Atlanta, Tampa, Philadelphia, Tulsa, and San Diego. Each project was different, but four out of five centered on public-housing complexes and developed "strategies that include an active role for both residents and management of the housing authorities" (p. 6).

The structure of the five programs is instructive: The police acted as organizer and broker and they formed a management committee or task force in which city agencies were represented. The Police Executive Research Forum supplied these task forces with a fulltime staff person, who was called a Field Technical Assistance Coordinator. With this staff person's help, each group embarked on a study of the drug problem in its area. This study included an inventory of available information and some original research:

> Project participants integrated existing data (from medical examiners, drug treatment facilities, hospitals, schools and other agencies) with information obtained through primary data sources such as community surveys,

environmental surveys, and jail debriefing forms. (Police Executive Research
Forum, 1989b, p. 6)

Based on the studies, the task forces defined drug problems they
wanted to address and strategies for addressing them. The strategies
included police units at the local level, who did studying and strategy
developing of their own. The local officers in turn involved citizens,
which meant that the approach was collaborative at every level.

In San Diego one of the strategies used was to deploy a group of foot
patrol officers for "high visibility and aggressive enforcement" (p. 8).
These officers were trained in problem-oriented policing, starting with
small-scale survey research. They discovered through surveys that residents felt afraid, helpless, and impotent, which led them to

a plan of action that would specifically address this problem: restore a "sense
of control" to residents as a means to reduce high levels of fear. Since church
affiliation of residents was their strongest organizational link, police planned
to use churches as an instrument to organize the community and restore a
sense of control. (p. 9)

A Philadelphia team did a different survey, which mapped the
physical environment of drug dealing, including "hot spots" that
seemed to facilitate dealing or promote fear. Another team in Philadelphia set up "drug-free zones" for residents who wanted to cooperate
with the police to control the drug problem in their neighborhoods.

One aspect of these projects that is interesting is that they combine
central and decentralized problem solving; the program is a two-tier
arrangement for problem-oriented policing. The task forces are groups
that study citywide problems. They can thereby ascertain, for example,
that resource allocation to a given housing complex makes sense. The
activity is then mostly carried out by teams of officers. These teams
study the strategic hot spots nominated by the task force and zero in on
what goes on there. They make a second set of decisions about what to
do and how to do it. These decisions include steps to mobilize citizens
and community resources, which become partners of the police.

The structure improves on most problem-oriented policing because
it examines the problem (in this case, drugs) on two levels with the
involvement of people who are concerned with the problem at that level.
It protects local actors from having minutely detailed policies imposed
on them and ensures that central planning occurs but that those at the
frontline do not have their discretion preempted by decisions at headquarters. By the same token, headquarters becomes permeable and
democratized. This makes democracy a nonzero-sum game and lets
everyone get involved in setting policy.

The two-tier system offers a substantial advance on community-oriented policing, which is typically microcollaborative. In most community-oriented policing projects, neighborhood residents relate to police officers. In good projects they influence what these local officers do, but they cannot influence headquarters policy. This limitation is part of the price the officers pay for decentralization and the autonomy they prize.

Citizens in the drug-fighting program become involved with the police at all levels. And they are involved as fellow problem solvers, which is different from being listened to or met with. Problems that are addressed in this way are by definition community problems and their solutions are community solutions, even where the police do much of the work. This arrangement may be helpful with most problems, but particularly so where targets (problem persons) are the peers of victims (persons with problems) and can become victims themselves. This offender–victim continuum matters, but it can escape even community police, who best know their communities. Such police often boast about the "rapport with citizens" that helps them "develop information." Here, "information" means that someone has located an offender or identified his offense. Such informing can be best done by a peer of the offender, who the offender trusts. But where this is the case, the "source" becomes a fink and no one (including finks) likes the connotations of finking.

It is different where police and citizens are collaborators who must decide what to do about offenders who are objects of their shared concern. In doing this kind of problem solving, data that are relevant to the problem (such as, what sort of nuisance is the offender?) must be available to those who define the problem so they can solve it. If A and B are partners, A and/or B will supply information and they jointly examine the facts and determine what to do. This is different from A supplying information so B can decide a course of action—allegedly, on A's behalf, but without A's participation.

In a problem-solving context, the citizen may say, "We have a problem with Jones, who trades crack in apartment 36, solicits children, and plays loud rock on a low-quality stereo. Jones is a sadist and bully and unremitting disgrace to our people, who should be broiled over a slow-burning fire. But Jones has a dear elderly mother who is a saint and depends on him for her livelihood. We must deal with Jones in a way such that no harm comes to his mother." The citizen provides information about what the citizen thinks is a problem. The citizen also discusses a solution (deleting Jones) and cites its drawbacks (what about Jones's mother?)

A possible outcome of the group discussion that may ensue would be for a police raid to occur in tandem with a welfare intervention that would address the citizens' ancillary concerns. This police action (the raid) is a standard enforcement step, but in this case citizens have helped to plan it. It follows that citizens now would be its proud beneficiaries rather than its ambivalent spectators.

One could legitimately argue that the way we wage the war on drugs is critical to its outcome, because the police–citizen alliances we could forge isolate the enemy and deprive it of support. Police actions requested by citizens can make best use of scarce resources, since the choice of targets (which is otherwise endless) is narrowed to those of most concern. Where persons who are intimately tied to neighborhoods help the police to shape interventions, this can also make police more sensitive to those who are targetted: it could reduce the harm we may do to persons who are innocent, salvageable, redeemable, or susceptible to less punitive solutions.

SEQUENCING

The police are the tentacles of the criminal justice system and they feed suspects into the system. With respect to drugs, police must arrest persons who deal in drugs and malefactors who commit drug-related offenses. The second category of arrest is less distinct, because drug offenders are hard to distinguish from other offenders the police arrest, such as burglars and robbers who do not steal to sustain drug habits, but who often ingest drugs.

As long as drug enforcement and the war on drugs are defined as synonymous, the police are fated to carry the burden. But if the war on drugs transcends enforcement, the police are not necessarily its central figures. Many activities that are subsumed under an expanded war — such as education and the treatment of addicts — have not much to do with police, but look just as important to the war effort. Why, then, should police still convene local councils of war and preside over them? Why is the war not fought under the auspices of schools or hospitals as problem-oriented education or treatment? Why should police be its catalysts and not mayors or city managers or other municipal agencies?

There are several reasons why police seem to be assigned a persistently seminal role. Among these reasons are (1) that people do not in fact believe the war on drugs is anything other than enforcement; (2) that police carry clout, so that a meeting called by a chief becomes compelling (see Chapter 9); (3) police are on-call all the time and other public servants are not; (4) police are multiservice providers; (5) most money for drug fighting tends to be allocated to the police; and (6) police want to be problem oriented more than do other human service workers.

The last reason (police interest) may be more important than one thinks, and two other reasons seem equally important: (1) many interventions require threat as a backup, and (2) it is difficult to work where things are in chaos. The three reasons translate into ways in which crime fighting and problem orientation dovetail:

1. Problem-oriented approaches become inviting where crime-fighting strategies have been tried without making a dent on the problem. For anyone other than the police to suggest this would be ungrateful, but the police can do so with credibility.
2. Drugs provide pleasure or profit, and alternatives (such as treatment, or a job) may look unattractive by comparison. These options can become attractive, however, when the alternative one faces is going to jail. For police, an arrest makes particular sense when the offender has been given a chance, but has rejected it.
3. Enforcement can be useful as a backup, but also as a preamble. Where a problem is out of control, arrests can reduce it to manageable proportions. They can also forestall the need for backup by demonstrating one's seriousness in advance, to both offenders and prospective allies, who might otherwise feel overwhelmed.

The police crime-fighting role is preserved in problem-oriented policing, but is invoked strategically rather than scattered and wasted. Arrests have become a tool because they have cleared the way for regenerative forces to achieve goals, which solidifies their impact. A street or school or housing development is recaptured, and its denizens have jelled into a potent, organized force. Kids with jobs are off the streets and are no longer available to gangs. Students are back in school.

The other side of the coin is that arrests have now reduced crime. Offenders have for once stayed away because raids have been followed by other activities, which make the environment inhospitable. Conventional drug sweeps, by contrast, are fleeting affairs, and offenders are back in harness within days, or, at most, weeks. The same occurs if drug sweeps are followed by problem-oriented talk but no action.

Choice of Problem-Oriented Interventions

A unique feature of the Police Executive Research Forum (five-city) program was that it provided for "cluster conferences" in which the projects could compare notes about what they had been learning. In that kind of setting, it seems important that two sorts of discoveries be made: (1) those that come from talking about *common denominators* of interventions and (2) those that come from discussing differences. The former discoveries build a science based on general principles, but so do the latter, once we go beyond the insight that "many roads can lead to Rome."

One principle has to do with a hierarchy of usable resources. As an example, assume two cities that have a drug problem involving truants from school. A partnership is easily formed in one city between the police and the school system, whose management is reform-minded and engaged in experiments that can readily include drug-related ones. The school works with parents, and the parents seem willing to consider the challenge of helping fellow parents restore control over straying offspring. The school also has peer counseling and thinks nothing of training dropouts as drug peer counselors to work on the problem of reintegrating ex-addicts through groups.

A second city tries working with schools but finds their staff cynical, obsessed with survival problems, and unhelpful. Meetings are called but unattended. When pressed, teachers talk of getting overtime pay. Parents declare themselves unavailable or fail to respond when contacted. It develops, however, that many of the same parents are up in arms as tenants of a local housing complex in which a child has been killed in crossfire. The management of the housing complex is similarly concerned and seems ready to work with tenants on the problem of drug gang infestation. Police cooperation in this endeavor is eagerly welcomed. The police respond, set up a storefront annex, and gather evidence that helps evict drug traders. The police also broach to the tenants the issue of truancy, which they had posed (unsuccessfully) to the schools. The tenants resonate to this problem, as do the managers, because truants "hang out" in the complex, attract bad company, and intimidate elderly residents. Responses the tenants feel they could use are discussed, including helping parents control wayward children and providing incentives for truants to go to school. These projects are tried at once and receive favorable publicity. The school administration is forced to notice and asks whether it can do something to help.

The goal has remained constant and the endgame is still comparable, but approaches have varied from one city to another because resources that were available in one community were unavailable in the another—at least, at first try. With rare exceptions, the police are forced to begin work with persons and agencies who are willing to commit time and energy because they are interested in promoting change. In return, the police can provide services of interest to their new partners, so as to cement the partnership. But as a first partnership bears fruit, less adventurous people may become willing to help address problems with the police. The process is incremental and depends on the readiness of citizens to become involved as the program gains respectability. This does not mean that police must compromise goals that are based on their study of problems. At worst, some problems will have been approached circuitously, through the back door rather than the front door. In the interim, community organization has taken place and group problem solving has been rehearsed.

One reason why it does not matter that approaches have to be modified to gain involvement of conservative elements is because resource development is critical to the problem-oriented approach. It is not enough for a problem to be tackled—even if this is done with success—if interest fades once the "project" is over. The development of problem solvers is a means to problem solving, but the reverse also holds. If we must fight a "war," we must have an "army" to fight it, and the best place to start is with patriotic volunteers.

Choice of Targets

We have noted (Chapter 1) that a problem can be defined as a pattern of who does what to whom. If this is so, a problem-oriented war on drugs deals with a more motley cast of characters. It accommodates activities that are purely victim centered (one could set up a prenatal clinic for crack-addicted mothers), some that are offender centered (sweeps of crack houses), but also some that are combinatory or difficult to classify (detoxification and treatment for addicted small-time dealers).

A community that studies any "drug problem" is bound to unearth patterns of facts that relate to offenders and offenses. Housing complexes, for example, are often multidrug emporia and places in which drug-motivated offenses occur. Schools can be sites of muggings that are perpetrated by drug-using teenagers. Neighborhoods can be battlegrounds of drug-trading gangs that fight for markets. In each case, there is a set of victims, such as persons who are mugged, stolen from, terrorized, or hounded into isolation. Interventions can follow an outline that dichotomizes the problem into victim problems and offender problems.

Solutions that respond to these patterns may be "hard," "soft," or "balanced." A hard solution is one that addresses the problem by pursuing and/or arresting perpetrators, thereby easing the fate of victims, to the extent to which offense rates can be reduced. Soft solutions can be victim centered and/or offender centered. Victim-centered solutions often presuppose that fear or suffering can become autonomous of their origins and that they can be ameliorated by working with victims. Soft offender-centered programs are programs that try to sidetrack or sideline offenders and use arrests sparingly as last resorts.

"Balanced" programs are most popular, and they combine hard and soft interventions. The accent in balanced programs can vary from hard to soft, depending on the political context. But politics is not a coherent framework that gives us a solid reason for balanced interventions. The best such reason is the fact that persons who are involved with drugs tend to be both perpetrators and victims, and cannot be properly targeted except with a balanced program.

One paradox, for example, is that addiction is by definition a disease that compromises volition, but that addicts commit offenses for which they must be held responsible. Another complication is that drug trading is a way of making fast and easy money, but that many persons who trade in drugs are young children and unmarried mothers of young children and others are chronically unemployed, unemployable, male adults. One must also deal with facts such as that addicted delinquents are often violent and troublesome victims of child abuse who have learning disabilities and other problems. And one must recognize that victims may be the relatives of persons who are victimizers.

Where problem persons can simultaneously be defined as persons with problems, the question of causation and culpability are complicated questions. The solutions one thinks of after exploring such questions can also be complicated, and they often combine punitive and benevolent interventions. A person may be arrested, for instance, and then referred for treatment, or may be given welfare assistance (such as child care, remedial education, emergency benefits, or vocational training) as he is carted off to jail.

When one looks at drug-infested and crime-ridden neighborhoods, it is natural to start by dichotomizing the people who live in those neighborhoods. One thinks of populations that are made up of two groups: "good guys" and "bad guys." The goal of interventions then becomes to help the good guys get rid of the bad guys. This goal requires that one first organize the good guys, who have been isolated and intimidated by bad guys, who are organized and sophisticated.

This picture is useful as a working assumption, but even as a first approximation, it must accommodate exceptions. Some bad guys, for one, are badder than others and are more sophisticated and organized, and they may prove more violent. Morgues and emergency room surgeries, for example, are not populated by good guys, but by bad guys who have been bested by badder peers. Bad guys also have families, including dependents, who may be innocent of wrongdoing. Such persons can derive unwitting profit from drug trading, but they may be seriously harmed (through eviction, dispossession, and so forth) as bad guys are uncompromisingly pursued.

Bad guys can participate in many not-bad activities—they may be going to church, attending school, or working while they are not engaged in their felonious employment. The hold such persons have on the good-guy world may be tenuous, but it represents a bridge one may want to strengthen rather than weaken. It is even conceivable that a few bad guys who have leadership qualities could become real pillars of their communities (given time), if they are not permanently and irredeemably exiled.

Such ruminations may sound utopian, but doubts can begin to color our thinking as community interventions run their course, and the complexities of intervention outcomes manifest themselves in terms of implications for the postwar future.

The postwar world will be hard to achieve if we think of it as reserved for a select few among us who are left to watch the rest of us rot in jail when the war is over. Nor can the future be envisaged as one of "drug-free" oases surrounded by roaming outlaws who respect their borders. The future implies a need to reintegrate most of the persons who are now part of the problem (or their successors) into the community, which requires that we take a conciliatory stance toward them as our problem solutions mature. Fortunately, problem persons represent decreasing threats as problems become solved, and it becomes less necessary to personalize the threats these persons represent to mobilize community action. Moreover, as we succeed in rehabilitating or exorcizing more and more problem persons, they become available to us as fellow change agents who have power and credibility by virtue of who they are and what they know (see Chapter 10).

THE POLITICAL CONTEXT OF PROBLEM-ORIENTED DRUG POLICING

With nine out of ten Americans declaring that drugs are a nationwide "crisis" (Morin, 1989), no social problem has a higher priority on the domestic agenda than the drug problem. Any approach that is seen as helpful in attacking this problem can gain support and status, and this includes problem-oriented policing. The other side of the coin is the risk of working in an area that is politically charged, because policies in such areas are shaped by parochial sentiments.

It has been claimed that we have a "tough drug enforcement strategy," but the phrase is a misnomer. There are few stands one can take in the political arena that do not stir opposition, and politics leads to compromise. Compromise typically takes the form of a patchwork quilt of legislative actions that stand in disequilibrated contradiction to each other. One constituency may be satisfied because money is allocated to one set of programs (say, treatment) and another is appeased when money is assigned to a rival set (enforcement). Symbolic emphases matter, such as language used in preambles that has nothing to do with content.

Implemented programs become Rube Goldberg contraptions: harsh sentences fill all available prisons until space runs out. Strange new inventions come about as a result ("shock incarceration," for instance, or electronic surveillance), which sound tough but shorten sentences. Ritualistic drug sweeps overload the courts, which negotiate sentences of probation. These dispositions inflate probation caseloads to impossible levels, leading staff to violate offenders and send them to prison (Labaton, 1990).

When one runs a program, salvation is often seen in ambiguity. Different emphases are annunciated to different sponsors or to diverse publics until one can no longer be sure of one's goals. Is one "tough" or is one in fact "warm and gentle"? One cannot know, because it depends on whom one might offend by what one does. One hastily argues things like

- It may look like we fraternize with civilians, but we are developing informants.
- We may be evicting some drug dealers, but what we are doing is organizing tenants.
- We are sending lots of people to prison as the only way they'll get drug treatment.
- We give slumlords a rough time in order to "get" law-violating tenants.

Compromise is the hobgoblin of consistency, as with politicians who call for a tougher but kinder war on drugs. A recent (October 16, 1990) *New York Times* story carried the subtitle "Politicians Mix Familiar Fears with New Cares." The story begins quoting a candidate who

vows to double prison capacity and expand use of the death penalty.
"If you elect me...I am going to hurt some drug dealers."
But moments later he adopts a mellower tone and promotes a package of education programs that he says are intended to keep poor people from turning to crime. He concludes by proposing two years of free college tuition for the disadvantaged....Then changing gears again, he reassures his supporters by asserting that he will pay for his war on drugs by cutting other programs rather than raising taxes. (Suro, 1990)

The theme here is one of "stressing crime prevention, not just punishment" (Suro, 1990). By emphasizing the benefits of prevention *and* punishment (a.k.a., enforcement), a politician implies that different populations would be targetted, with a tough policy directed at malefactors and a kind one at as-yet-innocent citizens.

The implicit theory is enticing, but its implementation dubious. This is so because we cannot prevent an offense that no one will commit. As it happens, "poor people" do not "turn to crime." Similarly, school children are not incipient addicts, and drug-scare commercials memorized by honors students prevent nothing. Strategies such as these have their impact only at extremes. Anti-truancy programs do work when they intercept drug dealers commuting to work. Drug treatment programs prevent crime where those who are treated are persons who tend to commit addiction-related offenses.

Real targets of crime prevention are high risk persons who could just as well be punished or arrested. This means that we have to give up one goal if we decide to opt for the other, which is different from having one's cake and eating it too.

In more community-oriented contexts, "prevention" has another meaning. It means attempting social reform that ameliorates "root causes" of crime. The crime thus affected, however, is *future* crime. It is crime committed by those who grow up in a world that stands improved through reforms. Current crime would be unaffected, because today's offenders are products of yesterday's environments. This is another reality that lowers the political payoff of anti-crime programs. The public wants immediate results that are difficult to achieve, particularly through means which are kind but tough, quick, and inexpensive.

Problem-oriented policing cannot afford to be insensitive to public sentiment, but it must have faith in the process whereby its solutions are derived. The point of such faith is not to ignore popular opinion, but to subordinate getting along to doing right, where facts and fashions differ. The dangers of not doing so are illustrated by past experiences, such as the saga of team policing, which was often aborted (prematurely) because it had been instituted as a gambit and not as an intervention responsive to an analysis of needs. Sentiments (in the case of team policing, the fear of riots) are often evanescent, while needs (such as the slum conditions that sparked riots) stay around and remain unmet. The fact that problem-oriented policing is now "in" should please us, but we must not confuse this fact with the reasons why the reform makes sense, which existed before the strategy was "in" (as in Oakland in 1969) and should remain long after drug-related pressures subside.

NOTES

1. Our peer review panel model did not work in an experiment in Kansas City, where officers were enthusiastic about the group process but less sanguine about the desirability of behavior change in panel subjects. When one transplants an intervention from one setting to another, one must introduce variations to accommodate differences in force fields. The best way to do this is through local participation in the design of the intervention.
2. Police involvement with citizen groups not only protects against vigilante activities but suggests that they are unlikely to occur. Citizens take the law into their hands when they are concerned about crime but feel that the police are either unconcerned or unable to help them. Vigilante movements are therefore expressions of contempt for, and disappointment in, the police and the criminal justice system. (The greatest danger arises where police concur with this judgment as it applies to the rest of the system.) Vigilantism is also curbed because it reliably involves activities that break laws that the police are enjoined to enforce. This creates an antagonistic relationship between over-enthusiastic citizens and officers, unless the officers become vigilantes themselves.

Postscript

We have said that problem-oriented policing must limit its targets to what is possible. You cannot reduce poverty, but you can persuade a landlord to repair his building. You cannot attack the drug overlords, but you can get rid of the drug dealers who are making life impossible for the tenants living in a particular housing project. You change what you can and accept what you cannot.

We have also said that problem-oriented interventions must start with where the public is, with its perception of the problem. But it is worth noting that the process of participating in change efforts may well change the public's perception of a problem from one that bureaucracy must solve to one that offers targets for participatory action.

It is plausible that grass roots problem solving will not only bring serious thinking to bear on local problems but will also develop understanding, confidence, and competence in the participants in these efforts. This may help counteract the growing apathy, cynicism, and nonparticipation in the voting process that keeps the consumers of public services from having any impact on the decisions being made at all levels of government.

It is no accident that the police are involved in this movement. Recent changes in the world have confirmed that the effectiveness of a community or of a culture can be determined by the nature of its security: the less repressive and more open to development, the more effective the culture. In this sense, problem-oriented policing can show us that our own democracy may be coming of age.

Appendix

SESSION RATING FORM

Check (✔) the appropriate box

	Very High	High	Average	Low	Very Low
Productivity					
Interest					
Group Participation					
My Own Participation					
Group Morale					
My Own Morale					

CIRCLE THE ADJECTIVES THAT DESCRIBE TODAY'S SESSION:

Academic	Fun	Promising	Instructive
Enjoyable	Torture	Thought Provoking	Bland
Sick	Monotonous	Critical	Silly
Sensible	Relevant	Creative	Helpful
Beautiful	Wasteful	Phoney	Informative
Constructive	Pleasant	Puzzling	Frustrating
Challenging	Painful	Aimless	
Inconclusive	Unfair	Enlightening	Damaging
Slow	Immoral	Great	Confusing
Purposeful	Subversive	Nonsense	Encouraging
Uninformative	Strange	Weakening	Pointless
Valuable	Practical	Sane	
Hopeless	Sad	Weird	
Rambling	Honest		
Annoying	Exasperating		
Inspiring	Tense		
Irritating	Dry		

USE BACK OF PAGE FOR ANY ADDED COMMENTS:

References

American Bar Association Project on Standards for Criminal Justice. *Standards Relating to the Urban Police Function.* New York: Institute of Judicial Administration, 1973.

Angell, J. E. Toward an alternative to the classic police organizational arrangements: A democratic model. *Criminology,* 1971, *19,* 185–206.

Argyris, C. *Personality and Organization.* New York: Harper & Row, 1957.

Ayres, B. D. Neighbors unite and score a victory in Capital's drug war. *New York Times,* August 14, 1989.

Barclay, D. Black Panthers' rise shocked America. Albany *Times Union* (Associated Press), April 23, 1989.

Bard, M. Family intervention police teams as a community mental health resource. *Journal of Criminal Law, Criminology and Police Science,* 1969, *60,* 247–250.

Baxal, Y. *Closing Correctional Institutions.* Lexington, MA: Heath, 1973.

Bennis, W. *On Becoming a Leader.* Reading, MA: Addison-Wesley, 1989.

Bishop, P. Berkeley Journal: Finding the right dog for a left-leaning city. *New York Times,* May 2, 1990.

Bittner, E. The police on skid-row: A study of peace keeping. *American Sociological Review,* 1967, *32,* 699–715.

Brown, L., and Wycoff, M. A. Policing Houston: Reducing fear and improving service. *Crime and Delinquency,* 1987, *33,* 71–89.

Burgreen, R. W. Interview. *Law Enforcement News,* April 30, 1989, *15,* 12 ff.

Cooper, M. R., Morgan, B. S., Foley, P. M., and Kaplan, L. B. Changing employee values: Deepening discontent? *Harvard Business Review,* 1979, *57,* 117–125.

Cordner, G. W. Fear of crime and the police: An evaluation of a fear-reduction strategy. *Journal of Police Science and Administration,* 1986, *14,* 223–233.

Cumming, E., Cumming, I., and Edell, L. Policeman as philosopher, guide and friend. *Social Problems,* 1965, *12,* 276–286.

Davis, K. C., *Police Discretion.* St. Paul, MN: West Publishing Company, 1975.

Deutsch, M. *Distributive Justice: A Social–Psychological Perspective.* New Haven: Yale University Press, 1985.

Drucker, P. F. *Innovation and Entrepreneurship: Practice and Principles.* New York: Harper & Row, 1985.

Duckles, M. M., Duckles, R., and Maccoby, M. The process of change at Bolivar. *Journal of applied Behavioral Science,* 1977, *13,* 387–399.

293

Eck, J. E., and Spelman, W. *Solving Problems: Problem-Oriented Policing in Newport News.* Washington, D.C.: Police Executive Research Forum, 1987a.

Eck, J. E., and Spelman, W. Who ya gonna call? The police as problem-busters. *Crime and Delinquency,* 1987b, *33,* 31–52.

Editorial. *New York Times,* February 7, 1990.

Editorial. A Quick Fix: One-Man Patrol Cars. *New York Times,* September 24, 1990.

Egan, T. Seattle Journal. Drug war weapon: Manpower on bikes. *New York Times,* January 5, 1990.

Emsley, C. *Policing and Its Context, 1750–1870.* London: MacMillan, 1983.

Federal Bureau of Investigation. *Uniform Crime Reports, 1971–1975.* Washington, D.C.: U.S. Government Printing Office, 1976.

Gain, C. R. The state of the art. (The police: What we know). Paper presented at California Justice Research Conference, San Francisco, 1972.

Goldstein, H. Improving policing: A problem-oriented approach. *Crime and Delinquency,* 1979, *25,* 236–258.

Goldstein, H. Toward community-oriented policing: Potential, basic requirements and threshold questions. *Crime and Delinquency,* 1987, *33,* 6–30.

Goldstein, H. *Problem-Oriented Policing.* New York: McGraw-Hill, 1990.

Grand Rapids Press, August 10, 1981.

Graper, E. D. *American Police Administration: A Handbook on Police Organization and Methods of Administration in American Cities,* 1921. (Reprinted, Montclair, N.J.: Patterson Smith, 1969.)

Guest, R. H. Quality of work life—learning from Tarrytown. *Harvard Business Review,* 1979, *57,* 76–87.

Hackman, J. R., and Oldham, G. R. Motivation through design of work: Test of a theory. *Organizational Behavior and Human Performance,* 1976, *16,* 250–279.

Hackman, J. R., and Oldham, G. R. *Work Redesign.* Reading, MA: Addison-Wesley, 1980.

Herzberg, F. *Work and the Nature of Man.* Cleveland: World Publishing, 1966.

Hevesy, D. Huey Newton symbolized the rising black anger of a generation. *New York Times,* August 23, 1989.

Holyoke Police Department. *Policy and Procedure Manual, Model Cities Police Team Project, Holyoke, Massachusetts.* Holyoke, MA: Police Department, 1970.

Kansas City Police Department. *Response Time Analysis.* Washington, D.C.: U.S. Government Printing Office, 1980.

Kelling, G. L. Foot patrol. *Crime File Study Guide* (undated). Washington: National Institute of Justice.

Kelling, G. L. Police and communities: The quiet revolution, *Perspectives on Policing* (No. 1). Washington, D.C.: National Institute of Justice, 1988.

Kelling, G. L., Pate, T., Dieckman, D., and Brown, C. E. *The Kansas City Preventive Patrol Experiment: A Technical Report.* Washington, D.C.: Police Foundation, 1974.

Kelling, G. L., Wasserman, R., and Williams, H. Police accountabililty and community policing. *Perspectives on Policing,* (No. 7). Washington, D.C.: National Institute of Justice, 1988.

Labaton, S. Glutted probation system puts communities in peril. *New York Times,* June 19, 1990.

Malcolm, A. H. Cities try out new approach to police work. *New York Times,* March 29, 1989.

Malcolm, A. H. Police chiefs' objective: Greater responsiveness. *New York Times,* April 23, 1990.

Maslow, A. H. *Motivation and Personality.* New York: Harper, 1954.

Mastrofski, S. D. Community policing as reform: A cautionary tale. In J. R. Greene and S. D. Mastrofski (Eds.), *Community Policing: Rhetoric or Reality.* New York: Praeger, 1988.

McGregor, D. Conditions of effective leadership in the industrial organization. *Journal of Consulting Psychology,* 1944, *8,* 55–63.

McGregor, D. *The Human Side of Enterprise.* New York: McGraw Hill, 1960.

McKinley, J. C. Police face drug tests in New York. *New York Times,* September 6, 1989.

MacNamara, D. E. J. and Vollmer, A. August Vollmer: The vision of police professionalism. In P. J. Stead (Ed.), *Pioneers in Policing.* Montclair, NJ: Patterson Smith, 1977.

Monkkonen, E. H. *Police in Urban America, 1860–1920.* Cambridge: Cambridge University Press, 1981.

Morgan, G. *Riding the Waves of Change: Developing Managerial Competencies for a Turbulent World.* San Francisco: Jossey-Bass, 1988.

Morin, R. Many in poll say Bush plan is not stringent enough. *The Washington Post,* September 8, 1989.

Muir, W. K. *Police: Streetcorner Politicians.* Chicago: University of Chicago Press, 1977.

Mydans, S. Powerful arms of drug war arousing concern for rights. *New York Times,* October 16, 1989.

National Advisory Commission on Criminal Justice Standards and Goals. *Police.* Washington, D.C.: U.S. Government Printing Office, 1973.

Oettmeier, T. N., and Bieck, W. H. Developing a policing style for neighborhood oriented policing: Executive session No. 1. Houston Police Department, 1987.

Oettmeier, T. N., and Bieck, W. H. Integrating investigative operations through neighborhood oriented policing. Houston Police Department, May 1989.

Ouichi, W. *Theory Z: How American Business can meet the Japanese Challenge.* Reading, MA: Addison-Wesley, 1981.

Pearlmuter, L. C., and Monty, R. A. *Choice and Perceived Control.* Hillsdale, NJ: Erlbaum, 1979.

Peters, T. *Thriving on Chaos: Handbook for a Management Revolution.* New York: Knopf, 1988.

Police Executive Research Forum (PERF). *The Key Elements of Problem-Oriented Policing.* Washington, D.C.: Police Executive Research Forum, undated.

Police Executive Research Forum (PERF). Down it comes. *Problem Solving Quarterly,* 1989a, *2*(1), 6.

Police Executive Research Forum (PERF). *Taking a Problem-Oriented Approach to Drug Enforcement.* Washington, D.C.: Police Executive Research Forum, 1989b.

President's Commission on Law Enforcement and Administration of Justice, *The Challenge of Crime in a Free Society.* Washington, D.C.: Government Printing Office, 1967a.

President's Commission on Law Enforcement and the Administration of Justice. *Task Force Report: The Police.* Washington, D.C.: U.S. Government Printing Office, 1967b.

Reiss, A. J. *The Police and the Public.* New Haven, CT. Yale University Press, 1971.

Reuss-Ianni, E. *Two Cultures of Policing: Street Cops and Management Cops.* New Brunswick, NJ: Transaction, 1983.

Roethlisberger, F. J., and Dickson, W. J. *Management and the Worker.* Cambridge, MA: Harvard University Press, 1961.

Saint Louis Police Department. *The St. Louis Detoxification and Diagnostic Evaluation Center.* Washington, D.C.: U.S. Government Printing Office, 1970.

Sheppard, H. L., and Herrick, N. Q. *Where Have All the Robots Gone?* New York: Free Press, 1972.

Sherman, L. W. Middle management and police democratization: A reply to John E. Angell. *Criminology,* 1975, *12,* 363–377.

Sherman, L. W., Milton, C. H., and Kelly, T. V., *Team Policing: Seven Case Studies.* Washington, D.C.: Police Foundation, 1973.

Silberman, C. E. *Criminal Violence, Criminal Justice*. New York: Vintage Books, 1980.

Skogan, W. G. *Disorder and Decline: Crime and the Spiral of Decay in American Neighborhoods*. New York: Free Press, 1990.

Skogan, W. G., and Antunes, G. E. Information, apprehension and deterrence: Exploring the limits of police productivity. *Journal of Criminal Justice*, 1979, 7, 217–242.

Skolnick, J.H., and Bayley, D. *The New Blue Line: Police Innovation in Six American Cities*. New York: Free Press, 1986.

Special Task Force to the Secretary of Health, Education and Welfare. *Work in America*. Cambridge, MA: MIT Press, 1973.

Suro, R. An old issue, crime, resurges in 1990 races. Politicians mix familiar fears with new cares. *New York Times*, October 16, 1990.

Taft, P.B. *Fighting Fear: The Baltimore County C.O.P.E. Project*. Washington, D.C.: Police Executive Research Forum, 1986.

Taylor, F. Testimony and conference contributions. In *Addresses and Discussions at the Conference on Scientific Management Held October 12, 13, 14 Nineteen Hundred and Eleven*, Hanover, NH: Dartmouth College, 1912.

Taylor, F. Testimony before the special house committee (1912a). In *Scientific Management*. New York: Harper and Brothers, 1947b.

Taylor, F. W. *Principles of Scientific Management* (1911). In *Scientific Management*. New York: Harper and Brothers, 1947a.

Time, December 19, 1969.

Toch, H. *Violent Men: An Inquiry into the Psychology of Violence*. Chicago: Aldine, 1969.

Trojanowicz, R. C., and Banas, D. W. *Job Satisfaction: A Comparison of Foot Patrol versus Motor Patrol Officers*. East Lansing, MI: Neighborhood Foot Patrol Center, 1985.

Trojanowicz, R., and Bucqueroux, B. What community policing can do to help. *Footprints*, 1989, 2, 1–8.

Trojanowicz, R., and Bucqueroux, B. *Community Policing: A Contemporary Perspective*. Cincinnati, OH: Anderson Publishing Company, 1990a.

Trojanowicz, R., and Bucqueroux, B. Michigan's new statewide community policing ban. *Footprints*, 1990b, 3, 1–3.

Vansina, L., Hoebeke, L., and Taillieu, T. From sociotechnical toward purposeful viable systems design. In B.M. Bass and P.J.D. Drenth (Eds.), *Advances in Organizational Psychology*. Newbury Park, CA: Sage, 1987.

Vera Institute of Justice. *Community Patrol Officer Program: Problem-Solving Guide*. New York: Vera Institute, 1988.

Walker, S. *A Critical History of Police Reform: The Emergence of Professionalism*. Lexington, MA: Lexington (D.C. Heath), 1977.

Washington Post, July 25, 1989.

Wasserman, R., and Moore, M. H. Values in policing. *Perspectives in Policing* (No. 8). Washington, D.C.: National Institute of Justice, 1988.

Watts, G. QWL: CWA's position. *QWL Review*, 1983, 1(4), 12–14.

Weisburd, D., and McElroy, J. E. Enacting the CPO role: Findings from the New York City pilot program in community policing. In J. R. Greene and S. D. Mastrofski (Eds.), *Community Policing: Rhetoric of Reality*. New York: Praeger, 1988.

Westley, W. A. *Violence and the Police: A Sociological Study of Law, Custom and Morality*. Cambridge, MA: MIT Press, 1970.

Wilson, J. Q. *Varieties of Police Behavior*. Cambridge, MA: Harvard University Press, 1968.

Wilson, J. Q., and Kelling, G. L. The police and neighborhood safety: Broken windows. *Atlantic Monthly*, 1982, 127, 29–38.

Wilson, J. Q., and Kelling, G. L. Making neighborhoods safe. *The Atlantic Monthly*, 1989, 134, 46–52.

Wilson, O. W. *Police Planning.* Springfield, IL: C.C. Thomas, 1952.

Winick, C. The alcohol offender. In H. Toch (Ed.), *Psychology of Crime and Criminal Justice.* New York: Holt, Rinehart and Winston, 1979.

Wiseman, J. P. *Stations of the Lost.* Englewood Cliffs, NJ: Prentice-Hall, 1970.

Wycoff, M.A. The benefits of community policing: Evidence and conjecture. In J. R. Greene and S. D. Mastrofski (Eds.), *Community Policing: Rhetoric or Reality.* New York: Praeger, 1988.

Author Index

Subject Index